Health book

FamilyCircle

Good Health Cookbook

EDITORIAL

Editor, Family Circle Books: Carol A. Guasti
Assistant Editor: Kim E. Gayton
Project Editors: David Ricketts, Joanne Morici
Editorial Assistants: Kristen Keller, Molan Wong
Book Design: MBS&K
Typesetting: Gary Borden, Alison Chandler, Maureen Harrington

Cover Photo: Fran Brennan
Photographers: Fran Brennan, Constance Hansen, Ronald Harris, Michael Jensen, Rudy Muller, Carin Riley, Jerry Simpson, Michael Skott

Contributing Food Editors: JoAnn Brett-Billowitz, Virginia T. Elverson, Jim Fobel, Sandra Gluck, Ceri Hadda, Suzanne Hart, Carmen Jones, Aida Karaoglan, Michael Krondl, Susan Herrmann Loomis, Mary Brown Malouf, George O'Brien, Veronica Petta, Mary Nell Reck, David Ricketts, Mary Salloum, Richard Sax, Joan Scobey, Janice Schindeler, Catherine Vosecky

MARKETING:

Manager, Family Circle Books & Licensing: Margaret Chan-Yip
Promotion Fulfillment Manager: Pauline MacLean Treitler
Administrative Assistant: Lynne Bertram

Published by The Family Circle, Inc.
110 Fifth Avenue, New York, NY 10011

Marinated Fish Salad, Poached Halibut with Lemon Garlic Butter, Baked Tuna with Peppercorns, Sole with Plums and Apricots, Turkish Fish in Parchment and Sautéed Prawns with Garlic are recipes from *The Great American Seafood Cookbook*, copyright © 1988 by Susan Herrmann Loomis. Reprinted by permission of Workman Publishing Co., Inc.

Minty Yogurt Soup, Super Vegetable Soup, Chicken Chick Pea Soup, Fruit Pockets, Bulgur with Tomatoes, Yogurt Eggplant Purée, Chicken Rice Pilaf, Lamb Stuffed Zucchini, Sesame Sauce are recipes from *A Taste of Lebanon*, copyright © 1988 by Mary Salloum. Tomatoes with Garlic & Cilantro, Kidney Bean Salad, Eggplant Dip, Potatoes with Chick Peas, Zucchini Pilaf, Watercress Salad, Arugula Salad are recipes from *Food For the Vegetarian*, copyright © 1988 by Aida Karaoglan. Recipes reprinted by permission of Interlink Publishing Group, Inc.

Manufactured in the United States of America

10 9 8 7 6 5 4 3 2 1

Library of Congress Cataloging in Publication Data
Main entry under title:

Family Circle Good Health Cookbook
Includes index.

1. Cookery
Family Circle (Mount Morris, IL)

1989

ISBN: 0-933585-11-X

OTHER BOOKS BY FAMILY CIRCLE

The Best of Family Circle Cookbook
    1986 Family Circle Cookbook
    1987 Family Circle Cookbook
    1988 Family Circle Cookbook
    1989 Family Circle Cookbook

Family Circle Busy Cook's Book

The Family Circle Christmas Treasury
1987 Family Circle Christmas Treasury
1988 Family Circle Christmas Treasury

Family Circle Favorite Needlecrafts

Family Circle Hints, Tips & Smart Advice

To order **FamilyCircle** books, write to Family Circle Books,
110 Fifth Avenue, New York, NY 10011.

To order **FamilyCircle** magazine, write to Family Circle Subscriptions,
110 Fifth Avenue, New York, NY 10011.

TABLE OF CONTENTS

1
INTRODUCTION

Healthy eating. It seems to be on everyone's mind these days. But there's no reason to think that easy, nutritious foods never go beyond boring boiled chicken and bean sprouts graced with a thimbleful of mayonnaise. In fact, good health and good eating can, and should be, the same thing. The Family Circle Good Health Cookbook is filled with delicious recipes, smart cooking techniques and up-to-date health information to help you create and maintain a healthful diet.

The key to healthy eating is learning to balance your diet. This is *not* a diet book with restrictive recipes aimed at fast weight-loss. Our approach is to help you maximize your nutritional I.Q. so that meal planning includes a wide variety of foods. That's why every recipe in the Good Health Cookbook has a nutrient analysis and is marked with one or more of these nutritional flags: LOW-FAT, LOW-CALORIE, LOW-SODIUM or LOW-CHOLESTEROL. And because of today's busy lifestyle, we also flag recipes for your microwave oven.

Before you decide whether you are eating healthfully, take a look at your weight and the general state of your health. And closely examine your dietary habits: Do you eat foods that provide plenty of complex carbohydrates, such as whole grains, fruits and vegetables? Do you use lowfat milk products and eat breads made with whole-grain flour? Have you curbed your intake of sweet and salty snacks?

On the following pages you'll find guidelines that make sense out of health "hot potatoes"—cholesterol, sodium, and saturated vs. unsaturated fats. For a healthier, longer and happier life, it makes good sense to pay attention to what you eat. Medical evidence indicates that a diet low in fat, cholesterol and sodium may help prevent heart attacks, breast and colon cancer, high blood pressure, diabetes and a Pandora's box of other maladies. And there are three other factors to consider: A regular program of physical activity, managing stress and stopping smoking will also contribute to your general well-being. Here's to your health!

An abundance of healthful foods, including an assortment of fresh fruits and vegetables, plus Chili Corn Muffins (recipe, page 14), Gingered Soy Sauce (recipe, page 89), Creamy Tomato Dip and Creamy Caper Dressing (recipes, page 90)

The Committee on Dietary Allowances of the National Academy of Sciences/National Research Council publishes and frequently revises the Recommended Dietary Allowances (RDA) which set standards for the daily nutritional needs of healthy males and females at various stages in their lives. Consult the chart below for recommended dietary guidelines.

Calories

What *is* a calorie? The term "calorie" is used to describe the *measure of energy* derived from the foods we eat. When the number of calories consumed exceeds the amount needed by the body, the excess calories are transformed into fat. Stored fat may be used by the body during times of stress, but an overabundance of fat just sits in the body. In a well-balanced diet, about 8% to 12% of the calorie count should come from protein, no more than 30% from fat (primarily poly- or monounsaturated), and the rest should come from complex carbohydrates.

DAILY NUTRITION COUNTDOWN CHART

Refer to the nutrient value listings on each of our recipes and then use the following guidelines to ensure a well-balanced, healthful diet.

| | Average Healthy Adult | |
	Women	Men
Calories[1]	2,000	2,700
Protein[2]	44 g (176 cal)	56 g (224 cal)
Fat[3]	66g (594 cal)	90g (810 cal)
Sodium[4]	1,100-3,300 mg	1,100-3,300 mg
Cholesterol[5]	300 mg	300 mg

Calories that do not come from protein or fat should be derived from complex carbohydrates found in whole grains, fresh fruits, vegetables, pasta, etc.

[1]RDA [2](8%-12% of calories) RDA [3](30% of calories) Amer. Heart Assoc. and Nat'l Acad. of Science [4]USDA [5]Amer. Heart Assoc.

Protein

We know that a healthy diet must include protein. But how much protein should we eat? Nutritionists seem to agree that a diet high in complex carbohydrates, low in fats and with moderate consumption of protein is the ideal diet both for weight control *and* for good health.

A "protein" is a long chain of amino acids. Protein is a component of all body cells, antibodies and enzymes, and is essential for the growth, repair and maintenance of healthy cells. Proteins from most animal sources—meat, fish, eggs, poultry and dairy products—usually are "complete", meaning they have a complete chain of the amino acids needed for a healthy diet. Proteins from plant sources usually are incomplete and need to be paired with other complementary proteins to provide all the necessary amino acids—ie., rice with beans or peanut butter with milk.

Fat

Despite bad press, not all fat is bad. Fat provides energy, helps the body maintain its heat and assists in the absorption of fat-soluble vitamins, such as vitamin E. However, fat has more calories than a similar amount of either carbohydrates or protein, so a little goes a long way.

Fat is made up of three types of linked fatty acids: saturated, polyunsaturated and monounsaturated. Saturated fat is found primarily in animal sources, but also is present in some plant sources, such as palm and coconut oils—these are the high-cholesterol fats. Polyunsaturated fat is found primarily in vegetable sources and some fish sources such as herring, salmon and mackerel. Monounsaturated fat also is primarily from plant sources and is found in olive and peanut oils, for example.

What does all this mean? Evidence seems to suggest that polyunsaturated fats may help to reduce the amount of cholesterol by increasing the ratio of HDLs (high density lipoproteins) in the blood. These cholesterol-carrying particles actually help sweep excess cholesterol out of the bloodstream. Saturated fats, on the other hand, may increase the ratio of LDLs (low density lipoproteins) in the blood. These LDLs deposit excess cholesterol in the arteries, which may result in plaque on blood vessel walls, subsequent hardening of the arteries and cardiovascular disease. Monounsaturated fats also seem to have a slightly beneficial effect on cholesterol levels. Recent studies of Mediterranean populations where use of olive oil is common show the incidence of cardiovascular disease is very low in this region.

Carbohydrates

Let's hear it for carbohydrates! They provide efficient energy, are comparatively low in calories and leave you with a satisfied "full" feeling—great news for dieters.

All carbohydrates are composed of sugars, arranged in various combinations. Simple carbohydrates are made of three single sugars: glucose, fructose and galactose, found in fruits and cane sugars; or in combinations of two single sugars.

Complex carbohydrates are combinations of simple sugars arranged in long and intricate chains. They fall into three categories: starch, which is broken down by the body to use as its chief source of energy; glycogen, which is excess glucose that is stored in the liver; and cellulose, the woody, stringy part of plants known as fiber (essential to the proper functioning of the digestive tract). Potatoes, whole-grain breads and cereals, rice, pasta, legumes, fruits and vegetables are all good sources of "complex" carbohydrates.

There are no recommended levels of daily intake for carbohydrates. But it is believed that an increase of complex carbohydrates and moderation of simple sugars (such as honey and table sugar) is beneficial to the diet.

Sodium

All animals need salt, and humans are no exception. Sodium, which makes up 40% of the salt molecule, is a major component of the fluid surrounding the cells in the body. Sodium is necessary to regulate the balance of water in body tissues and is active in muscle contraction. It touches off the heartbeat and controls its rhythm. But as crucial as sodium is, we need surprisingly little of it to function.

Excess sodium in the diet is considered to be a contributing cause of high blood pressure, hypertension (a risk factor in strokes), heart disease and kidney failure. Processed foods generally contain very high levels of sodium and many people oversalt food both while cooking and at the table. With sodium, as with most minerals, moderation is the key.

The U.S. Dept. of Agriculture (USDA) recommends 1,100 to 3,300 milligrams (1.1 to 3.3 grams) of sodium a day for both the average healthy adult male and female.

Cholesterol

Cholesterol seems to be the buzz word of late; many people are concerned with its adverse effects. It may surprise you to learn that most of the cholesterol in your body is produced by your liver. Cholesterol is an essential part of cell membranes, is used in building nerve sheaths and is the raw material for manufacturing hormones.

According to Harvard Medical School research, the body is capable of producing all the cholesterol it needs—without getting it from food sources. Excess levels of cholesterol in the blood have been linked with the increased likelihood of heart disease, atherosclerosis (clogged arteries) and stroke. The most concentrated form of cholesterol is the egg yolk, as well as organ meats—liver, kidney, brains. Also, any whole-milk dairy product, most red meats and some seafood are culpable.

The American Heart Association recommends no more than 300 milligrams daily for both the average healthy adult female and male.

Guidelines For Good Eating

How do you balance all of this nutritional information? In addition to the RDA, the USDA and the U.S. Dept. of Health and Human Services have suggested several guidelines for a sensible eating plan. But as research continues, these guidelines, as well as the RDA, are subject to change. The best defense is a well-informed attack: keep up-to-date on the latest medical and nutritional findings. If you have specific dietary problems, or are taking any prescription medication, consult a physician before planning your diet.

Eat a wide variety of foods. Plan your meals around the basic food groups: breads, cereals and grains; meat, poultry and fish; milk and milk products; fruits and vegetables. Vary the selection daily to ensure that you are receiving all the necessary nutrients.

Maintain a desirable weight. Consult your physician to decide upon your optimum weight. If you need to lose weight, avoid fad diets which promise a rapid weight loss. Such radical changes in weight can be dangerous. Instead, aim for a 1 to 2 pound loss per week. Avoid obesity, which has been linked to cardiovascular diseases, diabetes and other diseases.

Avoid excess fat and cholesterol in your diet. Pay attention to hidden fats in your meal planning. Choose lean cuts of red meat, increase your use of poultry and fish, and explore methods of cooking that add little or no extra fats. Remember that legumes are an excellent, low-fat source of protein, especially when combined with other proteins, such as rice.

Milk and milk products are important for their calcium content, but use low-fat and skim varieties. Use your judgement with egg consumption: the cholesterol is almost entirely in the yolk, so try making an omelette with one whole egg and just the white of a second.

Try to avoid overuse of prepackaged, processed foods. You'll be saving yourself from extra sugars, salt, cholesterol and fats.

Select high-fiber foods. Foods high in complex carbohydrates, such as whole-grain breads and cereals, vegetables, fruits and legumes are an excellent source of vitamins, minerals and fiber, and will leave you with a well-satisfied, "full" sensation.

Avoid excess sugar. Any necessary sugars are easily obtained by eating fresh fruit. Excess sugar increases the risk of tooth decay and calorie overload.

Avoid excess sodium. Processed foods, cheeses, cured meats, snack foods, baking soda, baking powder and table salt all contain sodium. Salt added during cooking often is unnecessary (except when baking) and can easily be replaced with herbs and spices. Don't add salt at the table.

Study food labels. Every time you pick up a can or package of food, read the label to check the levels of added sugar and salt. Check the oils used in processing to avoid saturated fats.

If you drink alcoholic beverages, do so in moderation. Liquor is high in calories and low in nutrients.

Criteria For Low-Calorie, Low-Sodium, Low-Cholesterol and Low-Fat Dishes

The following are guidelines we've used in this book for categorizing different dishes. The limit goes up to and includes the number.

Low-calorie		Low-Sodium		Low-Cholesterol	
Main dish	350 cal.	Main dish	140 mg	Main dish	75 mg
Side dish	100 cal.	Side dish	100 mg	Side dish	15 mg
Snack	100 cal.	Snack	65 mg	Snack	7 mg
Condiment	25 cal.	Condiment	50 mg	Condiment	5 mg
Dessert	150 cal.	Dessert	50 mg	Dessert	25 mg

Low-Fat
No more than 30% of the calories in a dish should be attributable to fat. To calculate this, apply the following: Grams of fat in the recipe x 9 calories (9 calories in 1 milligram fat) divided by total calories in dish x 100 = percentage of calories attributable to fat.

Fat Fighting Cooking Techniques

Moist-Heat Cooking

Moist-heat cooking helps tenderize food, and keeps it juicy. Techniques include:

Poaching: Poached foods cook immersed in liquid—ie., water, defatted chicken stock — in a covered pan on the stove top. Herbs or spices can add flavor to the poaching liquid with no added fat. For maximum food tenderness, the liquid should simmer gently, not boil. As the food cooks, it adds flavor to the poaching liquid, which can be served as a broth after the food is removed. Or, after removing the poached food from the pan, you can reduce the liquid (by evaporating the water to concentrate the flavor) and stir in puréed vegetables to make a light sauce.

Steaming: This easy, healthful method is very speedy—most vegetables and fish steam in under 10 minutes. Steaming involves cooking food in a covered saucepan over a small amount of boiling water, usually in a colander or steamer basket. Steamed foods retain their flavors, vitamins, minerals, colors and shapes.

Braising: Braised foods are usually pan-browned, in minimal amounts of fat or nonstick cooking spray, then slowly oven-baked or simmered, covered, on the stove top in a small amount of liquid. This helps food retain its moisture, allows flavors to meld and creates a tasty sauce. Braising is ideal for less tender cuts of meat.

Dry-Heat Cooking

Grilling, broiling, baking and roasting are all methods of dry-heat cooking that don't require added fat. Ideally, dry heat sears food on the outside and leaves it juicy on the inside. However, dry-heat cooking does not reduce toughness, so it's best used with relatively tender foods, or foods that have been marinated first. Be careful not to overcook foods with dry-heat methods.

Grilling: The backyard barbecue provides its own delicious taste, but you can use a low-fat sauce or marinade to add extra flavor. Try puréed vegetables, or a low-calorie topping of lemon juice spiked with a mixture of fresh or dried herbs.

Broiling: Broiling can be considered an indoor version of grilling, but without the smoky flavor. Broiled foods also must be turned and watched carefully so they don't burn. Broil meats on a rack in a broiler pan so that the fat drains off.

Baking and Roasting: Set meats or poultry to be baked or roasted on a rack in a baking or roasting pan so that the fat drains off. Or use a gravy separator to isolate the fat and use the meat juices as a light sauce. Turning food during cooking is not necessary, although basting with pan juices or other liquids helps keep the food moist inside, crisp outside. If you wish, bake poultry or fish on a bed of vegetables, such as chopped celery, carrot and onion, to add flavor and retain moisture.

Low-Fat Frying

Strictly speaking, "frying" means cooking food in fat. The fat both provides flavor and prevents food from sticking to the pan. While fat-free, deep-frying has yet to be invented, two techniques provide alternatives to frying in grease.

Nonstick sautéing: Traditionally, sautéing means cooking food in a small amount of fat or oil. Nonstick pans, which minimize or eliminate the need for fat as a grease, are a godsend to the health-conscious cook. With a good nonstick pan, you can scramble an egg without butter or sauté chicken or fish in a few drops of oil.

Stir-frying: Food cut into uniformly small pieces and stirred constantly in a very hot wok or deep sauté pan, cook quickly with little fat. You can even "stir-fry" with fat-free chicken or beef broth instead of oil.

Microwaving

Microwaving is ideal for healthy cooking because it yields moist results without any added calories. Vegetables are especially suited to the microwave oven, because they retain maximum flavor, color and nutrients. Even eggplant, a notorious oil sopper, microwaves to juiciness with no added fat.

6

2

THE BREAKFAST CLUB

"Breakfast is the most important meal of the day." How many times did your mother say that to you? Well, Mom was telling the truth: after fasting for about 12 hours, you really *do* need high-quality fuel to get you going. Eating a healthy breakfast also helps you avoid that late-morning, low blood-sugar slump that usually results in empty-calorie snacking.

Breakfast-skippers lose out on a lot of valuable nutrients, especially the three "C's": vitamin C, calcium and complex carbohydrates. If you've always skipped breakfast because you're trying to watch your weight, consider this: Most people tend to be more active during the day, so you have a better chance of burning off breakfast calories than either lunch or dinner calories. The best plan of action is to aim for a waker-upper that's low in sugar, high in fiber and complex carbohydrates, and also provides a good boost of protein.

If you're trying to beat the breakfast time crunch, muffins are a fiber-rich choice, such as our Carrot Bran *(recipe, page 12)* or Pineapple Oatmeal *(recipe, page 13)*. Another quick-fix: a pumpernickel bagel with Confetti Ricotta *(recipe, page 16)*.

And when you *do* have time for a sit-down meal, start your day with Whole-Grain Pancakes with Strawberry Sauce *(recipes, page 8 and page 239)*. By making the batter and the sauce ahead of time, you can sit down to a delicious, nutrient-rich meal in minutes. Or entice your family with fragrant Corn Cakes and Turkey Sausages *(recipes, page 10)*.

So listen to your mother: Breakfast has never been better for you!

Corn Cakes (recipe, page 10) with fresh Peach Yogurt
Sauce and Raspberry Cassis Sauce (recipes, page 11),
Turkey Sausages (recipe, page 10), Carrot Bran Muffins
(recipe, page 12)

WHOLE GRAIN PANCAKES WITH STRAWBERRY SAUCE

These hearty pancakes are sure to be a favorite with the whole family — and the strawberry sauce will satisfy anyone's sweet tooth.

Makes 9 pancakes.

Nutrient Value Per 3 Pancakes (using ¾ cup milk): 278 calories, 11 g protein, 12 g fat, 33 g carbohydrate, 364 mg sodium, 94 mg cholesterol.

¾   to 1 cup nonfat milk
1   cup puffed whole grain cereal
½   cup plain nonfat yogurt
2   tablespoons safflower oil
1   egg
½   teaspoon vanilla

½   cup whole wheat flour
¼   cup all-purpose unbleached flour
1   tablespoon oat bran
1   teaspoon baking soda
    Strawberry Sauce (recipe, page 238)

1. Combine ¾ cup of the milk and the cereal in a medium-size bowl and let stand for 2 minutes.

2. Beat in the yogurt, oil, egg and vanilla. Add the remaining ¼ cup of milk, if necessary, to make a pourable mixture.

3. Stir together the whole wheat and all-purpose flours, the bran and baking soda in a small bowl. Add to the yogurt mixture and stir just until blended. (For thinner pancakes, add more milk to the batter.)

4. Heat a nonstick skillet over medium-high heat. Drop the batter, 2 tablespoons at a time, onto the hot skillet, spreading out the batter slightly. Cook the pancakes for about 2 minutes or until bubbles appear on the surface. Flip the pancakes with a pancake turner and let the second side cook until golden.

5. Spoon some of the Strawberry Sauce onto individual plates. Top with the pancakes, then with the reserved halved berries. Pass the remaining Strawberry Sauce.

HEALTH

How Much of a Good Thing?

Ideally, breakfast should supply one-fourth to one-third of the day's calories. For an average man, therefore, breakfast should provide 675-900 calories; for a woman, 500-660; and for a 6-year-old child, about 425-525. Naturally, these guidelines need to be modified to suit your size and activity level. If you start eating a larger breakfast, you'll need to balance the extra calories by having a smaller dinner or exercising more.

HOTLINE

CookSmart

The Stack Market

The batter for wheaty yogurt pancakes can be prepared the night before and refrigerated for easy morning pouring. Once cooked, the pancakes can be cooled, wrapped and frozen, then quickly reheated in the microwave or toaster oven.

Use the basic recipe on this page as a springboard for your own pancake variations. Oat bran, rolled oats or crushed shredded wheat can be added to the batter in place of puffed cereal. Fresh fruit, such as diced apples or peaches and whole blueberries, raspberries or blackberries, can be folded into the batter just before it's cooked.

BLUEBERRY PANCAKES

You can combine the dry ingredients and keep the "mix" on hand to save time in the morning.

Makes 12 pancakes.

Nutrient Value Per Pancake:
105 calories, 3 g protein, 6 g fat,
11 g carbohydrate, 174 mg sodium,
58 mg cholesterol.

½ cup whole wheat flour
⅓ cup all-purpose flour
2 tablespoons cornmeal
1 tablespoon light brown sugar
1½ teaspoons baking powder
¼ teaspoon baking soda
¼ teaspoon salt

2 tablespoons unsalted butter, melted
2 eggs, separated
1 cup buttermilk
1 cup blueberries
2 to 3 tablespoons softened butter

1. Combine the whole wheat and all-purpose flours, the cornmeal, brown sugar, baking powder, baking soda and salt in a medium-size bowl. Stir to mix all the ingredients well.
2. Combine the melted butter, egg yolks and buttermilk in a bowl and stir to mix.
3. Beat the egg whites in a small bowl until stiff peaks form. Stir the buttermilk mixture into the flour mixture until combined. Fold in the egg whites. Gently fold in the blueberries.

4. Heat a heavy griddle or large skillet until hot. Brush the griddle with some of the softened butter. Using a ¼-cup measure, ladle the batter onto the griddle, allowing spreading room between the pancakes. Cook until the edges look dry and bubbles form on the tops. Turn over the pancakes and cook until they are browned on the underside. Repeat until all the batter is used.
5. Stack the cooked pancakes on top of each other to keep warm, or place them on a baking sheet in a warm oven until all the batter is used.

HEALTH

Breakfast of Champions

You've heard it before, but breakfast is the most important meal of the day. You probably had dinner about 12 hours earlier, and your body needs some high-quality fuel to get going again. A study carried out by the University of Iowa Medical College found that both children and adults have quicker physical responses and think more clearly if they begin the day with a full, balanced breakfast. In contrast, breakfast skippers generally find themselves struggling to stay alert by late morning. Another study, carried out by the Massachusetts Institute of Technology, revealed that 9- and 10-year-olds who didn't eat breakfast had a harder time solving schoolwork problems than those who did eat breakfast.

HOTLINE

TURKEY SAUSAGES

Combining ground turkey and sausage meat reduces the amount of saturated fat and the calories in this hearty breakfast main dish.

LOW-CALORIE
LOW-CHOLESTEROL

Bake at 350° for 15 to 20 minutes.

Makes 6 servings (1 pound).

Nutrient Value Per Serving:
124 calories, 10 g protein, 9 g fat,
0 g carbohydrate, 262 mg sodium,
39 mg cholesterol.

½ **pound ground turkey**
½ **pound bulk sausage**

1. Preheat the oven to moderate (350°).
2. Combine the turkey with the sausage in a medium-size bowl just until blended. Form the mixture into small rolls or patties.
3. Place the sausages on an oven rack over a shallow baking dish so the fat drips away from the sausages.

4. Bake the sausages in the preheated moderate oven (350°) for 15 to 20 minutes or until they are brown on the outside and no longer pink on the inside.

CORN CAKES

Little golden pancakes that can be served with sweet or savory accompaniments.

LOW-FAT
LOW-CALORIE
LOW-SODIUM

Makes 12 corn cakes.

Nutrient Value Per Corn Cake:
67 calories, 3 g protein, 1 g fat,
12 g carbohydrate, 32 mg sodium,
46 mg cholesterol.

2 **cups cooked fresh or canned whole kernel corn, drained***
¼ **cup lowfat milk**
2 **eggs**
¾ **cup unbleached flour**
½ **teaspoon baking powder**
½ **teaspoon sugar**
Pinch ground or grated nutmeg

1. Place the corn, milk, eggs, flour, baking powder, sugar and nutmeg in the container of a food processor fitted with the metal blade. Cover and process for 15 seconds or until no lumps of flour remain. (Alternatively, combine the milk with the eggs in a medium-size bowl. Mix together the dry ingredients in another bowl. Add the egg mixture to the dry ingredients and stir just enough to dampen the dry ingredients. Add the corn and stir to combine.) Pour the batter into a bowl or pitcher. Cover the bowl and refrigerate the batter for at least 1 hour or for up to 2 days. (You also can freeze the batter.) Stir the batter before using.
2. At serving time, preheat the oven to slow (250°).

3. Place a large nonstick skillet or a skillet coated with nonstick vegetable cooking spray over medium heat until hot.
4. Drop large spoonfuls of batter into the skillet to form 2- to 3-inch circles. Cook until the tops look dry and full of holes, and the edges begin to turn light brown. Turn over the corn cakes with a spatula and cook briefly on the second side. Transfer the cooked corn cakes to a serving platter and keep them warm in the preheated slow oven (250°) while cooking the remaining cakes.

*****Note:** *Four ears of corn yield approximately 2 cups of shucked corn kernels.*

RASPBERRY CASSIS SAUCE

A simple combination that enhances the wonderful flavor of fresh raspberries.

Makes about 2 cups.

Nutrient Value Per Tablespoon:
9 calories, 0 g protein, 0 g fat,
1 g carbohydrate, 0 mg sodium,
0 mg cholesterol.

1   **pint fresh raspberries**
¼   **cup crème de cassis
    (black currant liqueur)**

Combine the raspberries with the liqueur in the container of a food processor or an electric blender. Cover and whirl until the mixture is puréed.

Transfer the sauce to a small bowl, cover and refrigerate until serving time.

FRESH PEACH YOGURT SAUCE

Use very ripe peaches for the sweetest results. Don't prepare this sauce too far in advance, or it will darken.

Makes about 2 cups.

**Nutrient Value Per Tablespoon
(with the optional maple syrup):**
9 calories, 0 g protein, 0 g fat,
2 g carbohydrate, 5 mg sodium,
0 mg cholesterol.

3   **ripe peaches**
1   **cup plain lowfat yogurt**
¼   **cup maple syrup OR: honey
    (optional)**

1. Drop the peaches into a saucepan of boiling water and simmer for 20 seconds. Immediately plunge the peaches into a bowl of ice and water to stop the cooking. Peel off the skins with a paring knife. Halve and stone the peaches.

2. Place the peaches, yogurt and, if you wish, maple syrup or honey in the container of a food processor fitted with the metal blade. Cover and process until the mixture is puréed. Transfer the sauce to a bowl, cover the bowl and refrigerate the sauce until serving time.

CookSmart

Breakfast on the Go

If you're too frazzled in the morning to eat breakfast, or if you need an hour of consciousness before thinking of food, try one of these on-the-go ideas:
● Sandwich 2 whole wheat pancakes or waffles with no-sugar apple butter or natural peanut butter and sprinkle with granola or wheat germ.
● Bake and freeze a batch of muffins; tote them to work with a separate container of lowfat cottage cheese or ricotta cheese.
● Keep unsweetened dry cereals in the office and supplement them with a ½-pint container of lowfat milk purchased each morning (drink the rest for the protein).
● Make careful selections from the coffee wagon or vending machine. Look for fresh fruit, lowfat yogurt or a bagel with little or no butter or cream cheese.

CARROT BRAN MUFFINS

A wonderful mix of grated carrot, honey and bran helps get you off and running in the morning.

Bake at 350° for 25 minutes.

Makes 12 muffins.

Nutrient Value Per Muffin:
151 calories, 4 g protein, 6 g fat,
21 g carbohydrate, 99 mg sodium,
46 mg cholesterol.

1½ cups unbleached all-purpose
    flour
2   teaspoons baking powder
1   teaspoon ground or grated
    nutmeg
¾ cup unprocessed wheat bran

1¼ cups skim milk
¼ cup safflower oil
2   eggs, slightly beaten
3   tablespoons honey
    OR: maple syrup
1   cup grated carrot

1. Preheat the oven to moderate (350°). Place paper liners in 12 muffin-pan cups.
2. Sift together the flour, baking powder and nutmeg into a medium-size bowl. Stir in the bran.
3. Combine the milk, oil, eggs and honey in a small bowl. Pour the liquid ingredients all at once into the dry ingredients. Add the carrot. Stir just until blended; do not overmix.

4. Spoon the batter into the prepared muffin-pan cups so that each is three quarters full.
5. Bake the muffins in the preheated moderate oven (350°) for 25 minutes or until the muffins are golden and pull away from the sides of the cups. Serve the muffins warm.

HEALTH

What's Up Doc?

By eating just three carrots a week, you fulfill your body's entire need for vitamin A — and protect yourself against cancer. Carrots contain beta-carotene, a substance used by the body to manufacture vitamin A. There is strong evidence that beta-carotene helps prevent the development of cancers in certain tissues of the body, including the breasts, lungs and digestive tract.

HOTLINE

ZUCCHINI DILL MUFFINS

These muffins are a great way to use up your end-of-summer zucchini surplus.

Bake at 400° for 23 minutes.

Makes 18 muffins.

Nutrient Value Per Muffin:
93 calories, 2 g protein, 4 g fat,
12 g carbohydrate, 210 mg sodium,
17 mg cholesterol.

1¾ cups unsifted all-purpose flour
3   tablespoons sugar
3   teaspoons baking powder
1   teaspoon salt
1   egg
¾ cup milk

¼ cup vegetable oil
3   tablespoons chopped fresh dill
    OR: 1 teaspoon dried dillweed,
    crumbled
1   cup grated zucchini

1. Preheat the oven to hot (400°). Grease only the bottoms of eighteen 2½-inch muffin-pan cups.
2. Mix together the flour, sugar, baking powder and salt in a large bowl.
3. Lightly beat the egg in a medium-size bowl. Stir in the milk, oil, dill and zucchini until thoroughly combined.
4. Pour the liquid ingredients all at once into the dry ingredients. Stir the mixture briskly with a fork until the ingredients are evenly moistened; do not overstir. The batter will look lumpy.

5. Fill each prepared muffin-pan cup two thirds full with the batter.
6. Bake the muffins in the preheated hot oven (400°) for 23 minutes or until the tops are golden and a wooden pick inserted in the centers comes out clean. Remove the pan to a wire rack. Remove the muffins at once and serve them hot.

STRAWBERRY CORN MUFFINS

LOW-FAT

Vary this recipe using other combinations of fresh fruit and yogurt, such as blueberries with lemon yogurt or blackberries with vanilla yogurt.

Bake at 400° for 15 minutes.

Makes 12 muffins.

Nutrient Value Per Muffin:
160 calories, 3 g protein, 4 g fat, 26 g carbohydrate, 193 mg sodium, 27 mg cholesterol.

½ **cup chopped fresh strawberries**
¼ **cup plus 1 tablespoon sugar**
1 **cup yellow cornmeal (preferably stoneground)**
1 **cup unbleached all-purpose flour**
1 **tablespoon baking powder**

1 **container (8 ounces) strawberry lowfat yogurt**
1 **extra-large egg**
3 **tablespoons safflower oil**
1 **teaspoon baking soda**
1 **teaspoon vanilla**

1. Preheat the oven to hot (400°). Place paper liners in 12 muffin-pan cups.
2. Toss together the strawberries and 1 tablespoon of the sugar in a small bowl.
3. Stir together the cornmeal, flour, baking powder and remaining ¼ cup of sugar in a medium-size bowl.
4. Beat together the yogurt, egg, oil, baking soda and vanilla in a small bowl. Add the strawberries with their juice.

Pour the liquid ingredients over the dry ingredients and stir with a large spoon just until blended; do not overmix. Spoon the batter into the prepared muffin-pan cups.
5. Bake the muffins in the preheated hot oven (400°) for 15 minutes or until the tops are golden and spring back when lightly pressed with your fingertip.

PINEAPPLE OATMEAL MUFFINS

LOW-CHOLESTEROL

Pineapple juice adds a tangy sweetness to the recipe. For sweeter muffins, add 2 tablespoons of sugar to the oat and flour mixture.

Bake at 400° for 25 minutes.

Makes 12 muffins.

Nutrient Value Per Muffin:
157 calories, 4 g protein, 5 g fat, 24 g carbohydrate, 251 mg sodium, 0 mg cholesterol.

1 **cup old-fashioned rolled oats OR: oat bran**
¾ **cup whole wheat flour**
¾ **cup all-purpose flour**
1 **tablespoon baking powder**
1½ **teaspoons ground ginger**
½ **teaspoon baking soda**

½ **teaspoon salt**
3 **egg whites**
1 **can (8 ounces) crushed pineapple in pineapple juice**
½ **cup skim milk**
2 **tablespoons corn oil**
½ **cup dried currants OR: raisins**

1. Preheat the oven to hot (400°). Place paper liners in 12 muffin-pan cups.
2. Stir together the oats or oat bran, the whole wheat and all-purpose flours, the baking powder, ginger, baking soda and salt in a medium-size bowl.
3. Combine the egg whites, pineapple with its juice, milk, oil and currants or raisins in a small bowl until well blended.

Pour the liquid ingredients over the dry ingredients and stir just until the dry ingredients are moistened. Do not overmix. Spoon the batter into the prepared muffin-pan cups.
4. Bake the muffins in the preheated hot oven (400°) for 25 minutes or until the tops are golden and spring back when lightly pressed with your fingertip.

CHILI CORN MUFFINS

Buttermilk and whole kernel corn make these savory muffins extra moist—jalapeño and red peppers spice them up!

Bake at 400° for 20 minutes.

Makes 12 muffins.

Nutrient Value Per Muffin:
123 calories, 3 g protein, 3 g fat,
20 g carbohydrate, 268 mg sodium,
24 mg cholesterol.

1 cup unbleached all-purpose
   flour
1 cup yellow cornmeal
1 tablespoon baking powder
1 teaspoon ground cumin
½ teaspoon baking soda
¼ teaspoon salt
1 cup buttermilk

½ cup drained canned whole
   kernel corn
⅓ cup chopped canned jalapeño
   pepper
¼ cup chopped sweet red pepper
2 tablespoons finely chopped
   onion
1 egg
2 tablespoons corn oil

1. Preheat the oven to hot (400°). Place paper liners in 12 muffin-pan cups.
2. Stir together the flour, cornmeal, baking powder, cumin, baking soda and salt in a medium-size bowl.
3. Beat together the buttermilk, corn, jalapeño and red peppers, onion, egg and oil in a small bowl until well blended. Pour the liquid ingredients over the dry ingredients and stir just until the dry ingredients are moistened. Do not overmix.

4. Spoon the batter into the prepared muffin-pan cups.
5. Bake the muffins in the preheated hot oven (400°) for 20 minutes or until the tops spring back when lightly pressed with your fingertip. Invert the muffins onto a wire rack and serve them warm.

CookSmart

Cereal Story

In general, the fewer ingredients listed on the back of a cereal box, the better. Keep an eye on levels of sugar, salt and saturated fat. Deceptively labeled "natural" or granola-type cereals may resemble packaged cookies more than wholesome food.
● When cooking hot cereal, cook raisins or other dried fruit with the cereal; they'll be plump and moist, and add natural sweetness.
● Boost the protein value of hot cereal by using skim or half skim milk in place of water for cooking.
● Add ground spices to the cereal as it cooks for more flavor.
● Cereal can be microwaved right in the bowl, which means fewer bowls to clean up! Check packages for specific instructions.
   If you have no time in the morning to cook, start making the cereal the night before: Bring the cereal and its liquid to a simmer over medium heat, stirring until the cereal thickens. Spoon into a warmed, wide-mouthed thermal container and cap tightly. In the morning, add liquid to the desired consistency.
● If you've added dried fruit to hot cereal, little or no sweetener is needed. A teaspoon of sugar, honey or maple syrup probably will be enough.
● Top cold cereals with fresh or dried fruit. Or simmer fresh or dried fruit in concentrated fruit juice to make a compote topping.

BANANA BRAN MUFFINS

One of the nicest ways to wake up: muffins fresh from the oven or microwave.

Bake at 400° for 20 minutes; or microwave at full power for 3 to 4 minutes.

Makes 30 muffins.

3   large eggs
2⅓ cups buttermilk
1   cup unsweetened apple juice
½   cup sugar
½   cup honey
¼   cup safflower or corn oil
1   medium-size ripe banana, sliced

Nutrient Value Per Muffin:
137 calories, 4 g protein, 3 g fat, 27 g carbohydrate, 206 mg sodium, 28 mg cholesterol.

1   tablespoon ground cinnamon
1½ teaspoons vanilla
3   cups bran cereal
½   cup raisins
2½ cups unbleached all-purpose flour
1   tablespoon baking soda

1. Place the eggs, 1 cup of the buttermilk, the apple juice, sugar, honey, safflower or corn oil, banana, cinnamon and vanilla in the container of a food processor. Cover and process until most of the banana is puréed.
2. Place the cereal in a large bowl. Add the egg mixture, the remaining 1⅓ cups of buttermilk and the raisins. Let the mixture stand for 15 minutes to soften the cereal.
3. Sift together the flour and the baking soda into the bowl. Stir the mixture with a large spoon until the flour is absorbed; do not overmix.
4. Use the batter at once, or scrape it into a container, cover the container and refrigerate the batter for up to 1 month.
5. At serving time, preheat the oven to hot (400°). Place paper liners in muffin-pan cups.
6. Spoon the batter into the prepared muffin-pan cups so that each is about three quarters full.

7. Bake the muffins in the preheated hot oven (400°) for 20 minutes or until the tops spring back when lightly pressed with your fingertip. Serve the muffins warm, or cool and refrigerate or freeze them.

Microwave Instructions *(for a 650-watt variable power microwave oven)*

Directions: Place paper liners in glass or ceramic ramekins, or in microwave-safe muffin-pan cups. Spoon the batter into the prepared ramekins so that each is about three quarters full. Microwave up to 6 muffins at a time at full power for 3 to 4 minutes or until the muffins look almost done (they will continue to cook after being removed from the microwave). Cool the muffins in the ramekins directly on a heatproof surface before unmolding them.

CONFETTI RICOTTA ON PUMPERNICKEL BAGEL

A deliciously different topping for your breakfast bagel — so simple it almost prepares itself.

Makes 1 serving.

Nutrient Value Per Serving:
250 calories, 14 g protein, 6 g fat, 36 g carbohydrate, 448 mg sodium, 20 mg cholesterol.

¼ cup lowfat ricotta cheese
1 tablespoon chopped tomato
1 tablespoon snipped chives
1 tablespoon chopped sweet red or yellow pepper

1 tablespoon chopped green onion
1 pumpernickel bagel
  Cracked pepper, to taste

1. Combine the ricotta cheese, tomato, chives, red or yellow pepper and the green onion in a small bowl. Cover the bowl and refrigerate the ricotta mixture overnight.

2. In the morning, halve the bagel and toast it. Spread the halves with the ricotta mixture. Sprinkle with the cracked pepper.

CookSmart

Protein: Spread's the Word

Made from cooked dried beans, lowfat dairy products, tofu or nuts, the following high-protein mixtures make great sandwich fillings, baked potato toppers or dips for crudités:

● Beans for spreads are easier to mash while still hot. For Chili Bean Spread, flavor mashed pinto or kidney beans with chili powder, green onion, vinegar and a bit of tomato purée. Add chopped tomatoes and sweet green peppers and a bit of shredded Cheddar cheese.

● Flavor hummus, the traditional Middle Eastern chick pea dip, with lots of fresh lemon juice, parsley and garlic. Serve with pita bread cut into triangles.

● Combine lowfat cottage cheese with shredded hard cheese for a spread that's lower in fat and cholesterol than regular cheese spreads. The spread can be flavored with calorie-cutting ingredients such as finely chopped fresh herbs, onion and spices.

● Transform nut and seed butters into sweet or savory spreads. Use them sparingly because they are high in fat and calories. For Honey Sesame Spread, mix together tahini (sesame butter), lightly toasted sesame seeds and honey or maple syrup. Add enough non-instant milk powder to make a good spreading consistency. For Peanut Fruit Butter, stir chopped raisins, dates and prunes into natural peanut butter (made without sugar, salt or hydrogenated fats).

● Mashed tofu is a neutral base for sweet or savory flavorings. Try tofu blended with chopped green onion, fresh dill, lemon juice and cracked pepper.

OATMEAL APRICOT ROLLS

Tempt your tastebuds with a sweet sensation — a burst of apricot in your morning roll.

Bake at 375° for 30 minutes.

Makes 32 rolls.

Nutrient Value Per Serving (2 rolls): 156 calories, 4 g protein, 1 g fat, 32 g carbohydrate, 143 mg sodium, 0 mg cholesterol.

1 cup apricot nectar
½ cup dried apricots, cut up
¼ cup honey
1 tablespoon corn oil
1 teaspoon salt
1 cup oat bran

2 packages active dry yeast
1 teaspoon sugar
¼ cup warm water (105° to 115°)
3 cups all-purpose flour
1 egg white
1 tablespoon water

1. Combine the apricot nectar, dried apricots, honey, oil and salt in a small saucepan. Place the saucepan over medium heat and cook until the nectar boils. Pour the hot mixture over the bran in a large bowl. Let the mixture stand for 10 minutes or until the mixture is lukewarm and the bran has absorbed some of the liquid.
2. Meanwhile, sprinkle the yeast and the sugar over the warm water in a cup and let stand for 5 minutes or until the yeast mixture foams. Add the yeast mixture to the bran mixture.
3. Stir in half the flour. Stir in enough of the remaining flour to make a firm dough. Turn out the dough onto a floured surface. Knead for 5 to 8 minutes or until the dough is smooth and elastic.
4. Place the dough in a lightly greased large bowl and turn the greased side up. Cover the bowl and let the dough rise in a warm place, away from drafts, for 1 hour or until doubled in bulk.

5. Punch down the dough and knead it a few times on a lightly floured surface. Let the dough rest for 15 minutes. Cut the dough into 32 pieces and shape the pieces into rolls. Place the rolls, 2 inches apart, on nonstick baking sheets. Cover the rolls and let them rise again until almost doubled in bulk.
6. Meanwhile, preheat the oven to moderate (375°). Mix together the egg white and the 1 tablespoon of water in a small cup. Brush the egg mixture over the rolls.
7. Bake the rolls in the preheated moderate oven (375°) for 30 minutes or until the rolls are golden and crusty.

CookSmart

Straight from the Heart: Oat Bran

Oat bran is the richest source of soluble fiber, and can be incorporated into your diet easily. Here's how:
- Use it along with or instead of flour in muffin recipes.
- Add it to meatloaf mixtures or bread and cookie doughs.
- Use it in pancake batters.
- Stir it into juice or applesauce.
- Prepare it as you would other hot cereals. When cooked, the recommended ½ cup portion of oat bran yields a generous bowl of hot cereal.
- Oat bran is coarser than flour but finer-textured than rolled oats. For an even finer texture, process the bran in an electric blender or a food processor.

CURRIED TOFU SALAD IN PITA

Soft tofu mashes to an egg salad consistency for an ideal quick breakfast. The salad can be refrigerated for a day or two.

LOW-FAT
LOW-CHOLESTEROL

Makes 4 servings.

Nutrient Value Per Serving:
137 calories, 8 g protein, 4 g fat,
17 g carbohydrate, 163 mg sodium,
1 mg cholesterol.

½ pound soft tofu
1 tablespoon plain nonfat
   yogurt
1 tablespoon reduced-calorie
   mayonnaise
2 green onions, chopped
2 teaspoons curry powder
1½ teaspoons lemon juice

   Freshly ground pepper,
     to taste
4 tomato slices
4 lettuce leaves
4 small whole wheat pita
     breads, cut in half
     but not split

1. Mash the tofu with a fork in a small bowl.
2. Add the yogurt, mayonnaise, green onion, curry powder, lemon juice and pepper. Stir until all the ingredients are well blended. Cover the bowl and refrigerate the salad.

3. Tuck a tomato slice and a lettuce leaf into each pita pocket. Spoon in the tofu salad.

CookSmart

Creative Juices

Fruit and vegetable juices refresh the palate while supplying important vitamins. If you're too rushed to prepare fresh juices yourself, choose from a wide array of pure, unsweetened frozen, canned or bottled fruit juices, as well as no-salt vegetable juices. Create your own special combinations by blending two or more flavors; add a squeeze of fresh citrus juice for tang and an extra hit of Vitamin C.

For a refreshing spritzer, pour 2 ounces of juice into a glass and fill the glass with no-salt seltzer.

SESAME GRANOLA BARS

LOW-FAT
LOW-CALORIE
LOW-SODIUM
LOW-CHOLESTEROL

Dried fruit, orange juice and a touch of honey supply the sweetness in these treats.

Bake at 400° for 10 minutes.

Makes 2 dozen bars.

Nutrient Value Per Bar:
74 calories, 2 g protein, 2 g fat,
15 g carbohydrate, 2 mg sodium,
0 mg cholesterol.

HEALTH

Catching Some CCC's

When you skip breakfast, you are shortchanging yourself on some crucial nutrients, especially calcium, complex carbohydrates and vitamin C.

HOTLINE

½   **cup quick-cooking oats**
2   **tablespoons wheat germ**
2½ **tablespoons sesame seeds**
1½ **cups dried apricots**

1   **cup raisins**
½   **cup sliced almonds**
¼   **cup honey**
2   **tablespoons orange juice**

1. Preheat the oven to hot (400°). Line a baking sheet with aluminum foil and lightly grease the foil.
2. Mix together the oats, wheat germ and sesame seeds on a second baking sheet and spread out the oat mixture into an even layer.
3. Toast the oat mixture in the preheated hot oven (400°) for about 10 minutes or until the mixture is golden (watch for burning).

4. Place the apricots, raisins and almonds in the container of a food processor. Cover and process until the mixture is fine. Transfer to a medium-size bowl. Add the honey and the orange juice and mix until blended. Press the fruit mixture in an even layer onto the greased baking sheet. Cover with the toasted oat mixture, pressing down firmly.
5. Refrigerate the granola mixture overnight or until firm. Cut into 2 dozen squares with a sharp, serrated knife.

3
SOUPS & SNACKS

They say that old friends are the best — and that's certainly true when it comes to soup. Soup can be the hero in your fight for good health.

As an appetizer, soup works to blunt the edge of your appetite, so you'll be satisfied with smaller portions of your favorite (but higher-calorie) dinner foods. We rate these soups as side-dishes — which means they qualify as "low-calorie" if they are 100 calories or less. Check out our Watercress Cream Soup at 98 calories *(recipe, page 29)* and our 52-calorie Tangy Gazpacho *(recipe, page 25)*. Some soups, however, are so robust they qualify as a main-dish — such as our Black Bean Soup with Roasted Peppers *(recipe, page 30)* or Baked Potato Chicken Soup *(recipe, page 34)*. As a main course, soup can be filling without being fattening *and* provide you with a full complement of nutrients. With soups such as these, just add a tossed green salad and you'll have a healthful meal any night of the week.

Oh no! You're having a "snack attack" and those cream-filled cupcakes are looking mighty good right now. Resist those cupcakes and check out our great selection of sane snacks instead. Healthful snacks can be used as a weapon against overeating, the same way soup can, by helping you control your appetite. The key is *what* you have for a snack.

By keeping our tangy Yogurt Beet Dip *(recipe, page 39)* and fresh veggies in the fridge, you can snack anytime. Delectable, chewy Fruit 'N Nut Granola Bars *(recipe, page 41)* will satisfy the most insatiable sweet tooth but still are low in fat, calories, sodium and cholesterol. And for the bread-lovers, what could be better than a single Yeast Mini-Loaf *(recipe, page 44)* to curb those in-between meal cravings. If you crave a milkshake, sip a blender-easy, snack-in-a-glass: Raspberry Banana Smoothie *(recipe, page 48)*.

With snacks like these, you'll never miss those cupcakes!

Baked Potato Chicken Soup (recipe, page 34),
Gingered Apple Butter Roll-Ups (recipe, page 40)

SOUP'S ON!

Chlodnik (recipe, page 23)

CHLODNIK

Originally from Poland, this soup is simple to put together, beautiful to look at and gets better as it chills. To avoid cooking altogether, use precooked shrimp.

Makes 8 servings (1½ quarts).

Nutrient Value Per Serving:
129 calories, 7 g protein, 8 g fat, 7 g carbohydrate, 761 mg sodium, 104 mg cholesterol.

1   cup dairy sour cream
1   can (16 ounces) sliced beets
1   can (13¾ ounces) chicken broth
3   tablespoons fresh lemon juice
1   tablespoon cider vinegar
    OR: red wine vinegar
¼   pound shelled and deveined cooked shrimp, chopped (double this amount for a heartier soup)
½   cup diced smoked ham (about 3 ounces)

1   large cucumber, peeled, seeded and cut into ½-inch cubes
2   hard-cooked eggs, chopped
¼   cup thinly sliced green onion
2   tablespoons finely chopped fresh dill OR: 1 teaspoon dillweed, crumbled
1   teaspoon salt, or to taste
¼   teaspoon freshly ground black pepper
    Dairy sour cream, for garnish (optional)
    Dill sprigs, for garnish (optional)

1. Whisk the sour cream in a large bowl until smooth. Place a wire sieve over a small bowl and drain the beets. Slowly whisk the beet juice into the sour cream. Dice the beets and add them to the sour cream mixture. Stir in the broth, lemon juice, vinegar, shrimp, ham, cucumber, eggs, green onion, dill, salt and black pepper. Cover the soup and refrigerate for at least 2 to 3 hours, or overnight.

2. To serve, ladle the soup into chilled individual soup bowls. If you wish, garnish each bowl with a dollop of sour cream and a small sprig of dill.

Note: *Leftover soup will keep in the refrigerator for 2 to 3 days.*

CookSmart

Cholesterol Quick-Change

To lower the level of fat and cholesterol in recipes calling for dairy sour cream, substitute lowfat or nonfat plain yogurt. In the above recipe, you can also eliminate the hard-cooked eggs for a cholesterol cut.

MINTY YOGURT SOUP

For a variation on the theme, try using fresh basil or cilantro in place of the mint.

LOW-FAT

LOW-CALORIE

LOW-SODIUM

LOW-CHOLESTEROL

Makes 6 servings.

Nutrient Value Per Serving:
154 calories, 11 g protein, 1 g fat,
24 g carbohydrate, 127 mg sodium,
49 mg cholesterol.

4   cups plain nonfat yogurt
4   cups water
½   cup uncooked rice
1   egg

    Salt, to taste
    Fresh or dried mint, finely
      chopped, to taste

1. Place the yogurt in a heavy saucepan and beat with a fork until smooth. Add the water and stir until the water is thoroughly incorporated.

2. Mix together the rice and the egg in a small bowl. Add to the yogurt and stir to combine. Place the saucepan over medium heat and bring the mixture to boiling, stirring constantly with a wooden spoon. Lower the heat slightly and cook for 15 to 20 minutes or until the rice is cooked.

3. Season the soup with the salt. Serve the soup hot or cold, sprinkled with the mint.

HEALTH

Here's Looking at Yogurt

Yogurt is made by adding certain bacterial cultures to milk. Per cup, whole milk yogurt has 155 calories and 8 grams of fat; lowfat yogurt, 143 calories and 3 grams of fat; nonfat yogurt, 127 calories and just a trace of fat. A cup of nonfat yogurt provides 50 percent of your daily calcium requirement.

HOTLINE

ICED LEMON BUTTERMILK SOUP

A quick, cool soup you can put together in 10 minutes, then just chill until dinner.

LOW-FAT

LOW-CALORIE

Makes 6 servings.

Nutrient Value Per Serving:
133 calories, 7 g protein, 3 g fat,
19 g carbohydrate, 196 mg sodium,
98 mg cholesterol.

2   eggs
5   tablespoons sugar
2   tablespoons lemon juice
2   teaspoons grated lemon rind

1   quart buttermilk
    Plain lowfat yogurt (optional)
    Wheat germ (optional)

1. Beat the eggs and sugar in a bowl with an electric mixer at high speed until light and fluffy, for about 5 minutes. Blend in the lemon juice and rind. Gradually beat in the buttermilk with the mixer at low speed.

2. Chill for several hours. Serve in chilled soup bowls; garnish with a dollop of plain yogurt and a sprinkling of wheat germ, if you wish.

TANGY GAZPACHO

A south-of-the-border sensation from the blender — low in calories but rich in flavor.

Makes 2 servings.

Nutrient Value Per Serving:
52 calories, 4 g protein, 1 g fat,
10 g carbohydrate, 457 mg sodium,
0 mg cholesterol.

2   large ripe tomatoes, peeled
½   sweet red pepper, seeded
½   yellow onion
½   cucumber, peeled and seeded
¼   cup red wine vinegar

1   clove garlic
1   cup tomato juice
    Pinch ground hot red pepper
    Pinch dried dillweed

1. Chop the tomatoes, red pepper, onion and cucumber.
2. Mix together the vinegar, garlic and tomato juice in a small bowl. Place the vinegar and vegetable mixtures together in the container of an electric blender. Cover and whirl until puréed. Transfer the soup to a serving bowl.

3. Stir in the ground hot red pepper and the dill. Chill the soup for at least 2 hours before serving.

COLD CANTALOUPE SOUP

Cool and refreshing, this elegant soup is a perfect start to a summer meal — or to cleanse the palate between courses.

Makes 4 servings.

Nutrient Value Per Serving:
126 calories, 2 g protein, 0 g fat,
30 g carbohydrate, 13 mg sodium,
0 mg cholesterol.

1   ripe cantaloupe (about 2 pounds)
3   cups orange juice
½   teaspoon ground cinnamon
2   tablespoons lime juice
    Fresh mint sprigs

1. Pare, seed and cut the melon into chunks. Place the melon chunks in the container of an electric blender or food processor with 1 cup of the orange juice; whirl until puréed.
2. Add the remaining orange juice, the cinnamon and lime juice; whirl for 30 seconds.

3. Refrigerate the soup until thoroughly chilled. Just before serving, pour the soup into bowls and garnish with fresh mint sprigs.

CHILLED DILLED BEET SOUP

A cool, colorful soup to start off a meal. You can reduce the amount of sodium by using defatted homemade chicken broth.

LOW-FAT

LOW-CALORIE

LOW-CHOLESTEROL

MICROWAVE

Makes 8 servings.

Nutrient Value Per Serving:
80 calories, 5 g protein, 2 g fat,
12 g carbohydrate, 490 mg sodium,
4 mg cholesterol.

3   cups chicken broth
1¾ pounds beets (about 8
      medium-size beets), stems
      removed, scrubbed, peeled
      and diced OR: 1 can (1
      pound) sliced beets, drained
      and liquid reserved
1¼ cups buttermilk
1¼ cups plain lowfat yogurt

1   tablespoon chopped fresh dill
1   tablespoon lemon juice
⅛ teaspoon freshly ground
      pepper
      Additional plain lowfat yogurt
      OR: dairy sour cream, for
      garnish (optional)
      Dill sprigs, for garnish
      (optional)

1. If using fresh beets, bring the broth to boiling in a large saucepan over high heat. Add the beets and return to boiling. Lower the heat, cover the saucepan and simmer for 25 minutes or until the beets are tender. If using canned beets, combine the reserved liquid from the can with enough of the broth to make a total of 3 cups. Combine this mixture with the beets in a bowl.
2. Place the beets with the broth, working in batches if necessary, in the container of an electric blender (for smoother consistency) or a food processor. Cover and whirl until the mixture is puréed.
3. Pour the purée into a large bowl. Whisk in the buttermilk, yogurt, dill, lemon juice and pepper until well blended. Cover the soup and chill for several hours or overnight.
4. Just before serving, whisk the soup a few times until it is blended and smooth. Pour the soup into chilled individual soup bowls. If you wish, garnish each bowl with a dollop of yogurt or sour cream and a fresh dill sprig.

Microwave Instructions *(for a 650-watt variable power microwave oven)*

Directions: Trim the greens from fresh beets to about 1 inch. Scrub the beets well and place them in a microwave-safe 1½-quart casserole dish. Pour in ½ cup of water and cover the casserole dish. Microwave at full power for 18 to 23 minutes or until the beets are tender. (If the beets vary in size, check periodically for the tenderness of the smaller ones.) Let the beets cool slightly. Trim the ends and slip off the skins. Coarsely chop the beets and place them in the container of an electric blender or a food processor. Add 2 cups of the broth. Whirl until the mixture is smooth and puréed. Pour the purée into a large bowl. Whisk in the remaining 1 cup of broth, the buttermilk, yogurt, dill, lemon juice and pepper. Cover the soup and chill. Serve as in Step 4 at left.

CookSmart

Go For the Yogurt!

Yogurt is a very adaptable food. Here are some tips for using yogurt in cooking:
● In coffee cakes, muffins and other baked goods, yogurt provides the same tanginess and tender crumbs that sour cream does — but at a fraction of the calories.
● Use yogurt blended with, or instead of, mayonnaise to cut fat, cholesterol and calories in dressings for tuna fish, potato salad and coleslaw.
● Top fruit desserts with lightly sweetened yogurt instead of whipped cream.
● Top bean or vegetable soups and stews with a dollop of plain yogurt.
● Use plain nonfat yogurt to top baked potatoes and garnish them with snipped fresh herbs.
● Substitute yogurt for sour cream in dips for fresh vegetables.

CUCUMBER BEET SOUP

Enhance the presentation of this soup by garnishing it with chopped fresh chives and/or fresh mint leaves.

Bake beets at 350° for 30 to 45 minutes; microwave beets at full power for 12 minutes.

Makes 16 servings (about 3½ quarts).

1½ to 1¾ pounds beets (about 6 beets), tops trimmed and beets scrubbed
6 cucumbers (about 3 pounds), peeled and halved lengthwise
1 tablespoon coarse (kosher) salt
1 tablespoon margarine
1 tablespoon corn oil
4 medium-size tart green apples, peeled, halved, cored and sliced into 1-inch pieces (about 1½ pounds)

1 cup scallions, chopped (about 6 to 8)
1 cup dry vermouth
½ cup medium-dry sherry
1 head iceberg lettuce, sliced into ¼-inch-thick strips
6 cups homemade chicken stock OR: good quality canned chicken broth
1 teaspoon salt
¾ teaspoon freshly ground black pepper
2 cups reduced-calorie sour cream

Nutrient Value Per Serving:
124 calories, 3 g protein, 5 g fat, 18 g carbohydrate, 717 mg sodium, 8 mg cholesterol.

1. Preheat the oven to moderate (350°).
2. Wrap each beet separately in aluminum foil. Arrange the wrapped beets on a baking sheet.
3. Bake the beets in the preheated moderate oven (350°) for 30 to 45 minutes or until the beets are tender; a knife will pierce the beets easily when they are cooked through.
4. When the beets are cool enough to handle, remove the aluminum foil. Peel the beets, coarsely chop them into 1-inch pieces and set them aside.
5. Meanwhile, remove and discard the seeds from the cucumber halves, using a melon baller or a small spoon. Set a colander over a large bowl or in the sink. Grate the cucumbers into the colander and sprinkle them with the coarse salt. Let the cucumbers drain for at least 30 minutes.
6. Squeeze the drained cucumbers in a large piece of cheesecloth or a large dish towel to remove the excess liquid. Set the cucumbers aside.
7. Heat the margarine and the oil in a large saucepan. Add the apples and the scallions and sauté over medium-high heat for 10 minutes or until the apples and the scallions are very soft; do not brown. Pour in the vermouth and the sherry. Bring the mixture to boiling and remove the saucepan from the heat.

8. Add the lettuce, beets and cucumbers. Pour in the stock or broth and season with the teaspoon of salt and the pepper. Refrigerate the mixture, covered, until cool.
9. Working in batches, purée the soup in the container of a food processor or an electric blender until the mixture is smooth. Transfer the puréed soup to a 4½- to 5-quart serving bowl (or 2 large bowls). Whisk in the sour cream. Refrigerate the soup, covered, until ready to serve.

Microwave Instructions *(for a 650-watt variable power microwave oven)*

Directions: Arrange the beets, without wrapping, in a single layer in a microwave-safe, 2-quart casserole dish. Pour in 2 tablespoons of water and cover the casserole dish with the lid. Microwave at full power for 12 minutes or until the beets are tender when pierced with a fork. Remove the casserole dish from the microwave, uncover the dish and let it stand until the beets are cool enough to handle. Peel and coarsely chop the beets into 1-inch pieces. Continue the recipe from step 5 at left.

STRAWBERRY SOUP

This dessert soup can be made with any fresh summer berries; blackberry and raspberry mixtures should be forced through a fine strainer to remove the seeds.

Makes 8 servings.

Nutrient Value Per Serving:
109 calories, 3 g protein, 1 g fat,
24 g carbohydrate, 70 mg sodium,
3 mg cholesterol.

2   pints strawberries
1½ cups orange juice
1   teaspoon grated lemon zest
    (yellow part of rind only)
1   tablespoon fresh lemon juice
2   cups buttermilk

¼   cup sugar (optional)
3   small cantaloupe melons (½
    pound each), cut into wedges
    or halved, for serving
6   thin lemon slices, for garnish
6   mint leaves, for garnish

1. Rinse and hull the strawberries; reserve 6 whole berries. Place the remaining berries in the container of an electric blender or a food processor. Cover and whirl until the berries are a smooth purée. Transfer the purée to a bowl.

2. Stir in the orange juice, lemon zest, lemon juice and buttermilk. Add sugar, if you wish.

3. Slice the reserved 6 whole berries into the soup. Cover the bowl and chill the soup for at least 8 hours.

4. Serve the soup with the melon wedges. Or cut off a thin piece from the round end of each melon half, so it won't wobble, and serve the soup in the melon halves. Garnish with the lemon slices and the mint leaves.

PLUM SOUP

In Scandinavia, sweet fruit soups often are served as a dessert, but you also can serve this soup before the meal.

Makes 6 servings.

Nutrient Value Per Serving:
112 calories, 1 g protein, 0 g fat,
27 g carbohydrate, 90 mg sodium,
0 mg cholesterol.

4   cups sliced fresh ripe plums
2   cups water
¼   teaspoon salt
¼   cup sugar

    Grated zest (yellow part of rind
    only) and juice of ½ lemon
1   cup orange juice
6   orange slices, for garnish

1. Combine the plums, water, salt and sugar in a heavy saucepan. Bring the mixture to boiling over medium heat, stirring once or twice. Cover the saucepan and cook for 10 minutes or until the plums are tender and the sugar is dissolved completely.

2. Force the cooked plum mixture through a food mill or sieve into a bowl. Stir in the lemon zest and juice and the orange juice. Cover the bowl and refrigerate the soup.

3. To serve, ladle the soup into individual soup bowls and float an orange slice in each.

Note: *The soup keeps well in the refrigerator for several days.*

DILLED ZUCCHINI SOUP

LOW-FAT
LOW-CALORIE
LOW-SODIUM
LOW-CHOLESTEROL

A taste of spring in a creamy soup — perfect served with lamb, fish or poultry.

Makes 6 servings.

Nutrient Value Per Serving:
135 calories, 8 g protein, 2 g fat,
22 g carbohydrate, 76 mg sodium,
9 mg cholesterol.

1 cup chopped onion (1 large onion)
2 cups sliced raw potato
4 zucchini, peeled or unpeeled, thickly sliced
3 cups water
1 medium-size cucumber
2 cups lowfat milk
1 cup plain lowfat yogurt

3 tablespoons chopped fresh dill OR: 1 tablespoon dried dillweed, crumbled
   Salt and freshly ground white pepper, to taste
   Sliced green onion, sliced cucumber and/or fresh dill sprigs, for garnish

1. Place the onion, potato, zucchini and water in a large saucepan. Bring the mixture to boiling over medium heat. Lower the heat and simmer for 15 minutes or until the potato is soft. Cool the mixture to room temperature (this can be done in the refrigerator).

2. Peel and seed the cucumber. Combine the potato mixture with the cucumber in the container of an electric blender or a food processor. Cover and whirl until the mixture is puréed. Transfer the mixture to a large bowl.

3. Whisk in the milk, yogurt and dill until well blended. Cover the bowl and refrigerate the soup until very cold.

4. Add the salt and white pepper. Serve the soup garnished with the green onion, sliced cucumber and/or fresh dill sprigs.

CookSmart

Squash, Anyone?

Cup for cup, you can substitute summer squash for any recipe that calls for zucchini.

BLACK BEAN SOUP WITH ROASTED PEPPERS

These beans also are wonderful served over steamed rice—just leave out the final cup of water.

Makes 8 servings (about 2½ quarts).

Nutrient Value Per Serving:
290 calories, 14 g protein, 8 g fat,
44 g carbohydrate, 556 mg sodium,
0 mg cholesterol.

1   pound dried black beans, soaked
2   quarts plus 1 cup water
1   medium-size onion, coarsely chopped
2   large cloves garlic, crushed but left whole
3   cups chopped onion (3 large onions)
4   large cloves garlic, finely chopped

1   sweet green pepper, halved, cored, seeded and chopped
¼   cup olive or vegetable oil
2   teaspoons salt
¾   teaspoon freshly ground pepper
½   teaspoon leaf oregano, crumbled
2   sweet red peppers
2   to 3 tablespoons red wine vinegar
    Dairy sour cream OR: plain nonfat yogurt (optional)

1. Drain the black beans and place them in a large saucepan. Add 2 quarts of the water, the coarsely chopped onion and the crushed garlic cloves. Bring the mixture to boiling over medium heat. Lower the heat, cover the saucepan and simmer for 1½ hours or until the beans are almost tender.
2. Meanwhile, sauté the chopped onion, chopped garlic and green pepper in the olive or vegetable oil in a large skillet, stirring often, until the vegetables are soft, for about 10 minutes.
3. Stir the onion mixture into the beans with the salt, pepper and oregano. Cover the saucepan and simmer for 1 hour more or until the beans are very tender.

4. Char the red peppers on all sides over a gas flame or under the broiler. Place the peppers in a paper bag for 5 minutes to loosen their skins. Peel, core and seed the peppers. Reserve about half a red pepper for garnish and coarsely chop the remainder.
5. Add the chopped red peppers to the beans along with 2 tablespoons of the vinegar and, if necessary, up to 1 cup of the remaining water to make a good soup consistency. Simmer the soup for 15 minutes more. Taste and adjust the seasonings, if necessary.
6. Garnish the soup with the reserved red pepper and, if you wish, serve with dollops of sour cream or yogurt.

CookSmart

Using Your Bean for Better Beans

You can take much of the "gas" out of beans by soaking them twice, for 4 hours each time, in plenty of water. Discard the soaking liquid and add fresh water before cooking the beans. Even if you're using canned beans, rinsing them under cold running water should help eliminate some of the gas.

CURRIED APPLE AND LIMA BEAN SOUP

The wonderful things you can do with apples! Here they're paired with lima beans and flavored subtly with curry and ginger.

Makes 6 servings (about 8 cups).

Nutrient Value Per Serving:
232 calories, 10 g protein, 6 g fat,
37 g carbohydrate, 665 mg sodium,
0 mg cholesterol.

8 ounces dried lima beans, soaked
1 quart water
1½ cups chopped onion (3 medium-size onions)
1 medium-size tart apple, peeled, cored and chopped
1 large clove garlic, finely chopped
1 tablespoon finely chopped, peeled fresh gingerroot

2 tablespoons vegetable oil
2 to 3 teaspoons curry powder
¼ teaspoon ground cumin
1 teaspoon salt
¼ teaspoon freshly ground pepper
1 can (13¾ ounces) chicken broth
1 large potato (8 ounces), peeled and diced
1 teaspoon cider vinegar
⅓ cup chopped green onion

1. Drain the lima beans, place them in a large saucepan and add the water. Bring the water to boiling over medium heat. Lower the heat, cover the saucepan and simmer for 45 minutes or until the beans are almost tender.

2. Meanwhile, sauté the onion, apple, garlic and ginger in the oil in a large skillet over medium heat, stirring often, until the onion and the apple are softened, for about 5 minutes. Add the curry powder, cumin, salt and pepper and sauté for 1 minute more.

3. Add the onion mixture, broth and potato to the lima beans. Cover the saucepan and simmer the mixture for 30 minutes or until the potato is soft. Let the mixture cool slightly.

4. Working in batches, remove the solids with a slotted spoon to the container of an electric blender or a food processor; add a little of the liquid. Whirl until the mixture is a smooth purée. Return the purée to the saucepan and mix with any liquid remaining in the saucepan. Stir in the vinegar and the green onion. Heat the soup gently to serving temperature.

SPINACH LENTIL SOUP

Lentils, unlike most dried beans, do not have to be soaked before being cooked, which cuts down on the total preparation time.

Makes 8 servings.

Nutrient Value Per Serving (without the optional salt):
203 calories, 16 g protein, 1 g fat, 36 g carbohydrate, 69 mg sodium, 0 mg cholesterol.

2   **cups dried lentils**
10   **cups water**
2   **cups chopped onion (2 large onions)**
1   **cup chopped celery Handful celery leaves**
⅓   **cup chopped carrot**
2   **cloves garlic, crushed**
1   **teaspoon leaf thyme, crumbled**

1   **pound fresh spinach OR: 1 package (10 ounces) frozen chopped spinach**
3   **ripe tomatoes, peeled, seeded and chopped OR: 1 can (1 pound) Italian plum tomatoes, chopped Freshly ground pepper and salt, to taste (optional)**

1. Wash and pick over the lentils. Place the lentils in a large saucepan and add the water, onion, celery, celery leaves, carrot, garlic and thyme. Bring the mixture to boiling over medium heat. Lower the heat and simmer the soup for 1 hour or until the lentils are tender.
2. If you are using fresh spinach, rinse it in several changes of warm water to remove all traces of sand. Chop the spinach into bite-size pieces.

3. Add the spinach and the tomatoes to the lentil mixture. Simmer for 20 minutes more; if you are using frozen spinach, break it up with a fork. Season the soup with pepper and salt, if you wish.

HEALTH

Popeye Had the Right Idea
One half cup of cooked spinach is rich in iron and has more than your daily need for vitamin A. It also gives you a good dose of vitamin C and calcium. Raw spinach is a great addition to salads — just toss it in with the other greens for an extra boost of nutrition.

HOTLINE

WATERCRESS CREAM SOUP

Watercress is a good source of vitamins A and C. To lower the sodium level, omit the salt in this recipe.

Makes 6 servings.

Nutrient Value Per Serving:
98 calories, 9 g protein, 0 g fat, 14 g carbohydrate, 868 mg sodium, 5 mg cholesterol.

2   **bunches watercress**
2   **tablespoons flour**
6   **cups skim milk**

2   **teaspoons instant minced onion**
2   **teaspoons salt**

1. Wash the watercress and dry on paper toweling. Set aside 6 sprigs for garnish; finely chop the remaining stems and leaves. (You should have about 3 cups.)

2. Combine the flour and about ¼ cup of the milk until smooth in a large saucepan; slowly stir in the remaining milk. Add the onion and salt. Cook, stirring constantly, until the mixture thickens slightly and bubbles for 3 minutes. Remove from the heat. Stir in the chopped watercress. Serve hot.

SUPER VEGETABLE SOUP

A complete meal in a bowl! Add whatever vegetables you happen to have on hand, such as diced zucchini or cubed winter squash.

Makes 6 servings.

Nutrient Value Per Serving:
316 calories, 31 g protein, 11 g fat, 23 g carbohydrate, 225 mg sodium, 58 mg cholesterol.

2½ **pounds beef or lamb shanks**
10 **cups water**
1 **cinnamon stick**
2 **tomatoes, diced**
1 **cup diced turnips**
1 **cup diced carrots**

1½ **cups fresh green beans, trimmed and chopped**
½ **cup uncooked rice**
⅓ **cup tomato paste**
Salt and freshly ground pepper, to taste
1½ **tablespoons finely chopped parsley, for garnish**

1. Bring the beef or lamb shanks and the water to boiling in a large stockpot and boil for 5 minutes. Skim off the foam. Lower the heat and cover the pot. Simmer until the meat is tender, for about 1½ hours.
2. Add the cinnamon stick, tomatoes, turnips, carrots, green beans and rice. Cover the pot and simmer over medium heat until the vegetables are almost tender and the rice is cooked, for about 25 minutes.

3. Add the tomato paste, salt and pepper. Cook for 10 minutes more. If possible, chill the soup so the fat will rise to the top and solidify for easy removal.
4. To serve, reheat the soup and garnish with the parsley.

CookSmart

Skimming Off the Top

To de-fat soups, stews and stocks, chill them until the fat rises to the top and solidifies. Then just scrape off the congealed layer. To de-fat canned chicken or beef broth, refrigerate the can for an hour before opening and, again, just skim off the fat.

BAKED POTATO CHICKEN SOUP

A new twist on the chicken soup Mom used to make! Serve with a small green salad and you have a warming meal.

LOW-CALORIE

LOW-CHOLESTEROL

Makes 6 servings.

**Nutrient Value Per Serving
(using unsalted chicken stock):**
223 calories, 15 g protein, 8 g fat,
21 g carbohydrate, 170 mg sodium,
37 mg cholesterol.

2   large baked potatoes, cooled
3   thick slices bacon, diced,
      for garnish
1   medium-size onion, chopped
4   cups chicken stock
1½ cups flaked cooked chicken

      Salt and freshly ground
       pepper, to taste
2   tablespoons plain lowfat
       yogurt, for garnish
1   tablespoon snipped fresh
       chives, for garnish

1. Cut the potatoes into quarters lengthwise; do not remove the skins. Cut each quarter into ¼-inch-thick slices, discarding the end slices, and set the potatoes aside.
2. Sauté the bacon in a deep saucepan over medium heat until crisp. Remove the bacon with a slotted spoon and drain on paper toweling. Pour off all but 1 tablespoon of the drippings..

3. Add the onion to the saucepan and sauté until translucent. Add the stock and bring to boiling.
4. Add the potatoes and the chicken. Simmer the soup for 5 minutes, stirring once or twice, to heat the chicken and the potatoes. Season the soup with the salt and pepper.
5. Garnish the soup with the bacon, yogurt and chives.

HEALTH

Potato Power

Ah, the perfect potato! These nutrient-rich vegetables are packed with protein and vitamin C, high in complex carbohydrates and contain some B vitamins, iron and potassium. They're also low in sodium and essentially fat-free. Eat the whole potato (washed, of course), skin and all—the skin is full of dietary fiber. At the least, cook potatoes in their skins or peel them very thinly to preserve the nutrients.

HOTLINE

CHICK PEA AND CHICKEN SOUP

LOW-CALORIE
LOW-CHOLESTEROL

A make-ahead marvel, this soup is packed with protein and is very satisfying.

Makes 6 servings.

Nutrient Value Per Serving:
264 calories, 23 g protein, 4 g fat,
33 g carbohydrate, 65 mg sodium,
51 mg cholesterol.

½ broiler-fryer chicken (about 2 pounds), skinned and cut into pieces
10 cups water
1 cup dry chick peas, soaked overnight and drained OR: 2 cups canned chick peas, rinsed and drained

½ cup uncooked rice
Salt and freshly ground pepper, to taste
½ teaspoon ground cinnamon

1. Place the chicken and the water in a large stockpot. Bring the water to boiling, skimming the foam from the top. If using soaked dried chick peas, drain and add them to the pot now. Lower the heat, cover the pot and simmer the beans for 1½ hours.

2. Add the rice, salt and pepper and cinnamon to the stockpot. If using canned chick peas, add them to the pot now. Cook until the rice is tender, for about 20 minutes more.

HEALTH

"Mother's Penicillin"

Chicken soup is an almost universal folk remedy for the common cold. And, according to a study conducted at the Mount Sinai Medical Center in Miami Beach, Florida, it's a sound prescription. It speeds up mucus flow even better than a cup of tea does. Although it's not clear *why*, it helps unclog a stuffy nose, too. It's a home cure that really works!

HOTLINE

ZUCCHINI CHICKEN SOUP

LOW-FAT
LOW-CALORIE
LOW-CHOLESTEROL

Homemade chicken broth imparts its wonderful flavor but adds no cholesterol to this savory soup.

Makes 8 servings.

Nutrient Value Per Serving:
40 calories, 2 g protein, 1 g fat,
6 g carbohydrate, 647 mg sodium,
0 mg cholesterol.

1½ pounds zucchini, sliced into ⅛-inch-thick rounds
½ teaspoon salt
2 medium-size onions, coarsely chopped
½ to 1 teaspoon reduced-calorie margarine

1 quart defatted homemade chicken broth OR: canned chicken broth
½ cup chopped seeded tomatoes
2 teaspoons lemon juice
½ teaspoon leaf tarragon, crumbled
¼ teaspoon leaf basil, crumbled

1. Place the zucchini in a colander in the sink. Sprinkle with the salt and toss. Let the zucchini stand for 20 minutes. Pat with paper toweling.
2. Sauté the zucchini and the onion in ½ teaspoon of the margarine in a large nonstick saucepan over medium-high heat for 5 minutes. (Add the remaining ½ teaspoon of margarine to prevent sticking, if necessary.)

3. Add the broth and the tomatoes. Bring to boiling; lower the heat and simmer for 10 to 15 minutes, or until the vegetables soften.
4. Season with the lemon juice, tarragon and basil. Serve hot.

TOMATO ORANGE SOUP

Bursting with flavor, this tangy soup is perfect to start a meal — or as an afternoon treat.

Makes 4 servings.

Nutrient Value Per Serving:
61 calories, 2 g protein, 0 g fat,
14 g carbohydrate, 145 mg sodium,
0 mg cholesterol.

2¼ pounds ripe Italian plum
     tomatoes, quartered OR:
     1 can (35 ounces) whole
     plum tomatoes, undrained
½   cup firmly packed fresh basil
     leaves
1   strip orange peel (3 x ½ inch)
2   tablespoons sliced green
     onion (white part only)

1   cup orange juice
1   tablespoon cornstarch
2   tablespoons chopped fresh
     parsley leaves
¼   teaspoon salt
⅛   teaspoon freshly ground pepper
     Dairy sour cream, for garnish
     (optional)

1. Combine the tomatoes, basil, orange peel and green onion in a medium-size saucepan. Cover the saucepan and bring the mixture to boiling. Lower the heat and simmer, covered, for 15 minutes. Remove the orange peel. Force the tomato mixture through a food mill into a bowl. Or whirl in an electric blender or a food processor and strain the mixture through a fine sieve. Discard the solids.

2. Return the liquid to the saucepan. Stir together the orange juice and the cornstarch in a small bowl until no lumps remain. Stir the cornstarch mixture into the tomato mixture. Cook the soup over medium heat, stirring constantly, until it thickens and comes to a boil. Cook for 1 minute more. Season the soup with the parsley, salt and pepper. Garnish each serving with a dollop of sour cream, if you wish.

HEALTH

That's Some Tomato!

Fresh, canned or cooked, one medium-size tomato delivers nearly half of your RDA of vitamins A and C, some niacin and fiber and only 30 calories. If you cook tomato sauce in a non-enameled cast iron pot, you'll also reap, for each ½-cup serving, your RDA of iron, a key mineral for keeping color high and bright (the acid in tomatoes draws out iron from the cast iron.)

HOTLINE

CookSmart

Zest for Cooking

Lemons, limes and oranges should be grated before squeezing when a recipe calls for both grated rind and juice. The same applies when zest is called for in a recipe. Carefully remove the zest using a very sharp paring knife or a vegetable parer — then squeeze for the juice.

JAPANESE CLAM SOUP

Geoduck (pronounced "gooey duck") is a giant Pacific clam that can weigh up to 5 pounds. Abalone or steamed and shucked clams work equally well.

Makes 4 servings.

Nutrient Value Per Serving:
85 calories, 13 g protein, 1 g fat,
9 g carbohydrate, 7 mg sodium,
19 mg cholesterol.

½ pound geoduck siphon and
    breast meat (¼ pound each)
    OR: ½ pound abalone
    OR: 25 small, 15 medium-size
    or 12 large clams, scrubbed
1½ pounds spinach, washed well
    and stems removed
4 cups loosely packed
    watercress, washed and
    stems removed

One 6 x 2-inch piece kombu*
12 small mushrooms, trimmed,
    wiped and halved
2 tablespoons soy sauce
½ teaspoon grated, peeled fresh
    gingerroot
2 tablespoons fresh lime juice
    Salt, to taste
1 green onion, finely chopped,
    for garnish

1. Thinly slice the geoduck or abalone, or steam the clams just until they open. Set aside.

2. Cook the spinach and the watercress together in a separate large saucepan of boiling salted water just until they are wilted. Immediately remove the greens with a slotted spoon or strainer and transfer them to a large bowl of ice and water, to stop further cooking and preserve their color. Let the greens cool. Drain the greens and squeeze them to extract as much water as possible. Coarsely chop the greens and divide them among 4 individual soup bowls.

3. Place 4 cups of water in a large saucepan, add the kombu and bring the water to boiling. Add the sliced geoduck or abalone and simmer for 2 minutes, until lightened in color. (Or add the clams and simmer for 30 seconds.) Remove the geoduck, abalone or clams with a slotted spoon and divide it among the soup bowls. Remove and discard the kombu.

4. Add the mushrooms and the soy sauce to the cooking liquid. Bring to boiling. Add the ginger and the lime juice. Cook for 1 minute more. Taste and add the salt, if necessary.

5. Pour the soup into the individual bowls. Garnish with the green onion and serve at once.

__Note:__ Kombu is plain kelp and is available in Oriental food stores.

SNACK
ATTACK

Yogurt Beet Dip (recipe, page 39),
Chili Corn Muffins (recipe, page 14)

YOGURT BEET DIP

Quick and easy to make, this colorful dip tastes great with your favorite raw vegetables.

Makes about ⅔ cup.

Nutrient Value Per Tablespoon:
12 calories, 1 g protein, 0 g fat,
2 g carbohydrate, 24 mg sodium,
1 mg cholesterol.

HEALTH

The Calcium Connection

Yogurt is a potent weapon against osteoporosis, the bone-weakening calcium-deficiency disease that afflicts nearly half of all American women in their later years.

HOTLINE

6 slices (about ⅓ cup) drained
    canned or cooked beets
¼ small onion, peeled
⅔ cup plain lowfat yogurt

1. Place the beet slices and the onion in the container of a food processor. Cover and whirl until the vegetables are very finely chopped.

2. Add the yogurt to the container. Cover and process until the mixture is smooth. Transfer the dip to a small bowl, cover the bowl and refrigerate the dip.

CHILI SPICED POPCORN

Move over, pricey gourmet popcorns! Here's a do-it-yourself version that'll knock your socks off.

Makes 2 quarts.

Nutrient Value Per Cup:
59 calories, 1 g protein, 4 g fat,
6 g carbohydrate, 19 mg sodium,
0 mg cholesterol.

2 tablespoons corn oil
2 tablespoons chili powder plus
    more for sprinkling

   Salt (optional)
2 quarts fresh popcorn

1. Heat the oil in a small saucepan over medium-low heat. Add the chili powder and, if you wish, salt and cook for 1 minute.
2. Drizzle the chili oil over the popcorn in a large bowl, tossing to blend well. Sprinkle with additional chili powder and salt, if you wish.

Note: *For an even lower-calorie snack, spray a hot air corn popper container with nonstick vegetable cooking spray, sprinkle with the chili powder and add the unpopped corn.*

GINGERED APPLE BUTTER ROLL-UPS

Use this technique with a variety of other fillings, such as prune or dried apricot purée.

Bake at 300° for 20 to 25 minutes.

Makes 8 rolls.

Nutrient Value Per Roll:
89 calories, 2 g protein, 1 g fat,
18 g carbohydrate, 148 mg sodium,
0 mg cholesterol.

8   **slices oatmeal bread**
½   **cup unsweetened apple butter**
½   **teaspoon ground ginger**

1. Preheat the oven to slow (300°). Use a nonstick baking sheet or lightly grease a regular baking sheet.
2. Trim the crusts from the bread. Flatten the bread slightly with a rolling pin.
3. Combine the apple butter with the ginger in a small bowl. Spread 1 tablespoon of the apple butter mixture on each slice of bread.

4. Roll up the bread, jelly-roll style, and trim the ends to expose the filling. Place the rolls, seam side down, on the prepared baking sheet.
5. Bake the rolls in the preheated slow oven (300°) for 20 to 25 minutes or until they are golden. Cool the rolls on a wire rack and store them in a container with a loose-fitting lid.

CookSmart

Super Snacks: No Baloney!

Try these nutritious nibbles in brown bag lunches. (Of course, they're great at home, too!)
● Core an apple and generously stuff the cavity with natural peanut butter or soft cheese.
● Mix natural peanut butter with honey, raw peanuts and a tablespoon or so of wheat germ for a powerhouse sandwich spread.
● Mix softened lowfat cream cheese with chopped apples, walnuts and green peppers; spread the mixture on whole wheat bread.
● Snack, California-style: Add fresh fruit to a container of plain lowfat yogurt and eat a bran or whole-grain muffin on the side.
● Snack, Continental-style: Chunks of cheese, whole-grain rolls and small bunches of grapes.
● Soak carrot sticks in unsweetened pineapple juice before packing.
● Peel and cut fruit into small pieces to make it more appealing. Immediately dip the pieces in lemon juice to prevent browning.
● Try unbuttered popcorn with a small thermos or bowl of soup.
● Blend water-packed tuna with lemon juice and chopped celery, carrots and parsley.

FRUIT 'N NUT GRANOLA BARS

Try these as drop cookies, too. Allow the bars (or drops) to soften in an airtight container for several days to a week.

Bake at 350° for 10 to 15 minutes.

Makes 10 bars or 24 drops.

Nutrient Value Per Bar (per drop in parentheses): 175 (73) calories, 4 (2) g protein, 5 (2) g fat, 29 (12) g carbohydrate, 51 (27) mg sodium, 27 (11) mg cholesterol.

½ **cup unbleached all-purpose flour**
½ **cup whole wheat flour**
1 **teaspoon baking powder**
1 **egg**
⅓ **cup honey**
2 **tablespoons corn oil**

1 **teaspoon vanilla**
1½ **cups Fruit 'N Nut Granola (recipe, page 42) OR: 1½ cups unsweetened or lightly sweetened granola**

1. Preheat the oven to moderate (350°). For the bars, line a 9-inch baking pan with aluminum foil and lightly grease the foil. For the drops, line and grease a baking sheet.
2. Sift together the all-purpose and whole wheat flours with the baking powder onto wax paper.
3. Beat together the egg and the honey in a medium-size bowl with an electric mixer at high speed until well blended. Reduce the mixer speed to slow. Beat in the oil and the vanilla. Then beat in the sifted dry ingredients just until they are absorbed. Stir in the granola.

4. For the bars, press the granola mixture into the prepared 9-inch pan. For the drops, roll the granola mixture, 1 tablespoon at a time, into balls and place them 1 inch apart on the prepared baking sheet. Slightly flatten the balls with the bottom of a glass.
5. Bake the drops in the preheated moderate oven (350°) for 10 minutes, the bars for 15 minutes, or until they are golden. Remove the drops with a spatula from the baking sheet to a wire rack to cool. Cool the granola mixture in the 9-inch pan on the rack and cut into 10 bars with a serrated knife.

FRUIT 'N NUT GRANOLA

This granola has significantly less oil and honey than most versions. Nibble a small amount as a snack before working out, mix it with milk for breakfast or use it in baking.

Bake at 250° for 1 hour.

Makes 12 cups.

Nutrient Value Per ⅓ Cup:
145 calories, 4 g protein, 4 g fat,
23 g carbohydrate, 2 mg sodium,
0 mg cholesterol.

18	ounces rolled oats (not quick-cooking)
⅓	cup corn oil
½	cup honey
1	tablespoon ground cinnamon
½	cup whole hazelnuts
1	cup uncooked hot wheat breakfast cereal
1	cup oat or wheat bran
1	cup wheat germ
1	cup chopped pitted prunes
1	cup raisins

1. Preheat the oven to very slow (250°). Place the oats in a 13 x 9 x 2-inch baking pan.
2. Beat together the oil, honey and cinnamon in a small, deep bowl until well blended. Pour the mixture over the oats and stir until the oats are evenly coated.
3. Place the hazelnuts in a second baking pan.
4. Bake the oats and the hazelnuts separately in the preheated very slow oven (250°) for 20 minutes or until the hazelnuts are toasted and their skins have cracked. Remove the hazelnuts from the oven.

5. Bake the oats for 20 minutes more, stirring 2 or 3 times.
6. Meanwhile, rub the hazelnuts in a tea towel to remove as much of the skins as possible. Coarsely chop the nuts.
7. Add the cereal, oat or wheat bran and the wheat germ to the oats and stir to mix. Continue baking and stirring for 20 minutes more or until the mixture is golden.
8. Stir the hazelnuts, prunes and raisins into the hot granola. Cool the granola completely before storing in an airtight container.

CookSmart

Prunes and Prejudice

Pity the prune; it enjoys none of the favorable connotations that its younger brother, the plum, has. Yet once you overcome prune prejudice, you'll find this dried fruit to be delicious and versatile.

As plums are dried, the water in them evaporates and the sugars are concentrated, resulting in a pleasantly chewy, naturally sweet snack that has the added advantages of being high in fiber and iron. Prunes can be eaten straight from the box as a snack or added to a number of recipes:

● Stew prunes and dried apricots in a little water with orange and lemon slices and a cinnamon stick until the prunes are tender. Eat the cooked fruit warm or cold.
● Use chopped, pitted prunes as a substitute for raisins in a favorite cookie or muffin recipe.
● Add chopped, pitted prunes to hot or cold cereal or stir them into plain nonfat yogurt.
● Substitute orange juice for water when cooking rice and add ½ cup of chopped, pitted prunes to the rice as it cooks. Garnish with shredded orange zest and toasted almonds.
● Make your own trail mix by combining chopped, pitted prunes, sunflower seeds or chopped nuts and dry cereal or unbuttered popcorn.

OATMEAL FRUIT BARS

You can use a variety of dried fruits, such as chopped prunes or apricots, in place of the dates in this recipe.

Bake at 400° for 25 minutes.

Makes 40 bars.

Nutrient Value Per Bar:
88 calories, 1 g protein, 2 g fat,
17 g carbohydrate, 26 mg sodium,
0 mg cholesterol.

HEALTH

The Snack Sack

Portability is the key when you're too hurried to sit and eat one of the high-carbohydrate snacks that experts recommend having before and after a workout. If you constantly are on the run, you might want to carry a handy snack bag stocked with an apple, some nuts and dried fruits, homemade granola bars and perhaps a bagel.

HOTLINE

Raisin and Date Filling:
1½ cups raisins
1½ cups chopped, pitted dates
¾ cup orange juice
¾ cup water
1 tablespoon grated orange zest

Nonstick vegetable cooking spray

Crust:
½ cup soft corn oil margarine, chilled
½ cup firmly packed light brown sugar
1½ cups unbleached all-purpose flour
½ teaspoon baking soda
1 cup old-fashioned rolled oats OR: oat bran

1. Prepare the Raisin and Date Filling: Combine the raisins, dates, orange juice and water in a medium-size saucepan. Bring the mixture to boiling over medium heat, stirring occasionally. Continue to boil, stirring so the mixture does not stick, for 10 minutes or until the mixture thickens and becomes pastelike. Remove the saucepan from the heat and stir in the orange zest. Let the mixture cool completely.
2. Preheat the oven to hot (400°). Line a nonstick 13 x 9 x 2-inch baking pan with aluminum foil and spray the foil with nonstick vegetable cooking spray.

3. Prepare the Crust: Combine the margarine with the brown sugar in a medium-size bowl until well blended. Beat in the flour, baking soda and the oats or oat bran until the mixture is crumbly.
4. Press half the oat mixture into the prepared pan. Spread the filling in an even layer over the oats. Sprinkle the remaining oat mixture over the filling and press down lightly.
5. Bake the mixture in the preheated hot oven (400°) for 25 minutes or until the top is golden. Cut into 40 bars while still warm. Cool the bars completely and store them in an airtight container.

YEAST MINI-LOAVES

What could be better than a fresh loaf of bread? A whole batch of mini-loaves, in an assortment of shapes and flavors!

LOW-FAT

LOW-CALORIE

Bake at 400° for 15 minutes.

Makes 2 dozen mini-loaves.

Nutrient Value Per Mini-Loaf:
80 calories, 3 g protein, 0 g fat,
16 g carbohydrate, 126 mg sodium,
11 mg cholesterol.

1 **package active dry yeast**
1¼ **cups warm water (105° to 115°)**
3½ **to 4½ cups all-purpose flour**
    (not unbleached)
2 **teaspoons coarse (kosher)**
    salt

1 **egg**
1 **tablespoon water**
    Poppy, sesame or other seeds,
    for garnish (optional)

1. Sprinkle the yeast over ¼ cup of the warm water in a measuring cup. Gently mix to moisten the yeast and let the mixture stand for 10 minutes to soften. Combine 3½ cups of the flour with the salt in a bowl and stir to mix well.
2. Pour the yeast mixture into the flour mixture. Add the remaining 1 cup of warm water. Stir to form a ball. Add a little water if the dough is too dry, or flour if too wet. Knead the dough on a lightly floured surface with the heel of your hand, stretching the dough away from you.
3. Fold the dough back over on itself. Turn the dough a quarter turn. Repeat the kneading, folding and turning until the dough is smooth and elastic, for 10 to 15 minutes.
4. Lightly grease a bowl with butter or margarine. Place the dough in the greased bowl and turn the greased side up. Cover the bowl with a clean towel or plastic wrap.
5. Let the dough rise in a warm place, away from drafts, until doubled in bulk, for 1½ to 2 hours. To test, lightly stick your finger in the dough. The dent should fill in slowly when your finger is removed.

6. Punch down the dough and divide it in half. On a lightly floured surface, roll one half into a 12-inch-long rope and cut the rope into twelve 1-inch lengths. Repeat with the other half. To make baguette, crescent, cheese or whole wheat versions, or a large loaf, see the opposite page.
7. Cup your hand over one of the pieces of dough. Roll the dough into a smooth ball on the lightly floured surface. Repeat the rolling and shaping with the remaining pieces of dough to form a total of 24 mini-loaves.
8. Place the mini-loaves on lightly greased baking sheets. If you wish, cut slashes in the top of each loaf with a single-edged razor blade or thin knife. Cover the baking sheets and let the dough rise again in a warm place, away from drafts, until doubled in bulk, for 20 to 30 minutes.
9. Preheat the oven to hot (400°).
10. Combine the egg with the 1 tablespoon of water in a small cup. Brush the glaze over the mini-loaves. If you wish, sprinkle with poppy, sesame or other seeds.

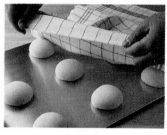

11. Bake the mini-loaves in the preheated hot oven (400°) for 15 minutes or until they are golden brown and crusty. Remove the mini-loaves with a spatula to a wire rack to cool briefly. Serve with butter, if you wish.

To Make One Large Loaf: Roll the dough into a 12 x 8-inch rectangle. Roll up the rectangle from the short side. Press the ends to seal them, then fold them under the loaf. Place the loaf in a greased 8½ x 4½ x 2⅝-inch loaf pan, seam side down. Cover the pan and let the dough rise again in a warm place, away from drafts, until doubled in bulk, for about 1 hour. Bake in the preheated hot oven (400°) for 30 minutes. Brush the top with 1 tablespoon of melted butter. Bake for 10 minutes more or until the loaf sounds hollow when tapped with your fingertips. Brush with another tablespoon of melted butter. Remove the loaf from the pan to a wire rack to cool.

Crescent or "Baguette" Variation: After halving the dough in Step 6 above, roll one half into a 6-inch-long rope. Divide the rope into thirds and shape the thirds into crescents or cigar shapes. Repeat with the other half. Place the crescents or baguettes on lightly greased baking sheets. Cover the baking sheets and let the dough rise again in a warm place, away from drafts, until doubled in bulk, for 30 to 40 minutes. Bake in the preheated hot oven (400°) for 25 minutes.

Whole Wheat Variation: Combine 1 cup of all-purpose flour with 2½ cups of whole wheat flour and substitute this mixture for the 3½ cups of all-purpose flour in Step 1 on the opposite page: Continue with the recipe.

Cheddar Cheese Variation: After punching down the dough in Step 6 on the opposite page, knead in ¾ cup of shredded Cheddar cheese. Continue with the recipe.

BAKED POTATO WITH DILLED YOGURT

By using lowfat or nonfat yogurt in place of sour cream as a potato topping, you get great taste but almost no fat or cholesterol.

Bake at 375° for 45 minutes.

Makes 1 serving.

1   medium-size baking potato
¼   cup plain lowfat yogurt
2   tablespoons chopped tomato

Nutrient Value Per Serving:
211 calories, 8 g protein, 1 g fat,
43 g carbohydrate, 61 mg sodium,
3 mg cholesterol.

1½ tablespoons chopped fresh
    dill
    Cracked black pepper

1. Preheat the oven to moderate (375°).
2. Bake the potato in the preheated moderate oven (375°) for 45 minutes or until it is soft.
3. Meanwhile, combine the yogurt, tomato and 1 tablespoon of the dill in a small bowl.

4. Slit the potato and top with the yogurt mixture. Sprinkle with the black pepper and the remaining dill.

HEALTH

Fuel to Burn

Before a workout, you should eat a high-carbohydrate snack or a very little bit of lean protein; avoid fats and sugars. Portions should be small, just enough to give your body a little fuel. Some examples of smart snacks:
—Small whole wheat, oat or corn waffle (go easy on eggs and oil)
—Banana or other piece of fruit
—Toast spread with a smear of lowfat cottage cheese
—Half a whole wheat bagel
—Tiny piece of chicken or tofu
—Small amount of lowfat yogurt or yogurt drink
—Yogurt dip and crudités
—Small blender shake made with banana or other fruit and juice or skim milk
—Small handful of homemade granola
—Small homemade granola bar
—Whole-grain or corn muffin

HOTLINE

FRUIT POCKETS

A refreshing snack, deliciously different breakfast dish or perfect picnic fare. Fill the pockets just before serving so they don't become soggy.

Makes 4 sandwiches.

Nutrient Value Per Serving:
181 calories, 5 g protein, 1 g fat, 40 g carbohydrate, 205 mg sodium, 1 mg cholesterol.

3½ cups mixed fruits chunks, such as watermelon cubes, banana slices and papaya cubes
½ cup plain nonfat yogurt

2 tablespoons shredded fresh coconut (optional)
2 large pita breads, halved OR: 4 small pita breads

Combine the fruit, yogurt and, if you wish, coconut in a medium-size bowl. Fill the pita pockets with the fruit mixture.

HEALTH

Replenish Your Resources

After a workout, drink plenty of fluids and eat a high-carbohydrate snack within an hour; portions should be larger than before exercising. If you eat a green salad, which is mostly water, supplement it with carbohydrates or a bit of lean protein. Good choices after exercising:
— Rice-stuffed grape leaves
— Taboulleh with chicken
— Couscous salad
— Devilled eggs (occasionally)
— Baked potato with yogurt
— Whole grain cereal and skim milk
— Bagel with a bit of margarine and low-sugar jam
— Salad with pasta or potatoes
— Chicken or fish
— Any cooked cereal
— Homemade granola bar
— Whole-grain bread
— A piece of any type of fruit
— Nuts and dried fruit
— Tofu salad
To quench your thirst after exercising and to begin replenishing fluids, drink water or fruit juice (or a combination of the two) within an hour of your workout. Try one of the many flavored or unflavored seltzers or mineral waters on the market. Don't drink alcohol or coffee — they tend to dehydrate you.

HOTLINE

RASPBERRY BANANA SMOOTHIE

A heavenly concoction for a hot afternoon — or anytime you need a little lift!

Makes 1 serving.

Nutrient Value Per Serving:
232 calories, 12 g protein, 3 g fat,
41 g carbohydrate, 152 mg sodium,
11 mg cholesterol.

¾ **cup plain lowfat yogurt**
¼ **cup skim milk**
1 **small ripe banana, cut**
   into chunks

⅓ **cup fresh raspberries**
3 **ice cubes**
1 **teaspoon sugar, honey or**
   maple syrup (optional)

Combine the yogurt, milk, banana, raspberries, ice cubes and, if you wish, sugar, honey or maple syrup in the container of an electric blender. Cover and whirl until the mixture is smooth and thick. Pour the smoothie into a glass.

HEALTH

Go Bananas!
Bananas are a rich source of potassium, a mineral crucial to the normal functioning of muscles, including the heart. Bananas are also a good source of thiamin, riboflavin, niacin and vitamins A and C.

HOTLINE

PAPAYA COOLER

Tempt your tastebuds with this tropical elixir—it's only a blender-whirl away!

Makes 2 servings.

Nutrient Value Per Serving:
151 calories, 5 g protein, 2 g fat,
31 g carbohydrate, 100 mg sodium,
7 mg cholesterol.

1 **very ripe papaya, peeled and cut into chunks**
½ **cup lowfat buttermilk**
½ **cup lowfat milk**
 Juice of 1 lime

1 **tablespoon honey**
¼ **teaspoon ground cinnamon**
3 **ice cubes**

Place the papaya, buttermilk, milk, lime juice, honey, cinnamon and ice cubes in the container of an electric blender. Cover and whirl until the mixture is smooth. Pour the cooler into 2 glasses.

PEACHY ORANGE BUTTERMILK

Buttermilk is low in calories and has a pleasant tartness. Its slightly thick consistency adds a smooth texture to blended drinks.

Makes 2 servings.

Nutrient Value Per Serving:
142 calories, 5 g protein, 1 g fat,
29 g carbohydrate, 130 mg sodium,
5 mg cholesterol.

1 **cup cold buttermilk**
1 **cup peeled and sliced peaches***
¼ **cup frozen orange juice concentrate**

Combine the buttermilk, peaches and orange juice concentrate in the container of an electric blender. Cover and whirl until the mixture is smooth and frothy. Serve in chilled glasses, if you wish.

***Note:** Peeled and sliced nectarines or mangos may be substituted for the peaches in this recipe.*

4

THE SALAD BAR

Gone are the days when a "salad" was iceberg lettuce with a tomato and some cucumber. From curly endive to peppery watercress, marinated chicken to lean beef, a salad is what you make it: side dish, main dish or snack.

When it comes to green cuisine, take advantage of the variety in the markets by trying salads such as Mâche and Bibb Lettuce with Balsamic Vinaigrette *(recipe, page 53)* and Arugula with Mustard Lemon Dressing *(recipe, page 55)*.

While there's nothing new about chicken salad, there's a lot to report on headliners such as Tropical Chicken Salad with Raspberry Dressing *(recipe, page 61)* or tasty Sesame Turkey Salad *(recipe, page 65)*. Even beef and lamb are on the salad circuit: Mexican Beef and Olive Salad *(recipe, page 70)* and Lamb and Mango Salad *(recipe, page 71)*.

And now, a quick salad quiz: What has no cholesterol, no fat and contains enough protein to make your salad hearty enough for a main dish? The answer: Beans. Try our Black Bean Salad *(recipe, page 76)* for a low-calorie, tangy treat. Bulgur Salad Primavera *(recipe, page 77)* mixes whole-grain bulgur, tomatoes, currants, sunflower seeds, carrots and assorted fresh herbs. And for a stick-to-your-ribs dish that's low in fat, calories, sodium and cholesterol, nothing beats Lentil, Pea and Corn Salad *(recipe, page 79)*.

"Dressing for success" takes on new meaning with our selection of salad dressings. Try our step-by-step Classic Vinaigrette *(recipe, pages 82-83)*, or flavored vinegars, such as Tarragon Vinegar *(recipe, page 84)* or Mint Vinegar *(recipe, page 85)*.

Now *that's* dressing with style!

Strawberry Soup (recipe, page 28), Corn and Pepper Salad (recipe, page 74), Mexican Turkey Salad (recipe, page 62), Mexican Beef and Olive Salad (recipe, page 70)

51

GREEN SALADS

*Mâche and Bibb Lettuce with
Balsamic Vinaigrette (recipe, page 53)*

MÂCHE AND BIBB LETTUCE WITH BALSAMIC VINAIGRETTE

Mâche and Bibb lettuce have a very delicate flavor, so drizzle each salad with a very small amount of the vinaigrette. Serve this salad on special occasions, because mâche is very expensive.

Makes 6 servings.

Nutrient Value Per Serving:
146 calories, 2 g protein, 13 g fat,
7 g carbohydrate, 517 mg sodium,
0 mg cholesterol.

4 **cups loosely packed mâche (about ¼ pound)**
3 **heads Bibb lettuce**
4 **sun-dried tomatoes, packed in oil**
1 **green onion, white part only**

Balsamic Vinaigrette:
1 **tablespoon balsamic vinegar**
¼ **teaspoon salt**
⅛ **teaspoon freshly ground pepper**
1 **tablespoon plus 1½ teaspoons olive oil**
1 **tablespoon plus 1½ teaspoons vegetable oil**

1. Remove and discard any clumps of dirt or roots from the mâche. Gently rinse the mâche in several changes of cold water. Dry in a salad spinner, or gently blot dry with paper toweling, and set aside.
2. Remove and discard any bruised or blemished leaves from the Bibb lettuce. Remove the remaining leaves from the head and wash them in several changes of cold water. Dry the leaves in a salad spinner, or blot dry with paper toweling (you should have about 8 cups of leaves), and set aside.
3. Cut the tomatoes into very thin slices and set aside.
4. Cut the white part of the green onion lengthwise into very thin strips and set aside.
5. Prepare the Balsamic Vinaigrette: Combine the vinegar, salt, pepper and the olive and vegetable oils in a small screw-top jar. Cover the jar and shake until the vinaigrette is well blended. Set aside.

6. Arrange the mâche and the lettuce on 6 individual salad plates. Scatter the tomato and the green onion over the greens, dividing equally. Using a spoon, drizzle each salad with a very small amount of the vinaigrette, and serve.

Main Dish Salad With Goat Cheese:
Cut 8 ounces of goat cheese into thin slices. Drizzle the greens with the vinaigrette. Arrange the slices of goat cheese on top of the greens, then scatter each salad with the tomato and the green onion. Serve the salads with melba toast rounds, flat bread or crusty Italian bread.
Makes 4 servings.
Nutrient Value Per Serving:
174 calories, 4 g protein, 15 g fat,
7 g carbohydrate, 611 mg sodium,
0 mg cholesterol.

ENDIVE AND LETTUCE WITH CUMIN VINAIGRETTE

A delightful combination of tastes: pleasantly bitter Belgian endive, buttery Boston lettuce and an aromatic cumin dressing.

Makes 6 servings.

Nutrient Value Per Serving:
295 calories, 1 g protein, 31 g fat,
5 g carbohydrate, 193 mg sodium,
0 mg cholesterol.

1   head Boston lettuce
2   heads Belgian endive
      OR: 1 large bunch watercress
4   radishes
1   small avocado
1   tablespoon lime juice

Cumin Vinaigrette:
4   tablespoons lime juice
1   teaspoon ground cumin
½   teaspoon salt
¼   teaspoon freshly ground white
      pepper
¼   cup olive oil
2   tablespoons vegetable oil
½   teaspoon grated lime rind

1. Remove and discard any discolored or bruised leaves from the lettuce. Remove the remaining leaves from the head and wash them in several changes of cold water. Dry the leaves in a salad spinner, or blot dry with paper toweling (you should have about 8 cups), and set aside.
2. If using the endive, cut off the core end and remove the leaves. If using the watercress, remove and discard any blemished leaves and tough stems. Rinse the endive or watercress leaves in cold water. Dry the leaves in a salad spinner, or blot dry with paper toweling, and set aside.
3. Cut the radishes into thin slices and set aside.
4. Halve the avocado and remove the pit. Cut each half lengthwise into quarters and remove the skin. Cut each piece diagonally into small slivers. Toss the avocado with the 1 tablespoon of lime juice in a small bowl and set aside.
5. Prepare the Cumin Vinaigrette: Combine the lime juice, cumin, salt, white pepper, olive and vegetable oils and the lime rind in a small screw-top jar. Cover the jar and shake until all the ingredients are well blended.

6. On each of 6 individual salad plates, arrange the endive spears, if using, in a star pattern, with the core ends meeting in the center of the plate. Arrange the Boston lettuce leaves in a circular pattern on top of the endive. Top with the watercress, if using the watercress instead of the endive. Arrange the radish slices and the avocado pieces on top. Drizzle each salad with a little of the vinaigrette.

Main Dish Salad With Scallops:
Marinate 12 to 16 ounces of cooked scallops in the Cumin Vinaigrette for 30 minutes. (If using large sea scallops, slice the scallops in half horizontally.) Drain the scallops from the vinaigrette, reserving the vinaigrette. Arrange the scallops over the tops of the salads. Drizzle each salad with some of the reserved vinaigrette.
Makes 6 servings.
Nutrient Value Per Serving:
361 calories, 14 g protein, 32 g fat,
7 g carbohydrate, 315 mg sodium,
25 mg cholesterol.

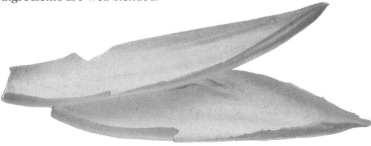

CookSmart

Keeping Greens in the Pink

● For the freshest flavor, use greens the day you purchase them.
● To store for a day or two, wrap whole heads of greens in plastic bags or paper toweling and refrigerate. With more tender mâche or arugula, wrap dampened paper toweling around the roots. Place watercress stems in a glass of water and wrap the leaves.

ARUGULA WITH MUSTARD LEMON DRESSING

LOW-SODIUM
LOW-CHOLESTEROL

The mustard lemon dressing is zesty enough to stand up to arugula's peppery taste.

Makes 4 servings.

Nutrient Value Per Serving:
145 calories, 3 g protein, 14 g fat,
4 g carbohydrate, 53 mg sodium,
0 mg cholesterol.

1   **pound arugula leaves,
     stems removed**
½   **cup lemon juice**
2   **cloves garlic, crushed**

1   **teaspoon dry mustard seeds**
¼   **cup good-quality olive oil**
    **Salt and freshly ground black
     pepper, to taste**

1. Wash the green arugula leaves very carefully in several changes of cold water, because arugula is very sandy. Dry the leaves in a salad spinner, or blot dry with paper toweling, and put them in a large salad bowl.
2. In a small bowl, whisk together the lemon juice, garlic and mustard seeds. Whisk in the oil until it is well blended. Season with the salt and black pepper.

3. Toss the arugula with the dressing in the salad bowl and serve.

WATERCRESS SALAD

LOW-CALORIE
LOW-SODIUM
LOW-CHOLESTEROL

To keep the watercress crisp, don't add the dressing until just before you are ready to serve.

Makes 4 servings.

Nutrient Value Per Serving:
74 calories, 2 g protein, 7 g fat,
2 g carbohydrate, 75 mg sodium,
0 mg cholesterol.

2   **bunches watercress**
3   **tablespoons lemon juice**
1   **clove garlic, crushed**

1   **teaspoon Dijon-style mustard**
2   **tablespoons olive oil**
    **Salt and freshly ground pepper,
     to taste**

1. Remove and discard any blemished or yellow leaves and tough stems from the watercress. Rinse the watercress leaves in cold water. Dry them in a salad spinner or blot dry with paper toweling. Break the leaves into pieces and refrigerate them until serving time.
2. For the dressing, whisk together the lemon juice, garlic and mustard in a small bowl. Add the oil, whisking to blend thoroughly. Season with the salt and pepper. Let the dressing stand for 30 minutes. Remove and discard the garlic. Toss the watercress with the dressing just before serving.

ARUGULA AND RED LEAF LETTUCE WITH RASPBERRY VINAIGRETTE

The bright green arugula leaves and the red leaf lettuce make this salad as colorful as it is delicious.

Makes 4 servings.

Nutrient Value Per Serving:
194 calories, 6 g protein, 14 g fat,
14 g carbohydrate, 202 mg sodium,
0 mg cholesterol.

2   bunches arugula
1   small head red leaf lettuce
1   head Bibb lettuce
1   medium-size sweet red
        pepper

Raspberry Vinaigrette:
¼   cup raspberry vinegar
¼   cup vegetable oil
¼   teaspoon salt
⅛   teaspoon freshly ground pepper

1   cup frozen lima beans, cooked
        according to package
        directions

1. Tear the tender green arugula leaves from the stems. Wash the leaves very carefully in several changes of cold water, because arugula is very sandy. Dry the leaves in a salad spinner, or blot dry with paper toweling (you should have about 5 cups of leaves), and set aside.

2. Remove and discard any discolored or bruised leaves from the red leaf lettuce. Remove the remaining leaves from the head and wash them in several changes of cold water. Dry the leaves in a salad spinner, or blot dry with paper toweling (you should have about 3 cups of leaves), and set aside.

3. Remove the leaves from the Bibb lettuce head and wash them in several changes of cold water. Dry the leaves in a salad spinner, or blot dry with paper toweling (you should have about 4 cups), and set aside.

4. Halve the red pepper lengthwise, core and seed it. Cut each red pepper half crosswise into halves. Cut each piece into thin slivers and set aside.

5. Prepare the Raspberry Vinaigrette: Combine the vinegar, oil, salt and pepper in a screw-top jar. Cover the jar and shake until the vinaigrette is well mixed.

6. Tear the greens into bite-size pieces and place them in a large salad bowl. Drizzle the greens with ¼ cup of the vinaigrette and toss to coat the greens with the vinaigrette. Arrange the red pepper slivers and the lima beans over the top. Pass the remaining vinaigrette with the salad.

Main Dish Salad With Pork: Cut 12 ounces of cooked pork (broiled thin loin pork chops work well) into thin pieces about ¾ x ¼ inch. Marinate the pork in the vinaigrette for about 30 minutes. Drain the pork, reserving the vinaigrette. Dress the salad as in Step 6 above. Arrange the meat on top of the salad.
Makes 4 servings.
Nutrient Value Per Serving:
424 calories, 38 g protein, 25 g fat,
14 g carbohydrate, 279 mg sodium,
97 mg cholesterol.

CookSmart

A-Cleanin' of the Greens

● To clean greens, discard any bruised, discolored or tough outer leaves. Remove the remaining leaves from the head, trim any tough core or rib, and wash the leaves gently in a sink or large bowl filled with water. Drain the leaves and rinse. (If the leaves are very sandy, wash them in several changes of water.)

● Dry the washed greens in a salad spinner or gently blot dry with paper toweling.

RADICCHIO AND ESCAROLE WITH TAMARI VINAIGRETTE

LOW-CHOLESTEROL

Radicchio has a small, firm head with ruby red leaves and a slightly bitter taste similar to endive — just a little can do a lot for your salad.

Makes 6 servings.

Nutrient Value Per Serving:
165 calories, 2 g protein, 16 g fat, 4 g carbohydrate, 157 mg sodium, 0 mg cholesterol.

¼ **pound snow peas**
1 **small head Boston lettuce**
¼ **head escarole**
1 **head radicchio**

Tamari Vinaigrette:
¼ **cup rice vinegar**
1 **teaspoon tamari soy sauce***
1 **teaspoon lemon juice**
½ **teaspoon freshly ground pepper**
6 **tablespoons vegetable oil**
2 **tablespoons olive oil**
½ **teaspoon Oriental sesame oil****
¼ **teaspoon salt**

1. String the snow peas and steam them just until they have lost their raw taste, for about 2 minutes. Rinse the snow peas in a colander under cold running water to stop the cooking. Blot them dry with paper toweling and set aside.
2. Remove and discard any bruised or blemished outer leaves from the Boston lettuce. Remove the remaining leaves from the head and wash them in several changes of cold water. Dry the leaves in a salad spinner or blot dry with paper toweling. Tear the leaves into bite-size pieces (you should have about 6 cups of leaves), and set aside.
3. Remove and discard any bruised or blemished outer leaves from the escarole. Remove the remaining leaves from the head and wash them in several changes of cold water. Dry the leaves in a salad spinner or blot dry with paper toweling. Tear the leaves into bite-size pieces (you should have about 2 cups of leaves), and set aside.
4. Remove and discard any bruised or blemished outer leaves from the radicchio. Remove the remaining whole leaves and wash them in several changes of cold water. Dry the leaves in a salad spinner, or blot dry with paper toweling (you should have about 4 cups of leaves), and set aside.
5. Prepare the Tamari Vinaigrette: Combine the vinegar, tamari soy sauce, lemon juice, pepper, vegetable and olive oils, Oriental sesame oil and the salt in a small screw-top jar. Cover the jar and shake until the dressing is well blended.

6. Toss the Boston and escarole pieces and the snow peas separately with some of the vinaigrette.
7. Arrange the radicchio leaves over half of each of 6 individual salad plates, with the stem ends toward the center of the plate and the leaves forming a basket. Place the Boston and escarole pieces on the radicchio leaves. Arrange the snow peas around the greens. Pass the remaining dressing.

*Note: *Tamari soy sauce contains less sodium than regular soy sauce.*
**Note: *Oriental sesame oil is richer in flavor and darker than regular sesame oil. It can be found in the Oriental food section of many supermarkets or in specialty food stores.*

Main Dish Salad With Chicken: Cut 12 ounces of cooked chicken meat into long thin pieces or shreds. Marinate the chicken in the Tamari Vinaigrette for 15 to 20 minutes, if you wish, then drain and reserve the vinaigrette. Arrange the chicken over the greens with the snow peas. Drizzle each salad with some of the reserved vinaigrette.
Makes 6 servings.
Nutrient Value Per Serving:
273 calories, 16 g protein, 20 g fat, 6 g carbohydrate, 205 mg sodium, 51 mg cholesterol.

WATERCRESS AND ENDIVE WITH GINGER VINAIGRETTE

This peppery salad is the perfect accompaniment to any stir-fried main dish.

Makes 4 servings.

Nutrient Value Per Serving:
250 calories, 2 g protein, 24 g fat,
8 g carbohydrate, 239 mg sodium,
0 mg cholesterol.

Ginger Vinaigrette:
2   tablespoons rice vinegar
2   tablespoons lemon juice
2   teaspoons Dijon-style mustard
1   teaspoon ground ginger
¼   teaspoon salt
¼   teaspoon freshly ground pepper
5   tablespoons vegetable oil
2   tablespoons olive oil

1   large bunch watercress
½   cucumber (halved crosswise)
1   navel orange
1   head Belgian endive
        OR: 2 bunches arugula
4   to 5 slices red onion,
        separated into rings

1. Prepare the Ginger Vinaigrette: Combine the vinegar, lemon juice, mustard, ginger, salt, pepper and the vegetable and olive oils in a screw-top jar. Cover the jar and shake until the ingredients are well mixed. Set aside.
2. Remove and discard any blemished or yellow leaves and tough stems from the watercress. Rinse the watercress leaves in cold water. Dry them in a salad spinner, or blot dry with paper toweling (you should have about 6 cups of leaves), and set aside.
3. Peel the half cucumber, halve it lengthwise and remove the seeds. Cut the cucumber quarters crosswise into thin slices and set aside.
4. Cut the peel, including the white pith, from the orange. Cut the orange crosswise into thin slices and cut each slice in half. Set aside.
5. If using the endive, cut off the core and cut the endive diagonally into thin slices (you should have about 2 cups). If using the arugula, tear the green leaves from the stems and wash them very carefully in several changes of cold water. Dry the leaves in a salad spinner, or blot dry with paper toweling, and set aside.

6. Place the watercress on 4 individual salad plates. Arrange the orange slices and the cucumber over the watercress. Scatter the onion rings over the top and arrange the endive or arugula around the edge of each salad. Drizzle the vinaigrette over the salads and serve.

Main Dish Salad With Shrimp:
Arrange 12 ounces of cold, cooked, shelled and deveined medium-size to large shrimp over or around the salads. *Makes 4 servings.*
Nutrient Value Per Serving:
347 calories, 23 g protein, 25 g fat,
9 g carbohydrate, 453 mg sodium,
193 mg cholesterol.

CookSmart

Secrets of Salad Success

● If you wish to store washed salad greens for an hour or two before using, layer the leaves with paper toweling in a plastic bag and refrigerate them.
● Most large greens should be torn — not cut — into bite-size pieces. Romaine and Belgian endive, on the other hand, can be cut crosswise into thin slices.
● For a well-dressed salad, toss the greens in a large bowl with a small amount of the dressing so the leaves are just lightly coated. Add more dressing, if you wish, but not so much that an excess gathers in the bottom of the bowl.
● Separately dress the heavier ingredients that could sink to the bottom of the bowl, such as radishes and cucumbers, and arrange them on top of the salad.
● If the salad already is arranged, drizzle it with a little dressing, gently toss the ingredients and pass the remaining dressing for each person to add.
● To keep the salad from getting soggy, add the dressing just before serving.
● Choosing a salad bowl: Glass bowls show off the colors of a salad. A ceramic or wooden bowl adds an earthy touch and brightly colored plastic is an attractive choice for a picnic or patio meal.

ROMAINE AND CURLY ENDIVE WITH MUSTARD ANCHOVY VINAIGRETTE

Distinctive and tangy, this salad combines some of the best ingredients from the Mediterranean. Try serving it with a glass of dry red wine.

Makes 6 servings.

Nutrient Value Per Serving:
291 calories, 6 g protein, 26 g fat,
10 g carbohydrate, 438 mg sodium,
7 mg cholesterol.

Mustard Anchovy Vinaigrette:
4   **canned anchovy fillets, chopped**
¼   **cup olive oil**
2   **tablespoons vegetable oil**
2   **tablespoons Dijon-style mustard**
3   **tablespoons red wine vinegar**

Garlic Croutons:
2   **slices day-old white bread**
¼   **cup olive oil**
1   **clove garlic, crushed**
1   **small head romaine lettuce**
1   **small head curly endive**
½   **cup grated Parmesan cheese**
6   **radishes, halved and thinly sliced (½ cup sliced)**

1. Prepare the Mustard Anchovy Vinaigrette: Combine the anchovy fillets with the olive and vegetable oils in a small saucepan. Heat the mixture over low heat, stirring with a wooden spoon to mash the anchovy and thoroughly incorporate it into the oil. Whisk in the mustard and the vinegar*. Remove the vinaigrette from the heat and set aside.
2. Prepare the Garlic Croutons: Remove the crusts from the bread and cut the bread into small cubes. Heat together the oil and the garlic in a medium-size skillet over medium-high heat. When the oil is hot, remove and discard the garlic. Add the bread cubes and toss until the cubes are toasted, for 3 to 4 minutes. Remove the skillet from the heat and set aside.
3. Remove and discard any bruised or discolored outer leaves from the romaine. Remove the remaining leaves from the head and wash them in several changes of cold water. Dry the leaves in a salad spinner or blot dry with paper toweling. Cut the leaves crosswise into ½-inch-wide strips (you should have about 6 cups of leaves), and set aside.
4. Remove and discard any bruised or discolored outer leaves from the endive. Remove the remaining leaves from the head and wash them in several changes of cold water. Dry the leaves in a salad spinner or blot dry with paper toweling. Tear the leaves into bite-size pieces (you should have about 6 cups of leaves).

5. Combine the greens with the Parmesan cheese in a large bowl.
6. Arrange the greens on 6 individual salad plates. Scatter the radish slices and the croutons over the greens, dividing equally. Drizzle the salads with the vinaigrette and serve.

*Note: *For a smoother dressing, mix together the dressing ingredients in a food processor or electric blender.*

Main Dish Salad With Tuna And Hard-Cooked Eggs: Drain a 6½-ounce can of water-packed tuna and flake or break the tuna into chunks. Cut 2 peeled hard-cooked eggs lengthwise into halves or smaller wedges. Arrange the eggs and the tuna on top of the salads. Drizzle the salads with the vinaigrette.
Makes 6 servings.
Nutrient Value Per Serving:
400 calories, 14 g protein, 34 g fat,
9 g carbohydrate, 524 mg sodium,
19 mg cholesterol.

MEAT
SALADS

Tropical Chicken Salad with
Raspberry Vinegar Dressing (recipe, page 61)

TROPICAL CHICKEN SALAD WITH RASPBERRY DRESSING

LOW-CALORIE
LOW-SODIUM
LOW-CHOLESTEROL

The dressing can be prepared in advance, but don't mix the salad ingredients until just before serving—the enzyme in papaya breaks down the fiber in chicken and makes it very soft.

Makes 6 servings.

Nutrient Value Per Serving:
248 calories, 13 g protein, 16 g fat, 16 g carbohydrate, 128 mg sodium, 32 mg cholesterol.

Raspberry Dressing:
7   teaspoons raspberry vinegar
10   teaspoons olive oil
1   teaspoon Oriental sesame oil*
1   teaspoon honey
¼   teaspoon salt
⅛   teaspoon liquid red pepper
      seasoning

Tropical Chicken Salad:
⅓   cup thinly sliced red onion
7   cups torn assorted salad greens,
      rinsed and dried
2   cups diced cooked chicken
      breast meat (about 12 ounces;
      from 2 whole breasts)
1½   cups bite-size mango pieces
1½   cups bite-size papaya pieces
⅓   cup pecan halves, toasted and
      sliced in half

1. Prepare the Raspberry Dressing: Whisk together the vinegar, olive and Oriental sesame oils, honey, salt and liquid red pepper seasoning in a small bowl until all the ingredients are well blended. Set aside.
2. Prepare the Tropical Chicken Salad: Place the onion slices in a bowl with cold water to cover and let them stand for 30 minutes. Drain the slices and pat them dry with paper toweling.
3. Place the greens, chicken, mango, papaya, onion and pecans in a large salad bowl. Pour the dressing over and toss to coat all the ingredients. Serve the salad immediately.

*Note: *Oriental sesame oil is richer in flavor and darker than regular sesame oil. It can be found in the Oriental food section of many supermarkets or in specialty food stores.*

SMOKED CHICKEN AND PEACH SALAD

Smoked chicken, available in many supermarkets, requires no additional cooking so this salad is a breeze to prepare.

Makes 4 servings.

Nutrient Value Per Serving:
207 calories, 25 g protein, 8 g fat,
12 g carbohydrate, 1,000 mg sodium,
35 mg cholesterol.

1 smoked chicken
   (about 1½ pounds)
24 radishes
2 ripe peaches
½ cup fresh mint leaves
   OR: 2 tablespoons leaf
   mint, crumbled

4 cups assorted lettuce greens,
   rinsed and patted dry
¼ cup Fresh Lemon Dressing
   (recipe, page 88)

1. Trim and discard the skin and fat from the chicken. Bone and shred the chicken meat and place it in a large salad bowl.

2. Wash, trim and thinly slice the radishes, and add them to the bowl. Halve and stone the peaches, and slice them into the bowl. Add the mint. Tear the lettuce into bite-size pieces and add it to the bowl. Very gently toss all the ingredients.

3. Add the Fresh Lemon Dressing to the bowl and toss very gently to combine all the ingredients.

MEXICAN TURKEY SALAD

Fragrant cumin, a primary ingredient in chili powder, flavors this salad. Jícama adds crunch.

Makes 8 servings.

Nutrient Value Per Serving:
147 calories, 17 g protein, 6 g fat,
6 g carbohydrate, 64 mg sodium,
44 mg cholesterol.

1¼ pounds boneless turkey
   breast
1 tablespoon cumin
2 teaspoons safflower oil
½ cup cider vinegar
   Grated zest (orange part of
   rind only) and juice
   of 1 orange

2 tablespoons safflower oil
1 cup diced celery
¼ cup finely chopped fresh
   cilantro OR: parsley
1 cup julienne-cut jícama
1 large red onion, diced

1. Cube the turkey and toss it with the cumin in a small bowl.

2. Sauté the turkey in the 2 teaspoons of oil in a large nonstick skillet over medium-high heat just until the meat is cooked through, for 4 to 6 minutes.

3. While the meat still is warm, toss it with the vinegar, the orange zest and juice and the 2 tablespoons of oil in a medium-size bowl. Let the mixture cool to room temperature.

4. Add the celery, cilantro or parsley, jícama and onion to the turkey mixture. Toss gently to combine all the ingredients. Cover the salad and refrigerate until serving time.

CHINESE CHICKEN SALAD

Jump aboard the Orient Express with this crunchy chicken salad. Remember that cellophane noodles expand 8 to 10 times in size during frying.

Makes 8 servings.

Nutrient Value Per Serving:
267 calories, 17 g protein, 18 g fat,
9 g carbohydrate, 320 mg sodium,
47 mg cholesterol.

Vegetable oil for frying
1½ ounces uncooked cellophane noodles, broken into 4-inch lengths
2 cups finely shredded romaine OR: leaf lettuce
4 cups shredded Chinese cabbage
4 stalks celery, diagonally sliced
3 green onions, finely chopped Freshly ground black pepper, to taste

3 cups cooked chicken chunks

Soy Vinaigrette:
1 large clove garlic, finely chopped
⅓ cup vegetable oil
2 teaspoons Oriental sesame oil*
2 tablespoons soy sauce
3 tablespoons cider vinegar
2 tablespoons water
½ teaspoon sugar

2 tablespoons sesame seeds

1. Pour the oil into a deep saucepan to a depth of 3 inches and heat it to 350° on a deep-fat frying thermometer. Add half the noodles all at once and fry for 30 seconds, turning once. Immediately remove the noodles with a slotted spatula to drain on paper toweling. Repeat with the remaining noodles.
2. Combine the lettuce, cabbage, celery and green onion in a large bowl. Season with the black pepper. Place the chicken in a medium-size bowl.
3. Prepare the Soy Vinaigrette: Whisk together the garlic, vegetable and Oriental sesame oils, soy sauce, vinegar, water and sugar in a small bowl. Add half the vinaigrette to the chicken and half to the lettuce mixture. Toss each mixture to combine its ingredients.

4. Layer the lettuce mixture, the noodles and the chicken on 8 individual salad plates. Sprinkle the salads with the sesame seeds, dividing equally.

__Note:__ Oriental sesame oil is richer in flavor and darker than regular sesame oil. It can be found in the Oriental food section of many supermarkets or in specialty food stores.

GAZPACHO SALAD WITH HAM AND CHEESE

With the addition of ham and cheese, the ingredients of a classic Spanish cold soup are turned into a colorful main dish salad.

Makes 10 servings.

Nutrient Value Per Serving:
318 calories, 14 g protein, 16 g fat,
30 g carbohydrate, 578 mg sodium,
33 mg cholesterol.

3⅓ cups water
1½ cups long-grain converted
    white rice
½ teaspoon salt
1 cup thinly sliced green onion
½ cup chopped parsley
½ teaspoon freshly ground pepper
1 large clove garlic
1 teaspoon sugar
¾ teaspoon leaf thyme,
    crumbled
¼ cup dry white wine
¼ cup white wine vinegar
    OR: cider vinegar
¼ cup olive oil

1 pound ripe tomatoes, halved,
    seeded and chopped
2 large cucumbers, peeled,
    halved, seeded and sliced
    ¼ inch thick
1 large sweet green pepper,
    cored, seeded and cut into
    ½-inch squares
¼ cup sliced almonds
1 tablespoon butter
8 ounces thinly sliced smoked
    ham
8 ounces thinly sliced
    Monterey Jack cheese

1. Heat the water to boiling in a medium-size saucepan over high heat. Stir in the rice and the salt and return the water to boiling. Reduce the heat to low. Cover the saucepan and cook for 20 minutes or until the rice is tender. Turn the rice into a large bowl and toss with the green onion, parsley and pepper.

2. Put the garlic through a garlic press, or finely chop the garlic with a knife, and place it in a medium-size bowl. Mash the garlic with a pinch of salt. Stir in the sugar, thyme, wine, white wine or cider vinegar and oil. Add the tomatoes and toss to coat. Stir the tomato mixture into the rice mixture, along with the cucumbers and the green pepper, until well mixed. Refrigerate the salad, covered, for at least 1 hour or overnight.
3. Sauté the almonds in the butter in a small skillet until golden. Set the almonds aside.
4. Spread the chilled rice mixture on a large platter. Arrange the ham and the Monterey Jack cheese on top. Scatter the almonds over the top just before serving.

SESAME TURKEY SALAD

*Look for dark sesame oil wherever Oriental food products are sold;
even a few drops impart a rich, nutty flavor.*

Makes 4 servings.

Nutrient Value Per Serving:
168 calories, 24 g protein, 3 g fat,
13 g carbohydrate, 375 mg sodium,
53 mg cholesterol.

HEALTH

Pumping Iron Intake

Although red meats remain the single best source of iron, eating any meat protein, including chicken and fish, especially in combination with other iron-rich foods, allows the small intestine to absorb iron more efficiently. For example, it was found that eating as little as one ounce of meat with rice, beans or other iron-containing foods can significantly increase iron absorption — by as much as 71%, according to animal studies.

HOTLINE

2 large carrots, trimmed
   and peeled
2 large cucumbers, peeled,
   halved and seeded
1 large sweet red pepper
¾ pound turkey breast
   OR: turkey tenderloin,
   poached and shredded

   Sesame Vinaigrette
   (recipe, page 81)
2 bunches watercress, rinsed
   and patted dry
2 tablespoons dry-roasted
   peanuts, for garnish
1 tablespoon toasted sesame
   seeds, for garnish*

1. Shave strips off the carrots, applying heavy pressure with a swivel-bladed vegetable peeler. Curl up the strips and drop them into a large bowl of ice and water. (The carrot curls can be made in advance and refrigerated until needed.)
2. Slice each cucumber half on the diagonal into ⅓-inch-thick crescents. Cut the red pepper in half and remove the seeds and ribs. Cut the pepper halves into small triangles.
3. Combine the turkey with the cucumber in a medium-size bowl. Add half the Sesame Vinaigrette and toss gently to coat the ingredients.

4. Combine the carrot curls, watercress and red pepper in a second medium-size bowl. Add the remaining vinaigrette and toss to coat the ingredients.
5. Place the watercress mixture on a serving platter or on 4 individual salad plates. Mound the turkey mixture on top. Garnish the salad with the peanuts and the sesame seeds.

*Note: *To toast sesame seeds, place them in a small, heavy skillet over medium heat and stir constantly until they are golden.*

INDIAN CHICKEN SALAD

Make this exotic salad your passage to India. Marinate the chicken in the refrigerator overnight so the tangy yogurt mixture can permeate the meat.

LOW-FAT
LOW-CALORIE
LOW-CHOLESTEROL

Broil the chicken for 8 minutes.

Makes 6 servings.

Nutrient Value Per Serving (without optional salt):
201 calories, 21 g protein, 6 g fat, 16 g carbohydrate, 193 mg sodium, 52 mg cholesterol.

2   cloves garlic, peeled
2   slices fresh gingerroot, peeled
1½ cups plain nonfat yogurt
3   green onions, trimmed
    Juice of 2 limes
1   teaspoon ground cumin
½ teaspoon ground coriander
½ teaspoon ground turmeric
¼ teaspoon ground hot red pepper
    Salt (optional)

2   whole chicken breasts (¾ pound each), skinned and boned
1   sweet red pepper, halved, seeded and cut into strips
1   cucumber, halved, peeled, seeded and sliced
¼ fresh pineapple, cut into chunks
¼ cup raisins
⅓ cup lowfat mayonnaise
    Lettuce leaves

1. With the food processor running, drop the garlic cloves, then the gingerroot, through the feed tube to chop them. Turn off the food processor. Add the yogurt, green onion, lime juice, cumin, coriander, turmeric, ground hot red pepper and, if you wish, salt. Cover and process until the yogurt mixture is smooth. Reserve and refrigerate ½ cup of the yogurt mixture.

2. Place the chicken breasts in a shallow glass or plastic container. Pour the remaining yogurt mixture over the chicken, tossing to coat the meat all over. Cover the container and refrigerate the chicken overnight.

3. Preheat the broiler.

4. Remove the chicken from the marinade and discard the marinade. Place the chicken on the broiler rack.

5. Broil the chicken 3 inches from the source of the heat for 4 minutes on each side or until the chicken is cooked through but still moist. When the chicken is cool enough to handle, cut it into chunks.

6. Place the chicken, red pepper strips, cucumber slices, pineapple chunks and raisins in a large bowl.

7. Mix together the reserved ½ cup of yogurt mixture and the mayonnaise in a small bowl. Pour the dressing over the chicken and vegetables and toss gently to combine all the ingredients. Refrigerate the salad until serving time.

8. To serve, line 6 individual salad plates with the lettuce leaves. Mound the chicken salad in the center of each plate.

STIR-FRIED CHICKEN SALAD

Tossing the warm marinade with the fresh salad greens adds a special touch to this salad.

Makes 6 servings.

Nutrient Value Per Serving:
243 calories, 20 g protein, 14 g fat, 10 g carbohydrate, 426 mg sodium, 43 mg cholesterol.

Marinade:
- ¼ cup dry white wine
- ¼ cup beer
- 2 tablespoons soy sauce
- 2 teaspoons olive oil
- 2 teaspoons peeled, finely chopped fresh gingerroot
- 1 teaspoon packed brown sugar
- 1 clove garlic, finely chopped
  Freshly ground white pepper, to taste
- 2 whole chicken breasts (¾ pound each), boned and skinned

- 5 tablespoons olive oil
- 1 firm, ripe tomato, peeled, seeded and cut into wedges
- 6 large mushrooms, sliced
- 1 small zucchini, cut into julienne sticks
- 1 stalk celery, cut into julienne sticks
- 1 small carrot, cut into julienne sticks
- ½ cup trimmed snow peas
- 8 cups mixed salad greens

1. Prepare the Marinade: Combine the wine, beer, soy sauce, oil, ginger, brown sugar, garlic and white pepper in a large, self-sealing plastic bag. Add the chicken and turn to coat it. Seal the bag, place it in a bowl and refrigerate it for 2 hours.
2. Remove the chicken and cut it into strips. Place the marinade in a small saucepan and simmer it over low heat.
3. Heat 1 tablespoon of the oil in a large, nonstick skillet over high heat. Add the chicken, tomato, mushrooms, zucchini, celery and carrot. Stir-fry the mixture for 8 minutes. Add the snow peas and stir-fry for 1 minute more.

4. Whisk the remaining 4 tablespoons of oil into the marinade in the saucepan and warm the mixture over low heat. Toss the marinade mixture with the greens in a large salad bowl. Top the wilted greens with the chicken mixture.

CookSmart

Handle With Care: Nonstick Pans

If you treat it properly, an inexpensive, nonstick pan will give you long and devoted service. Use only nylon, rubber or wooden utensils, never metal or anything that will scratch the nonstick surface. Clean the pan with a sponge and soapy water; don't use scouring pads.

BEEF AND CELLOPHANE NOODLE SALAD

Fresh ginger, jalapeño pepper and lots of lemon juice add a pungent note to this hearty salad.

Broil for 10 to 12 minutes.

Makes 8 servings.

Nutrient Value Per Serving:
245 calories, 17 g protein, 11 g fat,
21 g carbohydrate, 442 mg sodium,
44 mg cholesterol.

1½ **pounds flank steak**
1 **cup fresh lemon juice (4 lemons)**
1 **jalapeño pepper, seeded and chopped (wear rubber gloves)**
3 **tablespoons peeled, finely chopped fresh gingerroot**
3 **tablespoons soy sauce***
1 **package (3¾ ounces) cellophane noodles**

½ **pound snow peas, trimmed OR: ½ pound green beans, trimmed**
1 **red onion, thinly sliced**
1 **sweet red or green pepper, halved, seeded and thinly sliced**
2 **ripe tomatoes, sliced**
3 **tablespoons chopped fresh cilantro leaves**

1. Preheat the broiler.
2. Trim all the visible fat from the steak. Broil the steak 3 inches from the source of the heat for 5 to 6 minutes per side or until it is medium-rare.
3. Meanwhile, combine the lemon juice, jalapeño pepper, ginger and soy sauce in a small bowl. Transfer the broiled steak to a shallow container and pour the lemon dressing over the steak. Let stand while preparing the noodles and the vegetables.
4. Soak the noodles in very hot water in a bowl for 15 minutes. Drain well.

5. Meanwhile, cook the snow peas or green beans in a saucepan of boiling water for 1 minute. Drain the peas or beans and quickly plunge them into a large bowl of ice and water to stop the cooking. Let stand for 5 minutes, drain and pat dry.
6. Transfer the steak to a carving board and transfer the lemon dressing to a large bowl. Thinly slice the beef and add it to the dressing with the noodles, onion, red or green pepper, tomatoes and cilantro. Toss gently to combine all the ingredients.
7. To assemble the salad, arrange the snow peas or green beans around the edge of a serving platter or 8 individual salad plates. Top with the beef mixture.

***Note:** To reduce the amount of sodium, use reduced-sodium soy sauce, or a combination of half soy sauce, half water.*

SESAME BEEF AND NOODLE SALAD

The cut of steak for London broil is especially flavorful when marinated overnight.

Broil for 14 to 20 minutes.

Makes 8 servings.

Nutrient Value Per Serving:
225 calories, 22 g protein, 8 g fat, 15 g carbohydrate, 359 mg sodium, 53 mg cholesterol.

1½   **pounds top round for London broil**
3   **cloves garlic, finely chopped**
1   **cup beef broth**
¼   **cup Dijon-style mustard**
1   **tablespoon Oriental sesame oil***
1   **tablespoon honey**
¾   **teaspoon crushed red pepper flakes**
⅛   **teaspoon ground cinnamon**
3   **tablespoons coarse-grained mustard**
1   **package (3 ounces) cellophane noodles**
½   **pound snow peas**
2   **bunches watercress**
1   **tablespoon toasted sesame seeds****

1. Place the meat and the garlic in a large, self-sealing plastic bag.
2. Combine the broth, Dijon mustard, oil, honey, red pepper flakes and cinnamon in a small jar and shake to combine the ingredients. Pour ½ cup of the broth mixture into the bag. Cover and refrigerate the remaining broth mixture. Close the bag tightly and turn it several times to coat the meat all over. Place the bag in a bowl or other container, and refrigerate the meat for 4 hours or overnight.
3. Preheat the broiler. Remove the meat from the marinade, reserving ¼ cup of the marinade. Combine the coarse mustard with the reserved marinade in a cup.
4. Place the meat on the broiler rack and brush with part of the marinade-mustard mixture.
5. Broil the meat for 7 to 10 minutes, brushing once with the marinade. Turn the meat and brush again with the marinade. Broil for 7 to 10 minutes more or until done as you like steak. Remove the steak to a carving board and let rest for 10 minutes. Slice the steak in half lengthwise, then slice each half crosswise on the diagonal.
6. Soak the cellophane noodles in a large bowl of hot water for 10 minutes, following the package directions. Drain the noodles and return them to the bowl. Add cold water to cover the noodles.

7. Trim the snow peas and drop them into a large saucepan of boiling water. Boil for 30 seconds or until the peas are bright green but still crisp. Drain and immediately place the peas under cold running water. Drain the peas well.
8. Remove and discard any blemished or yellow leaves and tough stems from the watercress. Cut the stalks in half. Rinse the watercress in cold water and dry it in a salad spinner, or blot dry with paper toweling.
9. Drain the noodles very well and place them in a bowl or deep serving platter. Top with the watercress, snow peas and sliced steak. Drizzle the remaining broth mixture over the salad. Sprinkle with the sesame seeds and toss to combine all the ingredients.

***Note:** Oriental sesame oil is richer in flavor and darker than regular sesame oil. It can be found in the Oriental food section of many supermarkets or in specialty food stores.*
****Note:** To toast sesame seeds, place them in a small, heavy skillet over medium heat and stir constantly until they are golden.*

CookSmart

Pasta vs Noodle: What's in a Name?

In accordance with U.S. law, anything officially labeled pasta must contain wheat, while anything named noodle must have at least 5 percent egg solids. Nomenclature aside, pastalike products that contain ingredients such as rice, buckwheat or even seaweed are worth exploring. For example, cellophane noodles, made from high-protein mung beans (and used in the Sesame Beef and Noodle Salad on this page), are fast food par excellence: All they need is a brief soak in hot water before they're ready to use.

MEXICAN BEEF AND OLIVE SALAD

The salad should marinate for at least 2 hours. Deli roast beef works very well in this recipe.

Makes 8 servings.

Nutrient Value Per Serving:
171 calories, 17 g protein, 10 g fat,
3 g carbohydrate, 172 mg sodium,
46 mg cholesterol.

1   **pound cooked lean roast beef, cut into julienne sticks**
⅓   **cup pimiento-stuffed olives, sliced**
1   **red onion, cut into rings**
½   **sweet red pepper, seeded and cut into strips**
½   **sweet green pepper, seeded and cut into strips**

1   **teaspoon leaf oregano, crumbled**
3   **tablespoons safflower oil**
    Grated zest (green part of rind only) of 1 lime
    Juice of 3 limes
1   **tablespoon grated onion**

Combine the roast beef, olives, red onion, red and green peppers, oregano, oil, lime zest, lime juice and onion in a large bowl until well blended. Cover the bowl and let the salad marinate in the refrigerator for at least 2 hours.

ITALIAN SALAD

A hearty salad that can be layered ahead, covered with plastic wrap and refrigerated for up to 1 day. Just toss before serving.

Makes 8 servings.

Nutrient Value Per Serving:
221 calories, 12 g protein, 16 g fat
8 g carbohydrate, 272 mg sodium,
34 mg cholesterol.

Creamy Italian Dressing:
1   **clove garlic**
¼   **cup mayonnaise**
½   **cup plain lowfat yogurt**
¼   **cup grated Parmesan cheese**
1   **tablespoon capers, drained**
1   **tablespoon marinade from artichoke hearts (see below)**
½   **teaspoon mixed Italian herbs**

1   **medium-size head romaine lettuce, shredded (10 cups)**

1   **can (6 ounces) marinated artichoke hearts, drained and each heart cut into thirds**
6   **cherry tomatoes, sliced**
3   **ounces pitted ripe black olives**
½   **medium-size red onion, thinly sliced (about ¾ cup)**
1   **bunch watercress, stems removed**
½   **pound cooked deli roast beef, sliced and cut into thin strips**
½   **pound Provolone, cut into ½-inch cubes**
4   **sesame breadsticks, broken up**

1. Prepare the Creamy Italian Dressing: Drop the garlic through the feed tube of a food processor with the motor running until the garlic is finely chopped. Add the mayonnaise, yogurt, Parmesan cheese, capers, reserved marinade and Italian herbs and process with pulses until the dressing is smooth and creamy.
2. Place the lettuce in a large bowl. Top with the artichokes, tomatoes, olives and red onion. Layer half of the watercress, the roast beef and then the remaining watercress. Spoon the dressing over the salad and sprinkle with the Provolone.
3. Sprinkle the breadsticks over the salad before serving. Gently toss to coat all the ingredients.

LAMB AND MANGO SALAD

Make this colorful dish the star of your next party. You can substitute cooked steak for the lamb in this recipe; for best results use medium-rare lamb or steak.

Makes 18 servings.

**Nutrient Value Per Serving
(with Mustard Dressing):**
263 calories, 21 g protein, 9 g fat,
27 g carbohydrate, 84 mg sodium,
64 mg cholesterol.

6 potatoes (about 2 pounds)
   Mustard Dressing
      (recipe, page 86)
2½ pounds cooked lamb
4 ripe mangoes

Ginger Mango Dressing:
   Trimmed mango, finely
      chopped (see Step 3)
1 cup plain lowfat yogurt

1 teaspoon peeled, grated, fresh
      gingerroot
12 cups shredded assorted lettuce
      greens
3 cups grated carrot
2 red onions, cut into thin rings
6 cucumbers, seeded and diced
2 carambola (star fruit), sliced
      and seeded

1. Cook the potatoes in a large pot of boiling water until they are tender, but not mushy. Peel and cut them into thin slices. While still warm, combine the potato slices with the Mustard Dressing in a large bowl and toss very gently to blend. Let the potatoes stand while preparing the remaining salad ingredients.
2. Trim any fat remaining on the lamb. Cut the lamb into strips and set aside.
3. To pit and skin the mangoes, use a sharp knife and cut as close, and parallel, to each pit as possible, scraping the blade against the pit to loosen the flesh. Repeat with a second cut on the other side of each pit. Trim any remaining flesh from the pits, working over a bowl to catch the juices. Finely chop this trimmed flesh and reserve it and the juices for the Ginger Mango Dressing. Slit each mango half lengthwise into 4 pieces and carefully cut away the flesh from the skin. Set aside the mango slices.

4. Prepare the Ginger Mango Dressing: Stir together the reserved chopped mango with its juices, the yogurt and ginger in a small bowl until they are well blended.
5. The salad may be assembled on a serving platter or on individual dinner plates. Spoon part of the Ginger Mango Dressing on the platter or plates and top with the lettuce. Remove the potato slices from the Mustard Dressing, reserving the dressing. Layer the slices evenly on top of the lettuce, extending them to the periphery of the plate.
6. Top the potatoes with the carrot, but do not cover the potatoes completely. Drizzle some of the reserved Mustard Dressing on the carrot, then top the carrot with the onion rings, cucumber and the mango slices. Spoon a little of the Ginger Mango Dressing on the mangoes. Arrange the lamb strips on top. Garnish with the star fruit. Pass any remaining dressings.

VEGETABLE, BEAN & GRAIN SALADS

*Green Apple and Jícama Slaw
(recipe, page 73)*

Good Health Cookbook

GREEN APPLE AND JÍCAMA SLAW

LOW-FAT
LOW-SODIUM
LOW-CHOLESTEROL

Tart green apples combined with crunchy jícama make a delicious chilled slaw.

Broil red pepper for 15 minutes.

Makes 6 servings.

1   **large sweet red pepper**
4   **medium-size green apples**
    (1½ pounds)
1   **medium-size jícama**
    (¾ pound)
1   **tablespoon chopped fresh**
    parsley

Nutrient Value Per Serving:
116 calories, 1 g protein, 1 g fat,
30 g carbohydrate, 5 mg sodium,
0 mg cholesterol.

6   **tablespoons rice vinegar**
    OR: cider vinegar
¼   **cup tarragon vinegar**
3   **tablespoons honey (optional)**
    Freshly ground white pepper,
    to taste

1. Preheat the broiler.
2. Broil the red pepper, turning it as needed, for 15 minutes or until it is charred all over. Let the pepper stand until it is cool enough to handle. Peel, core and seed the pepper, then cut it into matchstick-size pieces. Place the pepper in a large bowl.
3. Peel, core and cut the green apples into matchstick-size pieces. Peel and cut the jícama into matchstick-size pieces. Add the apples and the jícama to the bowl.

4. Add the parsley, rice or cider vinegar, tarragon vinegar, honey, if you wish, and the white pepper. Toss well to combine all the ingredients. Cover the bowl and refrigerate the slaw until serving time.

CookSmart

What's HE-kah-ma?

That's the way to pronounce jícama, a brown-skinned vegetable with white flesh. It is called the "Mexican potato" and has a slightly sweet flavor and distinctive crunch. Jícama can weigh up to 6 pounds, but 1 pound is the average weight. It is delicious served raw as a vegetable dipper. Jícama also can be grated and added to sautéed and stir-fried dishes.

ROAST PEPPER SALAD

The wonderful smoky flavor of roast peppers adds a different dimension to salads and sandwiches.

Broil peppers for 15 minutes.

Makes 4 servings.

Nutrient Value Per Serving (without added salt):
89 calories, 1 g protein, 7 g fat, 6 g carbohydrate, 3 mg sodium, 0 mg cholesterol.

6 sweet red, green and/or yellow peppers
2 tablespoons virgin olive oil
1 clove garlic, finely chopped
   Leaf marjoram, crumbled

**Salt and freshly ground pepper, to taste
Chopped fresh parsley, for garnish**

1. Preheat the broiler.
2. Place the red, green or yellow peppers on a baking sheet lined with aluminum foil.
3. Broil the peppers 3 inches from the source of the heat, turning them with tongs, for 15 minutes or until they are charred all over. Remove the peppers from the broiler and place them in paper bags. Let the peppers stand for 10 to 15 minutes (the steam trapped in the bags will loosen the skins and make them easy to remove). When the peppers are cool enough to handle, peel off the skins. Halve the peppers and remove the seeds.

4. Slice the peppers and place them in a bowl. Add the oil, garlic, marjoram and salt and pepper. Toss gently to combine all the ingredients. Let the salad stand for at least 1 hour.
5. To serve, sprinkle the salad with the chopped parsley.

CORN AND PEPPER SALAD

This deliciously spicy salad can be prepared a day ahead—perfect for a party or picnic.

Makes 8 servings.

Nutrient Value Per Serving:
80 calories, 2 g protein, 1 g fat, 20 g carbohydrate, 235 mg sodium, 0 mg cholesterol.

3 cups cooked fresh corn kernels (about 6 ears) OR: 2 cans (12 ounces each) corn niblets, drained
1 sweet green pepper, halved, seeded and chopped
1 carrot, shredded
1 red onion, finely chopped

1 fresh or pickled jalapeño pepper, chopped (wear rubber gloves)
½ cup cider vinegar
2 teaspoons chopped fresh cilantro OR: parsley
   Freshly ground black pepper, to taste

Mix together the corn, green pepper, carrot, onion, jalapeño pepper, vinegar, cilantro or parsley and the black pepper in a medium-size bowl. Cover the bowl and refrigerate the salad until serving time.

RAITA SALAD

LOW-FAT
LOW-CALORIE
LOW-CHOLESTEROL

Often served as a soothing complement to Indian food, this mixture of yogurt, cucumber and mint is great with any spicy food.

Makes 6 servings.

Nutrient Value Per Serving:
89 calories, 6 g protein, 2 g fat,
15 g carbohydrate, 67 mg sodium,
5 mg cholesterol.

2   **large cucumbers**
1   **pint plain lowfat yogurt**
2   **tablespoons chopped fresh
    mint**

**Pinch ground white pepper,
    to taste**
6   **large, ripe tomatoes, thickly
    sliced**

1. Peel, halve and seed the cucumbers. Using a food processor or a hand grater, grate the cucumbers and place them in a medium-size bowl.
2. Add the yogurt, mint and white pepper to the cucumber and stir to combine the ingredients. Cover the bowl and refrigerate the yogurt mixture until needed.

3. To serve, arrange each sliced tomato on an individual salad plate and top with the yogurt mixture.

SALSA WITH GARLIC AND CILANTRO

LOW-CALORIE
LOW-SODIUM
LOW-CHOLESTEROL

A deliciously different version of a Mexican favorite — serve as a salad, side dish, spread or dip.

Makes 6 servings.

Nutrient Value Per Serving:
53 calories, 2 g protein, 3 g fat,
7 g carbohydrate, 17 mg sodium,
0 mg cholesterol.

1   **bunch fresh cilantro**
3   **to 5 cloves garlic**
2   **pounds ripe tomatoes**
1   **tablespoon olive oil**

**Salt and freshly ground pepper,
    to taste**
**Pita bread, cut into triangles
    OR: fresh vegetable dippers
    (optional)**

1. Finely chop together the cilantro and the garlic with a chef's knife, or chop them in a food processor.
2. Bring a large pot of water to boiling. Add the tomatoes and cook until the skins just start to split, for about 30 seconds. Transfer the tomatoes with a slotted spoon to a bowl of cold water. Peel, core and chop the tomatoes.

3. Heat the oil in a nonstick skillet. Add the garlic-cilantro mixture and sauté over medium-high heat for 2 minutes. Add the tomatoes, reduce the heat to very low and cook for 15 minutes. Cover the skillet and simmer until the tomatoes are pulpy, for about 3 minutes more. Season the mixture with the salt and pepper, transfer it to a bowl and chill.
4. Serve the salsa with pita triangles or fresh vegetables for dipping, if you wish.

KIDNEY BEAN SALAD

For a no-cook salad, substitute 2 cups of rinsed and drained canned beans for the dried ones.

Makes 4 servings.

Nutrient Value Per Serving:
254 calories, 11 g protein, 11 g fat,
30 g carbohydrate, 17 mg sodium,
0 mg cholesterol.

1   cup dried kidney beans,
      soaked overnight
5   tablespoons lemon juice
      Salt and freshly ground pepper,
      to taste
3   tablespoons olive oil
      Lettuce leaves

1   sweet green pepper, cored,
      seeded and chopped,
      for garnish
¼   cup chopped green onion,
      for garnish
3   tablespoons chopped parsley,
      for garnish

1. Drain the kidney beans, place them in a saucepan and cover them with fresh water. Bring the water to boiling over medium heat. Lower the heat and simmer the beans for 1 hour or until they are tender but still whole. Drain the beans.
2. Whisk together the lemon juice and the salt and pepper in a small bowl. Whisk in the oil until it is blended. Toss the beans with the dressing.

3. Spoon the kidney beans into a salad bowl lined with the lettuce leaves. Garnish with the green pepper, green onion and parsley.

BLACK BEAN SALAD

This easy-on-you salad uses canned beans, which are marinated in a tangy citrus vinaigrette.

Makes 10 servings.

Nutrient Value Per Serving:
130 calories, 6 g protein, 4 g fat,
18 g carbohydrate, 350 mg sodium,
0 mg cholesterol.

2   cans (16 ounces each) black
      beans, drained
1   sweet red or green pepper,
      halved, seeded and diced
5   green onions, sliced
1   small red onion, sliced
      Juice of 2 lemons
      Juice of 2 limes

½   cup rice wine vinegar
      OR: cider vinegar
4   cloves garlic, finely chopped
3   tablespoons olive oil
      Few drops liquid red pepper
      seasoning
      Salt and freshly ground
      pepper, to taste

Combine the black beans, red or green pepper, green onion, red onion, lemon and lime juices, rice wine vinegar or cider vinegar, garlic, oil, liquid red pepper seasoning and salt and pepper in

a medium-size bowl. Taste and adjust the seasonings, if necessary. Cover the bowl and refrigerate the salad. Adjust the seasonings once more before serving, if necessary.

BULGUR WITH TOMATOES

Serve this stick-to-your-ribs salad on its own or use it to fill green or red peppers for baking.

Makes 8 servings.

Nutrient Value Per Serving:
246 calories, 9 g protein, 7 g fat,
38 g carbohydrate, 26 mg sodium,
21 mg cholesterol.

½ pound lean ground beef
1 medium-size onion, chopped
2 cups coarse-grained bulgur
3 large tomatoes, peeled and diced OR: ¼ cup tomato paste

5 cups water
Salt and freshly ground pepper, to taste

1. Sauté the meat and the onion in a large saucepan until the onion is translucent, for about 10 minutes. Stir in the bulgur, then add the tomatoes or tomato paste, the water, salt and pepper.

2. Bring the mixture to boiling over medium heat. Lower the heat and simmer, stirring occasionally, until the bulgur is cooked, for about 20 minutes.

BULGUR SALAD PRIMAVERA

A taste of spring that will satisfy the heartiest appetite in your household.

Makes 6 servings.

Nutrient Value Per Serving:
314 calories, 7 g protein, 16 g fat,
39 g carbohydrate, 679 mg sodium,
0 mg cholesterol.

1 cup bulgur wheat
2 cups water
1⅓ cups chopped tomato
½ cup dried currants
½ cup hulled, roasted sunflower seeds
⅓ cup shredded carrot
2 green onions, finely chopped
1 small clove garlic, finely chopped

2 tablespoons finely chopped fresh mint
1 tablespoon finely chopped fresh basil
Pinch leaf oregano, crumbled
¼ cup red wine vinegar
¼ cup tamari OR: regular soy sauce
¼ cup olive oil

1. Place the bulgur in a large, heatproof bowl. Bring the water to boiling in a small saucepan and pour it over the bulgur. Let the bulgur stand for 20 minutes. Drain the bulgur thoroughly and return it to the bowl.
2. Add the tomato, currants, sunflower seeds, carrot, green onion, garlic, mint, basil and oregano to the bulgur.

3. Whisk together the vinegar, tamari or regular soy sauce and the oil in a small bowl. Pour the dressing over the bulgur mixture and mix to combine all the ingredients well.

TUNA AND WHITE BEAN SALAD

Marinating the tuna with the white beans allows the flavors of this tasty salad to develop fully.

LOW-CALORIE

LOW-CHOLESTEROL

Makes 6 servings.

Nutrient Value Per Serving:
297 calories, 17 g protein, 15 g fat,
25 g carbohydrate, 657 mg sodium,
5 mg cholesterol.

8   ounces small dried white
       beans (pea beans), soaked
1½ teaspoons salt
1   jar (2 ounces) sliced
       pimiento, drained
1   small red onion, quartered
       and thinly sliced
1   can (7 ounces) water-packed
       tuna, drained and
       coarsely flaked
¼   to ⅓ cup red wine vinegar

2   tablespoons lemon juice
       (1 lemon)
½   teaspoon finely chopped
       garlic
⅓   cup olive oil
¼   teaspoon freshly ground pepper
2   tablespoons finely chopped
       parsley
       Lettuce leaves
       Lemon wedges, for garnish
       (optional)

1. Drain the white beans and place them in a medium-size saucepan. Add cold water to the saucepan to cover the beans by 2 inches. Bring the water to boiling over medium heat. Lower the heat, cover the saucepan and simmer the beans for 1 hour. Add 1 teaspoon of the salt. Cover and simmer for 30 minutes more or until the beans are tender but still hold their shape. Drain the beans and place them in a bowl.
2. Gently stir the pimiento, onion and tuna into the beans.

3. Combine ¼ cup of the vinegar, the lemon juice, garlic, oil, pepper and remaining ½ teaspoon of salt in a small bowl. Stir in the parsley. Pour the dressing over the bean mixture and toss gently to mix all the ingredients. Taste and add the remaining vinegar, if necessary. Cover the bowl and refrigerate the salad for at least 2 hours, or overnight, to blend the flavors.
4. Serve the salad on the lettuce leaves and, if you wish, garnish it with lemon wedges.

CookSmart

A Big Batch 'O Beans

Beans are very adaptable. Once cooked, beans will keep for a week in the refrigerator, or 4 to 6 months in the freezer, so you can cook a large batch to last several meals. To prepare beans for cooking, drain the soaking water to eliminate some of the gas-forming ingredients, refill the saucepan with fresh water and simmer gently until the beans are tender. Salt should not be added to the beans until at least halfway through the cooking time because it tends to toughen the skins. As the beans simmer, remove any residue that floats to the top of the water. Add water as needed to keep the beans covered. Most beans are cooked fully when the skin cracks as you blow on one. As with pasta, when you bite into a cooked bean, it should be *al dente*, tender but still firm enough to hold its shape. Reheat beans gently to retain their shape.

LENTIL, PEA AND CORN SALAD

Dried lentils and split peas cook more quickly than other dried beans, which makes this salad fast, easy and full of nutrition.

Makes 8 servings.

Nutrient Value Per Serving:
269 calories, 14 g protein, 8 g fat, 39 g carbohydrate, 81 mg sodium, 0 mg cholesterol.

1 cup dried lentils
1 cup split peas
6 cups water
1 large onion
1 clove garlic, crushed but left whole
¼ teaspoon salt
   Kernels from 3 ears of corn, shucked and cooked OR: 1 can (12 ounces) whole kernel corn, drained

⅓ cup red wine vinegar
2 tablespoons corn oil
2 tablespoons olive oil
½ teaspoon paprika
2 tablespoons chopped fresh basil OR: 2 teaspoons leaf basil, crumbled
2 cups cherry tomatoes, rinsed, hulled and halved
   Chopped fresh parsley, for garnish

1. Combine the lentils, split peas, water, whole onion, garlic clove and salt in a large saucepan. Bring the mixture to boiling over medium heat. Lower the heat and simmer for 30 minutes or until the lentils and peas are tender but still retain their shape. Drain the lentils and peas; discard the onion and the garlic clove.

2. Place the still-warm lentils and peas in a large bowl. Add the corn, vinegar, corn and olive oils and the paprika. If using the leaf basil, add it here. Toss the mixture gently to combine all the ingredients, and let it stand for at least 1 hour.

3. If using the fresh basil, add it to the cherry tomato halves. Add the tomatoes to the lentil pea mixture and toss gently to mix all the ingredients. Cover the bowl and refrigerate the salad.

4. To serve, sprinkle the salad with the parsley.

DIPS & DRESSINGS

Classic Vinaigrette (recipe, page 82)

SESAME VINAIGRETTE

LOW-CALORIE
LOW-CHOLESTEROL

Open the door to the exotic flavors of the Far East with this unusual salad dressing — or use it to marinate chicken or flank steak for grilling or stir-fries.

Makes about ¼ cup.

Nutrient Value Per Tablespoon:
15 calories, 0 g protein, 1 g fat,
1 g carbohydrate, 257 mg sodium,
0 mg cholesterol.

- ¼ cup red wine vinegar
- 1 tablespoon soy sauce
- 1 teaspoon dark sesame oil
- 1 teaspoon peeled, grated fresh gingerroot

Beat together the vinegar, soy sauce, oil and ginger in a small bowl with a wire whisk until all the ingredients are thoroughly combined. Beat the vinaigrette again just before using it.

ITALIAN VINAIGRETTE

LOW-CALORIE
LOW-CHOLESTEROL

A delightful dressing for crisp salad greens, or try using it as a marinade for poultry.

Makes about 1 cup.

Nutrient Value Per Tablespoon:
46 calories, 0 g protein, 5 g fat,
0 g carbohydrate, 42 mg sodium,
0 mg cholesterol.

- 6 tablespoons olive oil
- 3 tablespoons red wine vinegar
- 2 tablespoons tomato juice (shake well before adding)
- 1 clove garlic, pressed
- ¼ teaspoon salt
- ⅛ teaspoon freshly ground pepper
- ¼ teaspoon dried parsley flakes
- ¼ teaspoon leaf oregano, crumbled
- ½ teaspoon grated Parmesan cheese

Combine all the ingredients in a screw-top jar or any jar that can be tightly covered. Shake well. For the best results, make the vinaigrette a day ahead so the flavors can blend. Shake well before serving.

Note: *For a spicy version of Italian Vinaigrette, add Dijon-style mustard to taste, or substitute ground hot red pepper to taste for the black pepper. Or use crushed red pepper flakes.*

CookSmart

Back to Basics: Easy Vinaigrette

As basic as a black dress, and just as handy: Place the salad greens in a salad bowl. Drizzle the greens first with olive or vegetable oil (4 to 6 tablespoons for 12 cups of loosely packed greens), then with vinegar (2 to 3 tablespoons). Season to taste with salt and pepper and toss lightly to coat the greens. Voilá — the simple dress for success!

CLASSIC VINAIGRETTE

Garlic and mustard give this classic salad dressing extra flavor. For even more variety, choose from any of the different oils and vinegars listed in the tip boxes on pages 83 and 85.

Makes about 1 cup (use ½ cup to dress 12 cups of greens; refrigerate the remainder for up to 5 or 6 days).

Nutrient Value Per Tablespoon:
91 calories, 0 g protein, 10 g fat, 0 g carbohydrate, 87 mg sodium, 0 mg cholesterol.

4   tablespoons vinegar
2   teaspoons Dijon-style mustard
½   teaspoon salt
¼   teaspoon freshly ground pepper

1   clove garlic, unpeeled
6   tablespoons vegetable oil
6   tablespoons olive oil

1. To make the vinaigrette by hand: Whisk together the vinegar, mustard, salt and pepper in a small bowl until all the ingredients are well blended and the salt is dissolved.
2. Add the garlic, using any of the following methods: Peel the clove, cut parallel horizontal and vertical lines toward the root end and cut the clove crosswise into tiny pieces. Add the garlic pieces to the vinegar mixture.
3. Or place the unpeeled clove in a garlic press and squeeze. Scrape the garlic from the press with a small knife into the vinegar mixture.
4. Or lightly crush the peeled clove with the side of a knife and rub a salad bowl with the crushed clove.
5. Gradually whisk the vegetable and olive oils into the vinegar mixture until the vinaigrette is well blended and smooth. Use the vinaigrette immediately, or refrigerate for a day or two and whisk just before using.
6. To prepare the vinaigrette in a jar: Put all the ingredients in the jar, cover tightly with the jar lid and shake until all the ingredients are well blended.
7. To make the vinaigrette in a food processor or an electric blender: Drop in the garlic while the machine is running. Stop the machine and scrape the sides of the container with a spatula. Add the vinegar, mustard, salt and pepper. Whirl for 2 to 3 seconds.

HEALTH

We ♥ Italian Food
By using mono-unsaturated olive oil instead of butter and other saturated fats, you can lower the overall cholesterol level in your diet. There's also some evidence which indicates that garlic and onions, two other staples of Italian cooking, can help prevent the formation of blood clots, thus boosting your protection against heart disease.

HOTLINE

8. Gradually add the vegetable and olive oils through the processor feed tube or blender top while the machine is running, and blend for 1 to 2 seconds more.

9. To add fresh herbs: With scissors, snip enough fresh herbs (tarragon, oregano, dill) to equal 1 to 2 tablespoons. Add them to the vinaigrette just before serving.

10. To add dried herbs: Add about 1 teaspoon of leaf herbs to the vinegar and let steep for 5 to 10 minutes before mixing the vinaigrette.

11. For table presentation, pour some of the vinaigrette into a salad bowl. Cross the serving utensils across the bottom. Place the salad greens on the utensils. Gently toss the greens with the dressing. Pass the extra vinaigrette.

CookSmart

Oil You Need for Salads

● Olive oil can range in taste from very light and delicate to very fruity or peppery. The Mediterranean oils are graded extra-virgin, virgin and pure, based on their acidity, aroma and flavor.

● Vegetable oils usually are more bland than olive oil. They include safflower, peanut, sesame and corn oil.

● Nut oils, such as walnut and hazelnut, are strongly flavored and usually are mixed with a lighter vegetable oil. These oils have a tendency to turn rancid more quickly than others.

DILLED MUSTARD

A little of this condiment goes a long way. Try using the remainder on smoked salmon sandwiches.

Makes 1 cup.

Nutrient Value Per Teaspoon:
25 calories, 1 g protein, 1 g fat,
4 g carbohydrate, 95 mg sodium,
11 mg cholesterol.

1	cup dry mustard powder
1	cup cider vinegar
¾	cup sugar, or to taste
¼	cup water

2	teaspoons salt (optional)
2	eggs, slightly beaten
2	tablespoons chopped fresh dill

1. Blend together the mustard powder, vinegar, sugar, water and, if you wish, salt in a small bowl, beating with a wire whisk until the mixture is smooth. Cover the bowl and let the mustard mixture stand at room temperature for 4 to 6 hours.

2. Pour the mustard mixture into the top of a double boiler and place the top directly over low heat. Cook, stirring occasionally, until the mixture is hot. Remove the top of the double boiler from the heat.

3. Add the eggs, stirring constantly with a wire whisk. Place the top of the double boiler over simmering water. Cook, stirring constantly, until the mixture thickens slightly and is smooth. Remove the top of the double boiler from the heat and let the mixture cool. Stir in the dill. Place the mustard in a covered container and refrigerate.

TARRAGON VINEGAR

Use this basic recipe as a springboard for several types of herbal vinegar. Use it in salad dressings and to marinate fish or chicken.

Makes two 1-pint bottles.

Nutrient Value Per Tablespoon:
3 calories, 0 g protein, 0 g fat,
1 g carbohydrate, 0 mg sodium,
0 mg cholesterol.

1	cup fresh tarragon sprigs
3¾	cups white wine vinegar
2	large tarragon sprigs, for garnish

1. Place the 1 cup of tarragon sprigs in a clean quart jar and press them with a wooden spoon to crush them slightly.

2. Bring the vinegar just to boiling in a stainless steel or enamel saucepan. Immediately pour the vinegar over the tarragon sprigs. Cap the jar tightly and let the mixture steep for 2 weeks.

3. Place one of the large tarragon sprigs in each of 2 sterilized 1-pint bottles. Strain the vinegar into the bottles. Cork the bottles tightly and store them at room temperature.

Note: *For Basil Vinegar, substitute 1 cup of fresh basil leaves for the 1 cup of tarragon sprigs and 3¾ cups of red wine vinegar for the white wine vinegar. Tuck a sprig of fresh basil in each bottle before pouring in the strained vinegar. Basil vinegar is excellent for marinating ripe tomato slices, crisply cooked green beans and other summer vegetable salads.*

CookSmart

Mustard: Hot Stuff!

Add mustards to salad dressings to give "depth" or a fuller flavor. Try some of the following:

● Smooth Dijon-style mustard, which is made with white wine.

● Coarse-grained mustard, which contains mustard seeds that are not completely pulverized, thus giving it a crunchy texture and mild flavor.

● Chinese mustard, which has a pronounced fiery taste. A dab of honey stirred into it softens its bite.

● Herb mustards, which usually combine a Dijon base with puréed herbs.

MINT VINEGAR

In addition to its natural affinity with lamb, mint vinegar imparts a wonderful note of contrast when splashed onto fruit salads.

Makes two 1-pint bottles.

Nutrient Value Per Tablespoon:
8 calories, 0 g protein, 0 g fat,
2 g carbohydrate, 0 mg sodium,
0 mg cholesterol.

3¾ **cups cider vinegar**
1½ **cups fresh mint leaves**
½ **cup sugar**
2 **mint sprigs, for garnish**

1. Bring the vinegar to boiling in a stainless steel or enamel saucepan. Add the mint leaves and the sugar. Stir and press the mint leaves with a wooden spoon to extract their flavor. Simmer the mixture for 5 minutes.
2. Pour the vinegar-mint mixture into a clean quart jar. Cap the jar tightly and let the mixture steep for 2 weeks.

3. Place one of the mint sprigs in each of 2 sterilized 1-pint bottles. Strain the vinegar into the bottles. Cork the bottles tightly and store them at room temperature.

SPICY LIME DRESSING

A tart and spicy accent to add to your salads — or try as a marinade for fish or poultry.

Makes 1 cup.

Nutrient Value Per Tablespoon:
61 calories, 0 g protein, 7 g fat,
1 g carbohydrate, 140 mg sodium,
0 mg cholesterol.

CookSmart

A Variety of Vinegars

● Red or white wine vinegar, plain or flavored with fresh or dried herbs, most typically is used for vinaigrette dressings and marinades for meats or fish.
● Distilled white vinegar and cider vinegar lend sharp tastes to pickles, relishes and spiced fruits.
● Balsamic vinegar is a dark, red vinegar made from unfermented grapes, rather than from wine. This vinegar usually is imported from Italy.
● Fruit vinegars, such as raspberry or blueberry, can add a touch of tart-sweetness to salads.
● Barley-derived malt vinegar traditionally is paired with fish, but is also good with other dishes.
● Oriental rice vinegar (Chinese and its sweeter Japanese counterpart) is similar to distilled vinegar but is not as pungent.

½ **cup olive or vegetable oil**
⅓ **cup lime juice**
2 **tablespoons cider vinegar**
1 **teaspoon salt**

Combine the oil, lime juice, cider vinegar, salt, chili powder and liquid red pepper seasoning to taste in a screw-top jar with a tight-fitting lid. Shake well to blend. Let stand for several hours. Always shake just before using.

½ **to 2 teaspoons chili powder**
    Liquid red pepper seasoning, to taste

HERB VINAIGRETTE

An elegant dressing for a green salad. For a subtler flavor, substitute
a small shallot for the garlic.

LOW-CALORIE

LOW-SODIUM

LOW-CHOLESTEROL

Makes about 1½ cups.

Nutrient Value Per Tablespoon:
80 calories, 0 g protein, 9 g fat,
0 g carbohydrate, 26 mg sodium,
0 mg cholesterol.

½ cup Tarragon or Basil
    Vinegar (recipe, page 84)
    OR: Mixed Herb Vinegar
    (recipe, page 87)
¼ teaspoon salt
1 small clove garlic, bruised

½ teaspoon Dijon-style mustard
1 cup olive or vegetable oil

1. Combine the vinegar, salt, garlic and mustard in a small jar or bowl. Shake or stir until the mustard and the salt dissolve into the vinegar.

2. Add the olive or vegetable oil to the jar, cover the jar and shake it vigorously to mix all the ingredients. Or add the oil gradually to the bowl, stirring vigorously with a fork or wire whisk. Shake or stir the vinaigrette once more just before using.

MUSTARD DRESSING

Toss this tangy dressing with mixed greens or use it to marinate
flank steak for London Broil.

LOW-CALORIE

LOW-SODIUM

LOW-CHOLESTEROL

Makes about ¾ cup.

Nutrient Value Per Tablespoon:
44 calories, 0 g protein, 5 g fat,
1 g carbohydrate, 25 mg sodium,
0 mg cholesterol.

½ cup cider vinegar
¼ cup olive oil
2 tablespoons coarse-grained
    mustard

½ teaspoon leaf rosemary,
    crumbled OR: ½ tablespoon
    chopped fresh rosemary
    Freshly ground black pepper,
    to taste

Combine the vinegar, oil, mustard, rosemary and black pepper in a small jar. Cover and shake vigorously until all the ingredients are well blended. Shake the dressing once more just before using.

ROSEMARY VINAIGRETTE

Fresh rosemary has a fragrance like sun-warmed pine needles. This versatile herb is a natural with chicken or for use in tomato sauces.

Makes about 1¼ cups.

Nutrient Value Per Tablespoon:
28 calories, 1 g protein, 3 g fat,
1 g carbohydrate, 6 mg sodium,
0 mg cholesterol.

1 cup rice vinegar OR:
   cider vinegar
   Juice of 1 lemon
1 tablespoon chopped fresh
   rosemary OR: 1 teaspoon
   leaf rosemary, crumbled

2 teaspoons Worcestershire
   sauce
3 shallots, finely chopped
¼ cup corn oil

Beat together the vinegar, lemon juice, rosemary, Worcestershire sauce and shallots in a small bowl with a wire whisk. Slowly beat in the oil until it is well blended.

MIXED HERB VINEGAR

The combination of herbs, peppercorns and shallots makes this a wonderful marinade for grilled meat — adding flavor and, at the same time, tenderizing the meat.

Makes two 1-pint bottles.

Nutrient Value Per Tablespoon:
4 calories, 0 g protein, 0 g fat,
1 g carbohydrate, 1 mg sodium,
0 mg cholesterol.

½ cup fresh rosemary leaves
½ cup fresh thyme leaves
4 shallots, peeled and sliced
1 large sprig parsley

12 peppercorns
3¾ cups cider vinegar
2 rosemary sprigs OR: thyme
   sprigs, for garnish

1. Place the rosemary and thyme leaves, the shallots, parsley and peppercorns in a clean quart jar and press them with a wooden spoon to crush them slightly.
2. Bring the vinegar just to boiling in a stainless steel or enamel saucepan. Immediately pour the vinegar over the herb mixture. Cap the jar tightly and let the herb mixture steep for 2 weeks.

3. Place one of the rosemary or thyme sprigs in each of 2 sterilized 1-pint bottles. Strain the vinegar into the bottles. Cork the bottles tightly and store them at room temperature.

FRESH TOMATO DRESSING

This dressing also can be made with a food processor or an electric blender; it will be smoother in texture and not as vivid in color, but still delicious.

Makes 2½ cups.

Nutrient Value Per Tablespoon:
3 calories, 0 g protein, 0 g fat,
1 g carbohydrate, 2 mg sodium,
0 mg cholesterol.

2   ripe tomatoes, chopped
1   stalk celery, diced
1   carrot, grated
½   sweet red pepper, cored,
       seeded and diced
½   sweet green pepper, cored,
       seeded and diced

¼   cup sliced green onion
2   cloves garlic, finely chopped
¼   cup balsamic OR: red wine
       vinegar
2   tablespoons olive oil

Combine the tomatoes, celery, carrot, red and green peppers, green onion, garlic, balsamic or red wine vinegar and the oil in a medium-size bowl. Stir the dressing thoroughly just before using. Store any leftover dressing in the refrigerator for up to 3 days.

Note: *To prepare the dressing with a food processor, cut all the vegetables except the green onion into 2-inch pieces. Process the carrot and the garlic for 10 seconds. Add the celery and the peppers and process for 5 seconds more. Add the tomatoes, vinegar and oil and process until the mixture is smooth. Transfer the dressing to a bowl and stir in the sliced green onion.*

FRESH LEMON DRESSING

The tangy taste of lemon is a welcome addition to any dish. Try this as a marinade for chicken or fish, too.

Makes about ½ cup.

Nutrient Value Per Tablespoon:
50 calories, 0 g protein, 5 g fat,
1 g carbohydrate, 19 mg sodium,
0 mg cholesterol.

Grated zest (yellow part of rind
    only) of 1 lemon
¼   cup fresh lemon juice
       (1 lemon)
3   tablespoons olive oil

1   tablespoon coarse-grained
       mustard
2   cloves garlic, finely chopped
       Salt and coarsely ground
          black pepper, to taste

Mix together the lemon zest and juice, the oil, mustard, garlic and salt and black pepper with a wire whisk in a small bowl. Whisk the dressing once more just before using. Cover and refrigerate any leftover dressing.

GINGERED SOY SAUCE

This flavorful sauce can be made up to a week in advance and is great on salads, for dipping or in stir-fries.

Makes about 1 cup.

Nutrient Value Per Tablespoon:
10 calories, 1 g protein, 0 g fat,
2 g carbohydrate, 515 mg sodium,
0 mg cholesterol.

1   **clove garlic, finely chopped**
½   **cup soy sauce**
¼   **cup fresh lemon juice
      (1 lemon)**
¼   **cup water**
1   **tablespoon sugar**
2   **tablespoons peeled, grated
      fresh gingerroot**

1   **jalapeño or serrano
      pepper, seeded and thinly
      sliced (wear rubber gloves)
      OR: ½ teaspoon crushed red
      pepper flakes**

Combine the garlic, soy sauce, lemon juice, water, sugar, ginger and jalapeño or serrano pepper or red pepper flakes in a jar. Close the jar tightly and shake it to combine all the ingredients. Refrigerate the sauce until ready to use and shake it once more just before using.

MINTY PINEAPPLE LEMON DRESSING

A taste of the tropics — perfect for chicken salad or tossed with fresh fruit.

Makes 1 cup.

Nutrient Value Per Tablespoon:
93 calories, 0 g protein, 10 g fat,
1 g carbohydrate, 103 mg sodium,
0 mg cholesterol.

¾   **cup vegetable oil**
¼   **cup unsweetened pineapple juice**
1   **teaspoon grated lemon rind**
2   **tablespoons lemon juice**

1   **teaspoon leaf mint, crumbled**
¾   **teaspoon salt**
½   **teaspoon dry mustard**

Combine the oil, pineapple juice, lemon rind, lemon juice, mint, salt and dry mustard in a large jar with a tight-fitting lid. Shake well to blend. Let stand for several hours. Shake again just before serving.

CREAMY TOMATO DIP

Try this smooth dip to top baked potatoes or with fresh vegetable dippers. Make it a day ahead and store it in the refrigerator.

Makes about 3 cups.

Nutrient Value Per ¼ Cup:
26 calories, 1 g protein, 1 g fat,
4 g carbohydrate, 90 mg sodium,
0 mg cholesterol.

1 cup mixed vegetable juice
1 large tomato, finely chopped
    Juice of 2 lemons

1 teaspoon leaf basil, crumbled
½ cup plain nonfat yogurt
½ cup light sour cream

Mix together the vegetable juice, tomato, lemon juice, basil, yogurt and sour cream in a small bowl. Cover the bowl and refrigerate the dip until ready to use.

CREAMY CAPER DRESSING

Capers and anchovies lend their own distinctive flavors to this dressing. You can make this dip up to 4 days in advance.

Makes about 1 cup.

Nutrient Value Per Tablespoon:
55 calories, 1 g protein, 6 g fat,
1 g carbohydrate, 139 mg sodium,
5 mg cholesterol.

½ cup mayonnaise
½ cup plain lowfat yogurt
1 teaspoon dillweed,
    crumbled

1 anchovy fillet, finely chopped
1 dill pickle, finely chopped
2 tablespoons drained capers

Mix together the mayonnaise, yogurt, dillweed, anchovy, pickle and capers in a small bowl. Cover the bowl and refrigerate the dressing until ready to use.

HERB DIP

Plain lowfat yogurt easily replaces fattening sour cream in this dip.
Serve it with vegetable dippers or pita bread triangles.

Makes about 2 cups.

Nutrient Value Per Tablespoon:
9 calories, 0 g protein, 1 g fat,
1 g carbohydrate, 15 mg sodium,
0 mg cholesterol.

1   **recipe Very Green Sauce**
    (recipe, below)
½   **cup plain lowfat yogurt**

Blend the Very Green Sauce with the
yogurt in a small bowl until well mixed.
Cover the bowl and refrigerate the dip
until serving time.

VERY GREEN SAUCE

Make a double batch of this sauce — it pairs as well with swordfish as
it does with crudités.

Makes about 1½ cups.

Nutrient Value Per Tablespoon:
9 calories, 0 g protein, 1 g fat,
1 g carbohydrate, 16 mg sodium,
0 mg cholesterol.

6   **green onions (green part**
    only)
⅓   **cup finely chopped fresh**
    parsley
    Skin from 1 large zucchini*
1   **sweet green pepper, halved**
    and seeded

3   **cloves garlic**
3   **tablespoons cider vinegar**
1   **tablespoon olive oil**
1   **tablespoon drained capers**
1   **gherkin pickle**
    Salt and freshly ground
    pepper, to taste

Place the green onion, parsley, zucchini
skin, green pepper, garlic, vinegar, oil,
capers and pickle in the container of a
food processor. Cover and whirl until
the mixture is puréed. Add the salt and
pepper. Transfer the sauce to a jar,
cover the jar and refrigerate the sauce
for up to 5 days. Stir the sauce just
before using.

*Note: *Use a swivel-bladed vegetable*
peeler to remove the skin from the
zucchini.

5

THE GARDEN OF EATIN': Vegetables from A to Z

We'll bet that you know vegetables are full of fiber and complex carbohydrates, vitamins and minerals. We'll also bet that you know vegetables are generally low in calories, contain no fat and no cholesterol. But did you know that asparagus is a natural diuretic? Or that one potato contains protein, magnesium, folacin, phosphorous, copper, niacin, iron, iodine, B vitamins and vitamin C? You'll learn all that and more—plus great ways to prepare vegetables—in this chapter.

Let's begin with "A" for asparagus. How about some Grilled Asparagus with Lemon Vinegar *(recipe, page 95)*? Our deceptively rich Broccoli with Squash and Pine Nuts *(recipe, page 97)* actually is low in calories, sodium and cholesterol. Or sample our elegant Timbales of Mushrooms and Leeks *(recipe, page 106)*. Our point here: we've got a terrific array of healthful, delicious vegetable dishes.

While most of these recipes are cataloged as side dishes, vegetable dishes also can become a main course with the addition of some protein. For instance, the cheese in Asparagus, Gruyère and Watercress Sandwiches *(recipe, page 97)* helps to provide 14 grams of protein per sandwich. Just add a tossed green salad and you've got a light, nutritious meal. By including either cheese or legumes, recipes such as hearty Eggplant and Mozzarella *(recipe, page 104)* or Potatoes with Chick Peas *(recipe, page 112)*, can be the main dish on your menu.

So give in to temptation: make yourself at home in the garden of good health.

Mixed Vegetables with Garlic Sauce
(recipes, pages 122-123)

ASPARAGUS WITH YOGURT DRESSING

Cook the spears loose in a skillet, or in bundles standing up so the stems boil and the tips steam for uniform tenderness.

Makes 6 servings.

Nutrient Value Per Serving:
70 calories, 5 g protein, 3 g fat,
7 g carbohydrate, 285 mg sodium,
6 mg cholesterol.

2   **pounds asparagus of uniform diameter**
½   **teaspoon salt**

Yogurt Dressing:
1   **cup plain lowfat yogurt**
¼   **cup reduced-calorie mayonnaise**
3   **teaspoons grated orange zest (orange part of rind only), for garnish**

1. Gently bend each asparagus spear near the stem end until the spear snaps; the spear will break where the tender part ends. Remove the scales with a small knife. Wash the asparagus gently to remove any sand from the tips.
2. If the thick ends of the spears are tough and woody, peel off the outer layers with a swivel-bladed vegetable peeler or small paring knife. Peel just to the point where the outer flesh becomes tender. Save the peelings for the soup pot.
3. To cook the asparagus loose, fill a skillet with water, add the salt and bring to boiling. Add the asparagus and return to boiling. Cook, uncovered, until the spears are done *(see Step 6)*, for 5 to 8 minutes for medium-thick spears, 8 to 10 minutes for large spears.
4. To cook the asparagus in bundles, gather together one quarter of the spears. Place them in the center of a length of kitchen twine. Wind the twine around the bundle a few times and tie it. Repeat with the remaining asparagus.

5. Pour water to a depth of 2 inches into the bottom of a double boiler or tall narrow pot and add the salt. Bring the water to boiling. Carefully stand the bundles upright in the pan. Cover with the inverted double boiler top or pot lid, or make a dome cover with aluminum foil. Cook until done *(see Step 6)*, for 10 to 12 minutes; the bottoms will boil while the tops steam.
6. To test for doneness, lift the bundles with a large fork; the stalks should bend slightly. For either the bundle or the loose method, you should be able to insert the tip of a small, sharp knife easily into the thick ends.
7. If the asparagus was cooked in bundles, lay the bundles on a clean kitchen towel or paper toweling to drain. Cut the twine. If the asparagus was cooked in a skillet, remove the spears with a skimmer, tongs or spatula and place them on the towel to drain.
8. Prepare the Yogurt Dressing: Combine the yogurt with the mayonnaise in a small bowl. Spoon some of the dressing over each serving of asparagus and garnish with some of the orange zest.

HEALTH

Asparagus: Ban the Bloat

Did you know that asparagus is a natural diuretic? Asparagus also is a good source of vitamins A and C, potassium and dietary fiber, and it is low in sodium. More good news: Four spears of asparagus contain only about 15 calories.

HOTLINE

GRILLED ASPARAGUS WITH LEMON VINEGAR

Asparagus cooks very quickly, so be careful not to overcook the tender spears.

Grill or broil for 1 to 2 minutes.

Makes 6 servings.

Nutrient Value Per Serving:
39 calories, 5 g protein, 0 g fat,
7 g carbohydrate, 6 mg sodium,
0 mg cholesterol.

4   teaspoons cider vinegar
      Zest (yellow part of rind only)
        of 1 lemon
2½ pounds pencil-thin asparagus

1. Combine the vinegar with the lemon zest in a small dish and let the mixture stand for at least 2 hours.
2. Build a charcoal fire or preheat the broiler.
3. Trim the ends and, depending on their toughness, up to 3 inches from the bottoms of the asparagus. Strip off the tough outer portion of each spear with a swivel-bladed vegetable peeler or small paring knife.

4. Place the asparagus on the grill rack or broiler rack and grill, turning constantly, for 1 to 2 minutes or until they are tender. Place the asparagus on a serving platter and drizzle with the lemon vinegar.

CookSmart

Stalking the Asparagus

Domestic asparagus is grown primarily in California, Washington and New Jersey. It is most plentiful from February through June.

● Select straight, firm stalks with closed, compact tips. Open tips mean old stalks.

● Stalks should not appear dry or wrinkled.

● The diameter of the stalks is not related to the tenderness of the asparagus.

● About two-thirds of the stalk should be green.

● Store asparagus in a plastic bag in the refrigerator at about 36°. Do not wash it before storing. Or, stand the spears upright with their stems in a pan of water in the refrigerator and cover them with plastic wrap.

● Try to use asparagus within 2 to 3 days after purchase; it ages rapidly.

● One pound of fresh asparagus yields ½ to ¾ pound trimmed asparagus, or about 3 servings.

CHILLED ASPARAGUS WITH HORSERADISH VINAIGRETTE

A deliciously different way to serve asparagus — tossed in a tasty vinaigrette of horseradish, Oriental sesame oil and balsamic vinegar.

Makes 8 servings.

Nutrient Value Per Serving:
90 calories, 3 g protein, 8 g fat,
3 g carbohydrate, 140 mg sodium,
0 mg cholesterol.

2½ **pounds fresh asparagus**
½   **teaspoon salt**
¼   **cup olive oil**
¼   **teaspoon Oriental sesame oil***
1   **tablespoon balsamic vinegar**
    OR: white wine vinegar

1   **tablespoon bottled**
    horseradish, drained
⅛   **teaspoon freshly ground**
    pepper
2   **tablespoons coarsely chopped,**
    toasted pine nuts (pignoli)
    Lemon twists, for garnish
    (optional)

1. Wash, trim and, if you wish, cut the asparagus into halves or thirds. Bring 1 inch of water to boiling in a large skillet or Dutch oven. Add ¼ teaspoon of the salt and the asparagus. Cover the skillet and cook for 3 to 5 minutes or until the spears are crisp-tender. Drain the asparagus in a colander.
2. Combine the olive and Oriental sesame oils, balsamic or white wine vinegar, horseradish, the remaining ¼ teaspoon of salt and the pepper in a large bowl; whisk together vigorously until the ingredients are well blended. Add the asparagus and toss together until well combined. Cover the bowl and chill the asparagus for several hours, or overnight, tossing the asparagus occasionally.

3. To serve, place the asparagus on a serving platter and sprinkle the spears with the pine nuts. Garnish with lemon twists, if you wish.

***Note:** Oriental sesame oil is richer in flavor and darker than regular sesame oil. It can be found in the Oriental food section of many supermarkets or in specialty food stores.*

CookSmart

Bright Colors— Best Veggies

Choose brightly colored fruits and vegetables; they usually contain more vitamins than pale ones. To maximize the bright green color and vitamin-rich nature of broccoli, green beans or peas, steam the vegetables for about 5 minutes, then immediately plunge them into cold water, briefly, to stop the cooking.

ASPARAGUS, GRUYÈRE AND WATERCRESS SANDWICHES

The perfect dish for an elegant lunch. Try serving it with a tossed green salad and a light Chablis.

Makes 6 servings.

Nutrient Value Per Serving:
256 calories, 14 g protein, 11 g fat, 26 g carbohydrate, 474 mg sodium, 54 mg cholesterol.

1   pound asparagus
    Dilled Mustard (recipe, page 84)
6   slices pumpernickel bread

6   slices Gruyère cheese
½   bunch watercress, rinsed and patted dry

1. Trim the ends from the asparagus. If the spears are old, peel off the tough outer layer with a swivel-bladed vegetable peeler.
2. Steam the asparagus spears for 5 to 7 minutes, or until they are crisp-tender. Plunge the asparagus into a bowl of ice and water to stop further cooking. Drain the asparagus and gently pat them dry with paper toweling.

3. Spread 2 teaspoons of the Dilled Mustard on each slice of bread. Top with the asparagus spears, Gruyère cheese and watercress.

BROCCOLI WITH SQUASH AND PINE NUTS

Adding just a few pine nuts to this dish provides a lot of rich flavor, without a calorie overload.

Makes 4 servings.

Nutrient Value Per Serving:
90 calories, 5 g protein, 5 g fat, 10 g carbohydrate, 32 mg sodium, 0 mg cholesterol.

1   head broccoli, broken into flowerets
1   small red onion, diced
1   teaspoon olive oil
2   cloves garlic, sliced
1   tablespoon pine nuts (pignoli), toasted

2   small yellow squash, trimmed and grated, with the excess water squeezed out
    Salt and freshly ground pepper, to taste

1. Steam the broccoli just until it is crisp-tender.
2. Meanwhile, sauté the onion in the oil in a medium-size nonstick skillet over medium heat for 5 minutes or until the onion is tender. Add the garlic and the pine nuts and sauté for 2 minutes more, stirring constantly.

3. Add the squash and sauté for 2 minutes more or until the squash is barely tender. Add the salt and pepper.
4. Top the broccoli with the squash mixture and toss gently to mix.

CHEESE AND CUCUMBER BOATS

This dish is an entertainer's dream, because each "boat" is an individual serving.

Makes 4 servings.

Nutrient Value Per Serving:
283 calories, 23 g protein, 14 g fat, 17 g carbohydrate, 317 mg sodium, 49 mg cholesterol.

¾ **pound lowfat mozzarella cheese**
2 **carrots, trimmed and peeled**
8 **green onions**
2 **large sweet red and/or green peppers**

Tarragon Dressing (recipe, page 99)
4 **medium-size cucumbers**
Lettuce leaves and red onion rings, for garnish

1. Coarsely grate the mozzarella cheese and the carrots into a large bowl.
2. Trim and thinly slice the green onion. Halve, seed and cut the red or green peppers into small cubes. Add the green onion, peppers and Tarragon Dressing to the cheese-carrot mixture and toss gently to combine the ingredients. Let the mixture stand while preparing the cucumbers.
3. If the cucumbers are waxed, peel them. Otherwise, leave the skin on. Slice off lengthwise the top quarter of each cucumber. Shave off a small piece from the bottom so the cucumber doesn't roll on the platter. Scoop out the insides of the cucumbers with a grapefruit spoon or melon baller. Discard the seeds and save the flesh for another use.

4. Spoon the cheese-carrot mixture into the hollowed-out cucumbers. Place the cucumbers on a serving platter. Garnish the "boats" with the lettuce leaves and the red onion rings.

HEALTH

Carrot Complexion Connection
A gold mine of beta-carotene, which your body converts to skin-smoothing vitamin A, one carrot has double your RDA for vitamin A. It's also fiber-rich and virtually fat-free. One large carrot contains about 40 calories.

HOTLINE

CookSmart

More Than a Munchie
Steamed, then puréed carrots make a tangy, colorful side dish. Finely grated raw carrots in salad add a sweetness that's a nice accompaniment to a bold dressing. And washed, unpeeled carrots become condensed in flavor and creamy in texture when slowly roasted alongside meats. For a change of pace, substitute carrot juice for orange juice at breakfast once in a while.

TARRAGON DRESSING

LOW-CHOLESTEROL

This dressing also can be used on a green salad. Store leftover dressing, covered, in the refrigerator.

Makes about ⅔ cup.

Nutrient Value Per Tablespoon:
102 calories, 2 g protein, 11 g fat,
1 g carbohydrate, 90 mg sodium,
0 mg cholesterol.

6 tablespoons cider vinegar
¼ cup water
¼ cup chopped fresh tarragon
   OR: 4 teaspoons leaf tarragon, crumbled
2 tablespoons Dijon-style mustard

2 teaspoons chopped fresh dill
   OR: ½ teaspoon dried dillweed
⅛ teaspoon freshly ground black pepper
½ cup olive oil

Whisk together the vinegar, water, tarragon, mustard, dill and black pepper in a small bowl. Gradually whisk in the oil. Whisk the dressing again just before using.

GRILLED CUCUMBERS WITH FRESH BASIL

LOW-CALORIE
LOW-SODIUM
LOW-CHOLESTEROL

Once the grill or broiler is fired up, you can have this savory side dish on the table in less than 10 minutes.

Grill or broil for 2 to 4 minutes.

Makes 10 servings.

Nutrient Value Per Serving:
42 calories, 1 g protein, 3 g fat,
5 g carbohydrate, 7 mg sodium,
0 mg cholesterol.

5 cucumbers
2 tablespoons olive oil
4 leaves fresh basil, chopped

Juice of 1 lemon
Freshly cracked black pepper, to taste

1. Build a charcoal fire or preheat the broiler.
2. Peel the cucumbers and cut them crosswise into ¼-inch diagonal slices. Brush both sides of the slices with the oil.

3. Place the cucumber slices on the grill rack or broiler rack and grill for 1 to 2 minutes per side. Transfer the cucumber slices to a serving platter.
4. Sprinkle the slices with the basil, lemon juice and black pepper.

CookSmart

The Cool Cucumber

New hybrid varieties of cucumber have practically eliminated the common complaint, "Cucumbers make me burp!" There are even some named "burpless." If you detect a little bitterness in the flavor, peel off the outer green skin. This popular salad ingredient also can be steamed, sautéed or blanched. A ½ cup serving of sliced, raw cucumber contains only 7 calories.

GRILLED WHITE CORN WITH CRACKED PEPPER

*The flavor of corn on the cob is intensified by grilling it in the husk —
the cracked pepper adds pizzazz!*

Grill for 6 to 10 minutes.

Makes 6 servings.

Nutrient Value Per Serving:
158 calories, 6 g protein, 2 g fat,
35 g carbohydrate, 28 mg sodium,
0 mg cholesterol.

12 **ears white corn on the cob,
in the husk, silk removed**
1 **tablespoon freshly cracked
black pepper**

1. Build a charcoal fire. Soak the corn in
their husks in water while the fire heats.
2. Place the corn on the grill rack and
grill, turning every 2 to 3 minutes, for 6
to 10 minutes or until the husks are
black all over.
3. Remove the husks and sprinkle the
corn with the black pepper.

CookSmart

Kernals of Truth

The sooner you cook corn on the
cob after picking it, the better. If
the corn is freshly picked, the
stem on the cob will be pale green
and moist. After about a day, the
stem turns chalky white;
eventually it turns brown. One ear
of cooked corn contains about 80
calories. To keep the calorie count
low, avoid using melted butter
and try squeezing a little lemon
juice on the cob instead.

CORN WITH LEMON LIME BUTTER

LOW-SODIUM

A piquant butter flavored with fresh lemon and lime adds a special taste to corn on the cob.

Makes 12 servings.

Nutrient Value Per Serving:
147 calories, 3 g protein, 9 g fat,
18 g carbohydrate, 15 mg sodium,
21 mg cholesterol.

12	ears tender young corn, husked
½	cup (1 stick) reduced-calorie margarine

Juice of 1 lemon
Juice of 1 lime
Large pinch ground white pepper

1. Place about 1 inch of water in a large pot and bring it to boiling. Place the corn in the boiling water in the pot and cook for 2 to 6 minutes or until the corn is tender.

2. Melt the margarine in a small saucepan. Stir in the lemon and lime juices and the white pepper.
3. Place the corn on a serving platter and brush the lemon-lime mixture over the corn.

SPINACH SAUTÉ WITH GARLIC YOGURT

LOW-CALORIE
LOW-SODIUM
LOW-CHOLESTEROL

For perfect spinach, wash the leaves in several changes of water and cook them in nonaluminum containers.

Makes 4 servings.

Nutrient Value Per Serving:
86 calories, 3 g protein, 4 g fat,
12 g carbohydrate, 76 mg sodium,
1 mg cholesterol.

¼	cup plain lowfat yogurt
2	cloves garlic, mashed and divided
1	tablespoon olive oil
1	pound fresh spinach, washed well, with tough stems removed (let some water cling to the leaves)

Salt and freshly ground black pepper, to taste
¼ cup raisins, plumped*

CookSmart

Sensational Spinach

Spinach is delicious raw, steamed, blanched, sautéed or any other way you can think of cooking it. But remember, to avoid sandy grit, carefully wash spinach in several changes of cool water. One half cup of chopped, raw spinach contains only 6 calories, and ½ cup of cooked, drained spinach has about 21 calories. This leafy, dark green is rich in iron and is a good source of vitamin A, potassium and calcium.

1. Mix the yogurt with one of the garlic cloves in a small bowl and set aside.
2. Heat the oil in a very large nonaluminum skillet over medium heat. Add the remaining garlic clove and sauté for 10 seconds.
3. Add the spinach to the skillet and toss it frequently with 2 large spoons until it begins to wilt. (The large quantity of spinach will be cumbersome to deal with at first, but will significantly reduce in volume as it wilts.)
4. Cover the skillet and let the spinach steam for 1 minute or until it wilts but still is very bright green.

5. Transfer the spinach to a plastic or stainless steel colander set over a large bowl. Drain the spinach well. (Reserve the liquid for soup, if you wish.)
6. Place the spinach in a large serving bowl. Add the salt and pepper, and toss in the raisins. Top with the garlic yogurt.

*Note: *To plump raisins, place them in a small saucepan with water to cover. Bring the water to boiling. Then drain the raisins well.*

SPICY STRING BEANS

These bright green beans are delicious served hot or at room temperature. Offer them as an appetizer or use them as a side dish.

LOW-CALORIE

LOW-CHOLESTEROL

MICROWAVE

Microwave for 17 minutes.

Makes 6 side dish or 12 appetizer servings.

Nutrient Value Per Side Dish Serving (halve for appetizer serving): 50 calories, 2 g protein, 2 g fat, 7 g carbohydrate, 176 mg sodium, 0 mg cholesterol.

5 cloves garlic, mashed
2 slices peeled fresh gingerroot
2 green onions, trimmed and
    cut into ½-inch pieces (use
    both white and green parts)
1 tablespoon olive oil

1 pound fresh string beans,
    trimmed
1 tablespoon crushed red
    pepper flakes
1 tablespoon soy sauce

1. Place the garlic, gingerroot, green onion and oil in a food processor. Cover and process until finely chopped. Transfer the mixture to a microwave-safe 2-quart dish.
2. Microwave, uncovered, at full power for 2 minutes.

3. Add the string beans, red pepper flakes and soy sauce. Toss to coat the string beans well with the garlic mixture.
4. Microwave the string beans, covered and vented, at full power, stirring 4 times, for 8 - 11 minutes or until beans are just tender but still bright green.

CookSmart

The Jolly Green Bean

Young, tender green beans are delicious as a snack at only 17 calories per half cup. If briefly steamed or blanched, green beans become a deliciously simple side dish — replace fatty butter with a squirt of lemon juice on them.

GRILLED GREEN ONIONS

An easy-to-make side dish that's great with grilled poultry, meat or fish.

Grill or broil for 4 minutes.

Makes 6 servings.

Nutrient Value Per Serving:
16 calories, 1 g protein, 0 g fat,
4 g carbohydrate, 7 mg sodium,
0 mg cholesterol.

24 green onions
1   teaspoon chili powder

1. Build a charcoal fire or preheat the broiler.
2. Rinse and trim the root ends from the green onions. Sprinkle the green onions with the chili powder.

3. Place the green onions on the grill rack or broiler rack and grill, turning once, for 4 minutes or until the green onions are tender.

GRILLED EGGPLANT WITH BASIL

You can make this recipe with either regular-size eggplants or the more delicate baby eggplants.

Grill or broil for 6 minutes.

Makes 6 servings.

Nutrient Value Per Serving:
85 calories, 2 g protein, 5 g fat,
11 g carbohydrate, 7 mg sodium,
0 mg cholesterol.

2   medium-size eggplants
    OR: 12 baby eggplants
    Salt, to taste
2   tablespoons olive oil

½   teaspoon leaf basil, crumbled
1   clove garlic, finely chopped

1. If using medium-size eggplants, cut them into ½-inch-thick slices. If using baby eggplants, make several lengthwise cuts, ¼ inch from the top (keep the slices attached), to form fan-like shapes.
2. Build a charcoal fire or preheat the broiler.
3. Sprinkle the eggplant slices or fans with the salt. Place the slices or fans in a drain rack over the sink and let them stand for 20 minutes (this removes any potential bitterness). Rinse the eggplants under cool running water and pat them dry with paper toweling.

4. Combine the oil, basil and garlic in a small bowl and stir until they are well blended. Carefully brush the eggplant slices or fans all over with the flavored oil.
5. Place the eggplant slices or fans on the grill rack or broiler rack and grill for 3 minutes on each side or until they are tender.

CookSmart

Looking Through a Green Onion

A green onion really is nothing more than a mature scallion. The white part can be chopped and used raw for flavoring, or added to dishes to be cooked. The green part can be sliced or coarsely chopped to make an attractive garnish or for use in salads.

EGGPLANT AND MOZZARELLA

Unlike many eggplant dishes, this one, designed for the microwave oven, requires no oil. It can be served on a slice of toasted garlic bread, if you wish.

LOW-CALORIE

LOW-CHOLESTEROL

MICROWAVE

Microwave at full power for 3 minutes.

Makes 6 servings.

1   medium-size to large eggplant (about 1½ pounds)
1½ cups Quick Tomato Sauce (recipe, page 115)

Nutrient Value Per Serving:
165 calories, 11 g protein, 10 g fat, 11 g carbohydrate, 189 mg sodium, 22 mg cholesterol.

½   pound lowfat mozzarella cheese, cut into 6 slices
      Fresh basil sprigs, for garnish

1. Peel and cut the eggplant into 6 rounds approximately ¾ inch thick. Place the rounds in a single layer in a microwave-safe 12 x 7 x 2-inch baking dish. Cover the dish tightly with microwave-safe plastic wrap.
2. Microwave the eggplant at full power for 2 minutes.
3. Carefully pierce the plastic with the tip of a knife to release the steam. Uncover the dish carefully and pour off any liquid. Spread the Quick Tomato Sauce over the eggplant. Top with the mozzarella cheese.

4. Microwave at full power for 1 minute or until the cheese just begins to melt. Garnish the mozzarella cheese with the basil sprigs.

CookSmart

Hold the Oil!

The trick to cooking eggplant is to eliminate the excess moisture — eggplant that has been salted and drained will soak up less oil during cooking than unprepared eggplant will. If you broil eggplant slices, you can eliminate the oil altogether. One half cup of cooked, drained eggplant cubes contains about 13 calories.

EGGPLANT DIP

LOW-CHOLESTEROL

Also known as baba ghannuj, this dip is wonderful served with crusty French bread.

Bake eggplant at 400° for 1¼ hours.

Makes 6 servings.

Nutrient Value Per Serving (with optional olive oil):
80 calories, 3 g protein, 3 g fat, 14 g carbohydrate, 196 mg sodium, 0 mg cholesterol.

2　**medium-size eggplants**
½　**cup lemon juice (4 lemons)**
2　**tablespoons tahini (sesame paste)**
1　**clove garlic, finely chopped**

½　**teaspoon salt**
1　**tablespoon olive oil (optional)**
2　**tablespoons chopped parsley, for garnish**

1. Preheat the oven to hot (400°). Pierce the eggplants with a fork. Bake the eggplants in the preheated hot oven (400°) until the skins blister and the eggplants are tender, for about 1¼ hours. Cool the eggplants. Scrape out the flesh from the skins with a spoon and discard the skins.

2. Mash the flesh in a bowl with the lemon juice and the tahini. Stir in the garlic and the salt. Add a teaspoon or two of water, if necessary, to make the mixture a dipping consistency.
3. Taste and add more seasonings, if necessary. Transfer the dip to a serving bowl. Sprinkle the oil on top, if you wish. Garnish with the parsley.

YOGURT EGGPLANT PURÉE

LOW-CALORIE
LOW-SODIUM
LOW-CHOLESTEROL

Serve with pita bread triangles as an appetizer or as a side dish to meat courses.

Bake eggplant at 400° for 1¼ hours.

Makes 6 servings.

Nutrient Value Per Serving:
83 calories, 3 g protein, 5 g fat, 9 g carbohydrate, 27 mg sodium, 1 mg cholesterol.

1　**large eggplant**
3　**tablespoons lemon juice**
2　**tablespoons olive oil**
¾　**cup plain nonfat yogurt**

2　**cloves garlic, crushed**
　　Salt and freshly ground pepper, to taste
2　**tablespoons finely chopped fresh parsley, for garnish**

1. Preheat the oven to hot (400°). Cut the stem end from the eggplant and pierce the skin several times with a fork.
2. Bake the eggplant in the preheated hot oven (400°) until it is soft, for about 1¼ hours. Cool the eggplant.
3. Halve the eggplant lengthwise. Scrape out the flesh from the skin with a spoon into a small bowl and discard the skin.

4. Add the lemon juice, oil, yogurt, garlic and salt and pepper to the eggplant. Mash the mixture with a potato masher until it is puréed. (For a smoother texture, use a food processor or an electric blender.)
5. Place the purée in a serving bowl and garnish with the parsley.

TIMBALES OF MUSHROOMS AND LEEKS

This elegant appetizer requires metal dariole molds or individual porcelain ramekins, available at gourmet cooking shops.

LOW-FAT
LOW-CALORIE
LOW-CHOLESTEROL

Bake at 300° for 30 minutes.

Makes 8 servings.

Nutrient Value Per Serving (without optional salt):
77 calories, 5 g protein, 2 g fat, 12 g carbohydrate, 146 mg sodium, 0 mg cholesterol.

1½ pounds fresh spinach
   Nonstick vegetable cooking spray
3   slices whole wheat bread, crusts removed
⅓   cup skim milk
⅓   cup unsalted chicken broth
3   leeks, rinsed and chopped
⅓   cup chopped celery
1   tablespoon margarine
½   pound fresh mushrooms
2   egg whites
2   teaspoons chopped fresh oregano OR: 1 teaspoon leaf oregano, crumbled

1   tablespoon chopped fresh basil OR: 1 teaspoon leaf basil, crumbled
1   teaspoon chopped fresh rosemary OR: ½ teaspoon leaf rosemary, crumbled
   Salt and freshly ground pepper, to taste (optional)
   Herb Sauce (optional; recipe, page 107)
   Fresh herbs, for garnish
   Shredded carrot, for garnish

1. Rinse the spinach in several changes of cool water. Place the spinach, with the water still clinging to the leaves, in a large skillet or wok. Cover the skillet and cook the spinach, in batches if necessary, over medium heat for 1 to 2 minutes or until the spinach just wilts. Remove the spinach from the skillet and pat it dry with paper toweling.
2. Spray 8 dariole molds or individual 3-ounce ramekins with nonstick vegetable cooking spray. Use the spinach leaves to line the bottom and sides of each mold, leaving an overhang at the top.
3. Preheat the oven to slow (300°). Soak the bread in the milk and the broth in a pie plate for 10 minutes or until the bread is soft.
4. Sauté the leeks and the celery in the margarine in a large nonstick skillet over medium heat until the vegetables are soft and translucent. Remove the skillet from the heat.
5. Place the mushrooms in the container of a food processor. Cover and pulse-chop. Add the sautéed vegetables, the bread with its soaking liquid, the egg whites, oregano, basil and rosemary. Cover and process just until the ingredients are combined. Taste and season with salt and pepper, if you wish.

6. Spoon the mushroom mixture into the spinach-lined molds. Fold the spinach leaves over the tops. Place the molds in a baking pan and place the pan on an oven rack. Pour boiling water into the pan to come halfway up the sides of the molds.
7. Bake the molds in the preheated slow oven (300°) for 30 minutes or until the spinach shrinks from the sides of the molds. Remove the molds to wire racks and cool them for 5 minutes.
8. Carefully run a thin, sharp knife around the edge of each mold and invert the mold onto an individual dinner plate. Serve with fresh Herb Sauce, if you wish. Garnish with the fresh herbs and the shredded carrot.

CookSmart

Leek-ing Information

More subtle in flavor and more digestible than other members of the onion family, leeks can be boiled, braised, blanched, steamed — in fact, they are an incredibly versatile vegetable for cooking. (They're even worn in hats in Wales on St. David's Day!) One cooked leek contains about 38 calories and is rich in vitamin A and potassium.

HERB SAUCE

The sauce particularly enhances steamed vegetables, but it also is wonderful served over chicken or fish.

Makes 1½ cups.

Nutrient Value Per Tablespoon (without optional salt):
5 calories, 0 g protein, 0 g fat,
0 g carbohydrate, 10 mg sodium,
1 mg cholesterol.

1   cup plain nonfat yogurt
⅓   cup lowfat buttermilk
¼   cup reduced-calorie
       mayonnaise
¼   cup snipped chives
¼   cup chopped fresh basil
       OR: fresh parsley

2   teaspoons grated onion
2   teaspoons fresh lemon juice
       Salt and freshly ground white
       pepper, to taste (optional)

Combine the yogurt, buttermilk, mayonnaise, chives, basil or parsley, onion, lemon juice and, if you wish, salt and white pepper in a small bowl. Stir until all the ingredients are well blended. Cover the bowl and refrigerate the sauce until serving time.

RED PEPPER MARMALADE

Low-sugar apricot preserves provide both sweetness and texture to this condiment. Use with grilled and roasted meats or steamed vegetables — experiment!

Broil red peppers for 15 minutes.

Makes about 1¼ cups.

Nutrient Value Per Tablespoon:
37 calories, 0 g protein, 0 g fat,
10 g carbohydrate, 1 mg sodium,
0 mg cholesterol.

2   large sweet red peppers
½   cup bottled pimentos,
       drained
1   cup low-sugar apricot
       preserves
       Juice of 1 lemon

1. Preheat the broiler.
2. Broil the red peppers, turning, for 15 minutes or until they are black and blistered all over. Place the peppers in a brown paper bag and let them stand for 15 minutes. Peel, seed and cut the peppers into strips.
3. Place the pimentos in the container of an electric blender or a food processor. Cover and whirl until they are puréed.

4. Combine the red peppers, pimento purée and apricot preserves in a small saucepan. Bring the mixture to boiling. Lower the heat and simmer for 20 minutes or until the mixture thickens. Cool the marmalade. Stir in the lemon juice. Store the marmalade, tightly covered, in the refrigerator.

ZUCCHINI AND ORZO-STUFFED PEPPERS

Orzo is a variety of small pasta that resembles rice but cooks in far less time.

Bake at 350° for 15 to 20 minutes.

Makes 4 servings.

Nutrient Value Per Serving (without optional salt):
150 calories, 5 g protein, 5 g fat, 23 g carbohydrate, 52 mg sodium, 2 mg cholesterol.

4   medium-size sweet red, yellow or green peppers
1   cup chopped onion
1   teaspoon finely chopped garlic
1   tablespoon olive oil
1   medium-size zucchini, trimmed and shredded
1   cup finely chopped mushrooms
1   cup cooked orzo, tubettini or star pasta (cooked in unsalted chicken broth)
2   tablespoons grated Parmesan cheese
    Salt and freshly ground pepper, to taste (optional)

1. Cut off the top quarter of each red, yellow or green pepper and seed the pepper. Steam the peppers and their tops for 3 minutes or until they are barely cooked.

2. Preheat the oven to moderate (350°).

3. Sauté the onion and the garlic in the oil in a large nonstick skillet over medium heat for 5 minutes or until the vegetables are very soft and translucent. Add the zucchini and the mushrooms and sauté for 1 minute more. Remove the skillet from the heat. Stir in the pasta, Parmesan cheese and, if you wish, salt and pepper.

4. Place the peppers in a baking dish large enough to hold them upright in one layer. Stuff them with the pasta mixture. Replace the pepper tops.

5. Bake the peppers in the preheated moderate oven (350°) for 15 to 20 minutes or until they are tender and the stuffing is hot.

CookSmart

The Rainbow Coalition

Sweet peppers come in a veritable rainbow of colors: green, red, yellow and even purple. One raw pepper contains about 18 calories and is a good source of vitamins A and C and potassium. Sweet peppers can be served raw with dips, stuffed and baked, as a garnish and in a wide variety of dishes whenever you want to add a little zest to your food.

CHEESE-FILLED PEPPERS

LOW-CALORIE
LOW-CHOLESTEROL
MICROWAVE

This dish, reminiscent of chiles rellenos, uses long, pale green frying peppers. And it's ready in minutes using a microwave oven.

Microwave at full power for 3 minutes.

Makes 4 servings.

8   **frying or Italian peppers**
2   **tablespoons water**
½   **pound lowfat mozzarella cheese, cut into 8 sticks**
    Quick Tomato Sauce, heated (recipe, page 115)

Nutrient Value Per Serving:
164 calories, 15 g protein, 9 g fat, 6 g carbohydrate, 268 mg sodium, 0 mg cholesterol.

1. Slit each frying or Italian pepper lengthwise along one side. Wearing rubber gloves, remove and discard the stems, ribs and seeds.
2. Place the peppers in a microwave-safe 12-inch round dish or quiche pan. Add the water. Cover the dish tightly with microwave-safe plastic wrap.
3. Microwave the peppers at full power for 2 minutes.

4. Uncover the dish carefully and let it stand until the peppers are cool enough to handle. Stuff each pepper with a stick of the mozzarella cheese. Close the pepper over the mozzarella cheese and secure it with a wooden pick.
5. Microwave the stuffed peppers, uncovered, at full power for 1 minute or until the mozzarella cheese melts.
6. Remove the wooden picks. Serve the peppers with the Quick Tomato Sauce.

TWO-WAY NEW POTATOES

Some like it hot, some like it cold—here is a dish that is great either way. Though the recipe is designed for the microwave, the potatoes can be boiled in a large pot of water until tender.

LOW-SODIUM

LOW-CHOLESTEROL

MICROWAVE

Microwave at full power for 20 minutes.

Makes 12 servings.

3 **pounds small new potatoes, scrubbed and dried**
10 **cloves garlic, mashed**
½ **cup extra-virgin olive oil**
  Salt and freshly ground pepper, to taste

Nutrient Value Per Serving:
173 calories, 8 g protein, 9 g fat,
3 g carbohydrate, 8 mg sodium,
0 mg cholesterol.

Chopped parsley, for garnish (optional)

1. Place the potatoes in a microwave-safe 14 x 11 x 2-inch baking dish. Stir in the garlic and the oil. Cover the dish with microwave-safe plastic wrap.
2. Microwave the potatoes at full power, shaking the dish twice, for 20 minutes or until the potatoes are tender.
3. To serve as a hot side dish, season the potatoes with the salt and pepper and, if you wish, garnish with chopped parsley.

Potato Salad: Let the potatoes stand until they are cool enough to handle. Halve or quarter the potatoes, leaving the skins on, and place them in a salad bowl. Add ¾ cup of your favorite reduced-calorie vinaigrette dressing (bottled or homemade) and toss. Sprinkle the potatoes with ⅓ cup of snipped chives.

THYME POTATOES

Tender new potatoes, gently sautéed in olive oil with fresh thyme, are a welcome addition to any meal.

LOW-FAT

LOW-SODIUM

LOW-CHOLESTEROL

Makes 4 servings.

8 **tiny new potatoes (1 pound)**
8 **sprigs fresh thyme**
1 **tablespoon olive oil**
  Salt and freshly ground black pepper, to taste

Nutrient Value Per Serving:
120 calories, 2 g protein, 4 g fat,
21 g carbohydrate, 7 mg sodium,
0 mg cholesterol.

1. Scrub and dry the potatoes, leaving the skins on. With a paring knife, make a ¼-inch-deep cut in each potato. Fill each cut with a thyme sprig.
2. Heat the oil in a skillet. Add the potatoes and sauté for 2 minutes. Cover the skillet, lower the heat and cook for 10 minutes.

3. Uncover the skillet and raise the heat to medium. Sauté until the potatoes are tender. Add the salt and black pepper.

SAUTÉED NEW POTATOES AND GARLIC

Using only 2 teaspoons of butter, these sautéed potatoes are lightly crisp and golden.

Makes 6 servings.

Nutrient Value Per Serving:
106 calories, 3 g protein, 1 g fat,
21 g carbohydrate, 10 mg sodium,
3 mg cholesterol.

1½ **pounds medium-size new
    potatoes, scrubbed, skin on**
2   **teaspoons unsalted butter
    Salt and freshly ground black
    pepper, to taste**

2   **large cloves garlic, chopped
    Finely chopped parsley,
    for garnish**

1. Steam the potatoes over boiling water until they are tender, for about 15 minutes. Remove the potatoes from the heat.
2. When they are cool enough to handle, cut the potatoes into halves or, if they are large, into quarters.
3. Melt the butter in a large nonstick skillet over medium heat. When the butter is foaming, add the potatoes and cook, shaking the skillet occasionally so the potatoes are coated with butter on all sides, for about 4 minutes. Season the potatoes with the salt and black pepper. Add the garlic and continue cooking until the potatoes and the garlic are golden, for about 3 minutes more.

4. When the potatoes are golden, remove the skillet from the heat. Garnish the potatoes with the parsley and serve.

POTATOES WITH CHICK PEAS

A delicious main dish! A cup of canned chick peas, rinsed and drained, may be used instead of the dried beans.

LOW-FAT
LOW-CALORIE
LOW-SODIUM
LOW-CHOLESTEROL

Makes 6 servings.

Nutrient Value Per Serving:
231 calories, 7 g protein, 6 g fat, 39 g carbohydrate, 62 mg sodium, 0 mg cholesterol.

½ cup dried chick peas, soaked overnight and drained
2 tablespoons olive oil
2 large onions, sliced
3 cloves garlic
2 pounds potatoes, peeled and sliced
4 tomatoes, peeled, seeded and chopped
2 tablespoons tomato paste
2 tablespoons water
   Salt and freshly ground pepper, to taste

1. Cook the chick peas in unsalted water in a saucepan until tender, for about 1½ hours. Drain the chick peas.
2. Meanwhile, sauté the onions in the oil in a nonstick skillet over medium heat until golden, for about 10 minutes.
3. Add the chick peas and the garlic and sauté for 5 minutes. Add the potatoes and continue sautéing, stirring constantly, until the potatoes brown. Add the tomatoes, tomato paste, water, salt and pepper. Cover the skillet.

4. Simmer the mixture, stirring occasionally, until the potatoes are tender, for about 25 minutes. Serve the potato-chick pea mixture warm or cold.

HEALTH

Super Spuds

Though you may think of potatoes as "just starch," in fact they contain significant amounts of protein, vitamins, fiber and minerals. A 5-ounce potato supplies 6% of the day's recommended protein, 8% of magnesium, folacin and phosphorus, 10% of copper, niacin and iron, 15% of iodine, 20% of vitamin B$_6$, and 35% of vitamin C. And potatoes can't be beat for versatility. They're delicious in soups, salads, side dishes, entrées, and even breads. A medium-size, plain baked potato has about 100 calories. Bonus benefits: Potatoes are virtually fat-free and contain no cholesterol.

HOTLINE

GRILLED SWEET POTATOES WITH FRESH CILANTRO BUTTER

Potatoes in their skins usually are baked buried in the coals. Here they're sliced, grilled on the barbecue and brushed with flavored butter.

Grill or broil for 6 to 8 minutes.

Makes 6 servings.

2   tablespoons chopped fresh
      cilantro
3   tablespoons unsalted butter,
      melted

Nutrient Value Per Serving:
187 calories, 2 g protein, 6 g fat,
32 g carbohydrate, 18 mg sodium,
16 mg cholesterol.

6   sweet potatoes, peeled if
      desired, cut into
      ½-inch-thick slices

1. Build a charcoal fire or preheat the broiler. Stir the cilantro into the melted butter in a small saucepan and set aside.
2. Place the sweet potato slices on the grill rack or broiler rack and grill for 3 to 4 minutes per side or until the slices are soft but not too mushy.

3. Lightly brush the sweet potato slices on both sides with the cilantro butter, and serve.

GRILLED SUMMER SQUASH WITH TOMATO CORN RELISH

If you can find small young summer squash, halve them lengthwise instead of cutting them into circles.

Grill or broil for 4 minutes.

Makes 6 servings.

Nutrient Value Per Serving:
128 calories, 5 g protein, 4 g fat,
24 g carbohydrate, 24 mg sodium,
0 mg cholesterol.

1 bunch green onions, sliced
1 pound ripe tomatoes, chopped
5 radishes, shredded
1 cup cooked corn (from 2 ears
     fresh corn or a package
     frozen corn)
¼ cup chopped fresh cilantro
     OR: fresh parsley
     Juice of 1 lemon

2 teaspoons olive oil
3 cloves garlic, finely chopped
3 small summer squash,
     trimmed and cut into
     1-inch-thick circles
3 small zucchini, trimmed and
     cut into 1-inch-thick circles

1. Build a charcoal fire or preheat the broiler.
2. To prepare the relish, mix the green onion, tomatoes, radishes, corn, cilantro or parsley and the lemon juice in a medium-size bowl. Let the mixture stand while preparing the squash.
3. Mix together the oil and the garlic in a small bowl and brush the garlic oil onto the summer squash and zucchini circles.

4. Grill or broil the summer squash and zucchini circles for 2 minutes on each side or just until they are tender.
5. Serve portions of the squash topped with a spoonful of the relish. Pass the remaining relish.

TOMATOES PROVENCAL

A simple dish to prepare, with a striking presentation. If you wish to vary the recipe, thyme also will work well.

Makes 4 servings.

Nutrient Value Per Serving:
32 calories, 1 g protein, 0 g fat,
7 g carbohydrate, 11 mg sodium,
0 mg cholesterol.

4 firm, ripe tomatoes
1 sweet onion*
1 tablespoon red wine vinegar
2 tablespoons chopped fresh
     marjoram OR: fresh oregano

Salt and freshly ground
  pepper, to taste

1. Trim the tomatoes on both sides and cut each tomato into 3 or 4 half-inch slices.
2. Cut the onion into ¼-inch slices, leaving the rings together.
3. Alternate the tomato and onion slices on a serving platter. Sprinkle with the vinegar, marjoram or oregano and the salt and pepper. Refrigerate the tomatoes until serving time.

*****Note:** *If the onion is not sweet, slice and place it in a shallow dish. Cover the slices with a mixture of 1 tablespoon of sugar and ½ cup of water. Let the onions stand for at least 1 hour, then drain them.*

GRILLED RED AND GREEN TOMATOES

Balsamic vinegar's natural sweetness complements the tangy flavor of the tomatoes.

Grill or broil for 2 to 4 minutes.

Makes 10 servings.

5 **large red tomatoes**
5 **large green tomatoes**
   Freshly cracked black pepper, to taste

1. Build a charcoal fire or preheat the broiler.
2. Meanwhile, core the red and green tomatoes and slice them thickly.
3. Place the tomato slices on the grill rack or broiler rack and grill them for 1 to 2 minutes per side or until they are tender but not mushy. Remove the tomatoes with a spatula to a serving platter.

Nutrient Value Per Serving:
33 calories, 2 g protein, 0 g fat,
7 g carbohydrate, 16 mg sodium,
0 mg cholesterol.

2 **tablespoons balsamic vinegar**
   OR: red wine vinegar

4. Season the tomato slices with the freshly cracked pepper and drizzle with the balsamic or red wine vinegar.

QUICK TOMATO SAUCE

A flavorful red sauce that is made quickly in the microwave oven. Try it—you'll like it!

Microwave at full power for 11 minutes.

Makes 3 cups.

4 **large ripe tomatoes**
1 **small carrot, peeled and cut into thirds**
1 **stalk celery, cut into thirds**
1 **small onion, quartered**
2 **cloves garlic, mashed**

1. Drop the tomatoes into a large saucepan of boiling water and boil them for 1 minute or until the skins begin to loosen. Remove the tomatoes with a slotted spoon and plunge them into a bowl of ice and water to stop the cooking. Peel, seed and chop the tomatoes.
2. Chop the carrot, celery, onion and garlic with a knife or in a food processor. Place the vegetable mixture in a microwave-safe 1-quart baking dish. Stir in the oil.

Nutrient Value Per Tablespoon:
11 calories, 0 g protein, 1 g fat,
1 g carbohydrate, 2 mg sodium,
0 mg cholesterol.

3 **tablespoons olive oil**
½ **cup torn fresh basil**
   OR: 1½ tablespoons leaf basil, crumbled
   Salt and freshly ground pepper, to taste

3. Microwave, uncovered, at full power for 1 minute.
4. Add the tomatoes, basil and salt and pepper to the dish.
5. Microwave at full power for 10 minutes or until the sauce is thick.

COLLARDS WITH SUN-DRIED TOMATOES AND HOT PEPPERS

Sun-dried tomatoes lend a piquant accent and serrano peppers add pizzazz to steamed greens.

LOW-CHOLESTEROL

Makes 4 servings.

Nutrient Value Per Serving:
307 calories, 6 g protein, 25 g fat,
21 g carbohydrate, 1,258 mg sodium,
0 mg cholesterol.

2   pounds collards or kale,
    trimmed and cut into
    3-inch slices
2   serrano peppers, seeded and
    thinly sliced (wear rubber
    gloves) OR: ¼ to ½ teaspoon
    crushed red pepper flakes

5   sun-dried tomatoes in olive
    oil, drained and cut into
    ¼-inch slices
1   tablespoon olive oil from the
    tomatoes
1   teaspoon red wine vinegar
    Salt, to taste

1. Place the collards or kale on a steamer rack.
2. If using fresh serrano peppers, lay them, then the tomatoes, in an even layer on top of the greens. Bring 2 cups of water to boiling in the bottom half of the steamer. Place the vegetables over the water. Cover and steam until the greens have wilted and are deep green, for 10 to 15 minutes.

3. Meanwhile, blend together the oil and the vinegar in a large bowl. If using dried red pepper flakes, add them to the vinegar and oil. Season with the salt.
4. Transfer the cooked vegetables to the bowl with the dressing and toss the vegetables in the dressing to coat them.

TOMATO SORBET OLÉ

The combination of tomatoes, avocado and spicy seasonings makes a delicious sorbet. Try it as a refreshing side dish, salad or between-course dish.

Makes 8 servings.

Nutrient Value Per ½ Cup Serving:
90 calories, 2 g protein, 3 g fat,
15 g carbohydrate, 122 mg sodium,
0 mg cholesterol.

⅓ cup sugar
⅓ cup water
2 pounds very ripe tomatoes (about 6 medium-size tomatoes), coarsely chopped
1 ripe avocado (8 ounces), peeled, seeded and coarsely chopped
1 tablespoon Worcestershire sauce
1 tablespoon lime juice
½ teaspoon celery salt
½ teaspoon ground coriander
¼ teaspoon ground hot red pepper
   Tomato wedges, lime slices and parsley, for garnish (optional)

1. Heat together the sugar and the water in a small saucepan over medium heat until the sugar dissolves. Cool the sugar syrup.
2. Place the tomatoes and the avocado in the container of an electric blender or a food processor. Cover and whirl until the mixture is a smooth purée. Strain the purée, forcing it gently through a sieve with the back of a spoon. Discard the solids in the sieve. Stir in the Worcestershire sauce, lime juice, celery salt, coriander, ground hot red pepper and sugar syrup.
3. Freeze the tomato mixture in an ice cream maker, following the manufacturer's directions. Serve the sorbet immediately in tall champagne or other dessert glasses, or cover the sorbet and place it in the freezer for no more than 2 hours. Garnish the sorbet with tomato wedges, lime slices and parsley, if you wish.

Note: *If you do not have an ice cream maker, freeze the sorbet in a 9-inch square pan, covered with plastic wrap, until the sorbet is firm, for 3 to 6 hours. Break the sorbet into small pieces. Place the pieces in the container of a food processor, or use an electric mixer, and process or beat just until the sorbet is fluffy. Serve the sorbet immediately or return it to the freezer for no more than 2 hours.*

CookSmart

You Say To-may-to and I Say To-mah-to!

Any way you say it, this favorite fruit comes in three familiar shapes: the round tomato, good for a whole host of things; the plum tomato, particularly suited for canning, catsups, chutney or other recipes where a lot of pulp is necessary; and the small round cherry tomato, great in salads, as a garnish and for snacks. One round tomato has about 24 calories.

ZUCCHINI PILAF

If you prefer very crisp zucchini, don't add it to the pot until you add the rice.

Makes 8 servings.

Nutrient Value Per Serving:
175 calories, 4 g protein, 2 g fat,
35 g carbohydrate, 9 mg sodium,
0 mg cholesterol.

1 tablespoon olive oil
1 large onion, chopped (about 2 cups)
 Salt and freshly ground pepper, to taste
½ teaspoon cinnamon

4 medium-size zucchini, diced
3 ripe tomatoes, peeled, seeded and chopped
1½ cups uncooked rice
3 cups water

1. Rinse out a large deep pot with water. Add the oil and sauté the onion until it is golden, for about 10 minutes. Season with the salt and pepper and the cinnamon. Add the zucchini and sauté for 5 minutes more. Add the tomatoes and simmer for 5 minutes.·

2. Add the rice and the water. Bring the mixture to boiling and boil for 10 minutes or until the vegetables are tender and the rice has absorbed all the liquid.

ZUCCHINI AND OLIVE SAUTÉ

This savory sauté uses many of the ingredients indigenous to Italian cooking — try it as a side dish or an appetizer.

Makes 6 servings.

Nutrient Value Per Serving:
50 calories, 1 g protein, 4 g fat,
4 g carbohydrate, 48 mg sodium,
0 mg cholesterol.

3 large zucchini (1½ pounds)
1 tablespoon virgin olive oil
3 tablespoons lemon juice
1 clove garlic, finely chopped
2 teaspoons white wine vinegar
6 Kalamata or other black olives (¼ cup), pitted and finely chopped

1 plum tomato, finely chopped
1 teaspoon chopped fresh oregano OR: ½ teaspoon leaf oregano, crumbled
¼ teaspoon crushed red pepper flakes
1 tablespoon chopped parsley, for garnish

1. Trim the zucchini and cut them lengthwise into ¼-inch-thick slabs.
2. Mix together the oil, lemon juice and garlic in a small cup. Let the mixture stand to combine the flavors.
3. Sparingly brush half the oil mixture over the zucchini. Heat a nonstick skillet over medium heat. Add the zucchini and sauté for about 1 minute on each side or until they are golden. Transfer the zucchini to a shallow container.

4. Add the vinegar, olives, tomato, oregano and red pepper flakes to the remaining oil mixture and pour it over the zucchini. Let the zucchini mixture stand for at least 1 hour.
5. Sprinkle the parsley over the zucchini just before serving.

ZUCCHINI RELISH

This sweet-and-sour condiment makes good use of two prolific summer vegetables — zucchini and tomatoes.

Makes four 1-pint jars.

Nutrient Value Per Tablespoon:
9 calories, 0 g protein, 0 g fat,
2 g carbohydrate, 207 mg sodium,
0 mg cholesterol.

4   **cups finely chopped zucchini**
2   **cups finely chopped onion**
2   **cups finely chopped green tomatoes**
1   **cup finely chopped sweet green pepper**
1   **cup finely chopped sweet red pepper**

¼   **cup salt**
2   **cups cider vinegar**
1   **cup sugar**
1   **tablespoon dry mustard powder**
2   **teaspoons celery seed**
1   **teaspoon ground turmeric**

1. Combine the zucchini, onion, green tomatoes, green and red peppers and the salt in a large bowl. Cover the bowl and let the vegetable mixture stand overnight.

2. Drain the vegetable mixture in a colander over the sink, pressing out as much excess liquid as possible.

3. Combine the vinegar, sugar, mustard powder, celery seed and turmeric in a large stainless steel or other nonaluminum saucepan. Bring the mixture to boiling over medium heat, stirring occasionally.

4. Add the drained vegetable mixture to the saucepan. Bring to boiling. Lower the heat and simmer, uncovered, stirring occasionally to prevent burning, for 40 minutes or until the relish thickens.

5. Spoon the relish into four clean 1-pint canning jars, leaving ½ inch headroom. Wipe the rims of the jars and seal the jars tightly with lids and rims. Process the jars for 10 minutes in a hot water bath. Or store the relish in the refrigerator.

*Note: *To process the relish in a hot water bath, you will need a water bath canner — a pot large enough to accommodate a rack that holds the jars in one layer off the bottom of the pot, and deep enough so that the jars are covered by 1 inch of boiling water. Heat the water so it will be boiling when the relish is ready for processing. Place the jar lids and rims in the water. Wash the jars in hot soapy water, rinse them quickly and fill them with the relish to within ½ inch of the top. Wipe the rims and cap the jars tightly. Place the filled jars in the canner and begin counting the processing time when the water comes to boiling again. When the processing time is over, immediately remove the jars to a cloth towel. Cool and store the jars in a cool, dark place.*

STUFFED CROOKNECK SQUASH

For the best flavor and texture, look for small squash with a graceful curve to the neck.

Grill for 15 minutes, or bake at 350° for 20 minutes.

Makes 6 servings.

Nutrient Value Per Serving:
125 calories, 6 g protein, 5 g fat, 14 g carbohydrate, 8 mg sodium, 13 mg cholesterol.

6 **yellow crookneck or summer squash***
½ **sweet red or green pepper, finely chopped**
1 **teaspoon ground cumin**
1 **teaspoon safflower oil**
¾ **cup cooked brown rice**
¾ **cup shredded low-sodium Swiss cheese (3 ounces)**

1. Build a charcoal fire and set the grill rack 6 inches above the coals. Or preheat the oven to moderate (350°).
2. Slice the squash in half, lengthwise. Scoop out the insides of the squash halves with a melon baller or paring knife, leaving a ¼-inch shell. Finely chop the scooped-out flesh.
3. Sauté the chopped squash and the red or green pepper with the cumin in the oil in a large skillet over medium heat for 5 minutes, or until the vegetables are wilted. (If the vegetables stick to the pan, add 1 or 2 tablespoons of water to provide the necessary moisture during cooking.) Remove the skillet from the heat.
4. Add the rice and all but 3 tablespoons of the Swiss cheese to the sautéed vegetables. Toss to combine the ingredients. (The stuffing, extra cheese and squash halves may be covered and refrigerated overnight. Remove them from the refrigerator 1 hour before cooking.)

5. Stuff the squash halves with the rice mixture. Sprinkle the tops with the remaining 3 tablespoons of Swiss cheese. Wrap 2 halves each in a square of aluminum foil, leaving a little extra room at the top to prevent the cheese from sticking to the foil.
6. Grill the foil packets on the grill rack for 15 minutes or until the cheese melts and the squash are tender. Or bake the foil packets in the preheated moderate oven (350°) for 20 minutes or until the squash are tender.

*****Note:** *Small zucchini or patty pan squash can be substituted for the crookneck squash in this recipe.*

RATATOUILLE

Although the flavors of the vegetables meld together in the microwave, each vegetable retains its shape. To serve as an entrée, top with a poached egg or shredded Bel Paese cheese.

Microwave at full power for 6 minutes.

Makes 4 main dish servings.

3   tablespoons olive oil
1   large red onion, thinly sliced
4   cloves garlic, finely chopped
1   medium-size eggplant
      (1 pound), peeled, cut
      into 1-inch-thick rounds
      and diced
3   small zucchini, trimmed and
      cut into ½-inch-thick
      rounds

1   medium-size sweet green
      pepper, halved, seeded and
      cut into ½-inch strips
¼   cup chopped fresh basil
      OR: 4 teaspoons leaf basil,
      crumbled
      Freshly ground black pepper,
      to taste
2   large ripe tomatoes, cored
      and cut into wedges
      Salt (optional)

Nutrient Value Per Serving:
166 calories, 4 g protein, 11 g fat,
17 g carbohydrate, 15 mg sodium,
0 mg cholesterol.

1. Combine the oil, onion and garlic in a microwave-safe 2-quart baking dish. Do not cover the dish.
2. Microwave at full power for 2 minutes.
3. Stir in the eggplant, zucchini, green pepper, basil and black pepper. Cover the dish tightly.

4. Microwave the vegetables at full power for 3 minutes.
5. Uncover the dish carefully. Stir in the tomatoes. Recover the dish.
6. Microwave at full power for 1 minute.
7. Taste the ratatouille and, if you wish, add salt.

CookSmart

Expert Eggplant

To pick the perfect eggplant (which is actually a fruit), look for one that is firm and heavy in relation to its size, with a uniformly dark, rich purple color. Use it as quickly as possible after purchasing or, if necessary, store it in a plastic bag in the refrigerator for a day or two.

MIXED VEGETABLES WITH GARLIC SAUCE

Be inspired! This is a flexible recipe, so try a variety of whatever vegetables are fresh and available. (You can blanch or steam the vegetables to the degree of doneness you prefer.)

Microwave at full power for 2 to 3 minutes.

Makes 5 first course or 10 cocktail-size servings.

5   new potatoes (about ½ pound), scrubbed and halved
4   fresh beets (about 1 pound), scrubbed and quartered
4   turnips (about ¾ pound), scrubbed and quartered
½   pound French green beans (haricots verts) OR:
½ pound very thin green beans, trimmed

Nutrient Value Per First Course Serving (without Garlic Sauce):
112 calories, 4 g protein, 0 g fat, 26 g carbohydrate, 118 mg sodium, 0 mg cholesterol.

10   cherry tomatoes, hulled
Salt and freshly ground pepper, to taste
Garlic Sauce (recipe, page 123)

1. Use a 14 x 11 x 2-inch microwave-safe baking dish. Place the vegetables that require the longest cooking times (the potatoes, beets and turnips) around the perimeter of the dish. Place mounds of the French or very thin green beans at either end of the dish, within the border of the other vegetables.
2. If you like cherry tomatoes cooked, prick each of them twice with a wooden pick and place them in the center of the dish. (Otherwise, add them to the dish just before serving.) Cover the dish tightly with microwave-safe plastic wrap.

3. Microwave the vegetables at full power for 2 to 3 minutes or until the vegetables are cooked as you like them.
4. Pierce the plastic with the tip of a knife to release the steam. Uncover the dish carefully and season the vegetables with the salt and pepper. Serve the vegetables with the Garlic Sauce on the side as a first course, or use the sauce as a dip when serving them as a cocktail-size dish.

CookSmart

Can't Beet It!

Beets, aside from the vivid color they add to any dish, also are packed with vitamins A and C — and their greens are a good source of calcium. At about 40 calories per half cup, beets can be microwaved, grilled, steamed or served raw (try to leave the nutrient-rich stem intact).

GARLIC SAUCE

This creamy sauce, also known as aioli, adds character to simply prepared chicken or seafood as well as to vegetables.

Makes about 1½ cups.

Nutrient Value Per Teaspoon:
41 calories, 0 g protein, 5 g fat,
0 g carbohydrate, 32 mg sodium,
4 mg cholesterol.

HEALTH

Cloves of Protection

Use garlic generously. Scientific evidence suggests it may help to protect against heart attacks, cancer, infection and diabetes.

HOTLINE

1　whole egg
1　tablespoon white wine
　　vinegar OR: lemon juice
1　teaspoon salt
¾　cup olive oil

¾　cup corn or safflower oil
1　large or 2 small cloves garlic
　　Freshly ground pepper,
　　　to taste

1. Place the egg, vinegar or lemon juice and the salt in the container of a food processor. Cover and process for 2 to 3 seconds or until the mixture is blended.
2. With the motor still running, gradually add the olive oil and the corn or safflower oil through the feed tube. The mixture should thicken. Add the garlic through the feed tube and continue processing until the mixture is smooth.

3. Taste the sauce. Add the pepper and, if necessary, additional salt and vinegar.
4. Transfer the sauce to a bowl, cover the bowl and refrigerate the sauce for up to 1 week.

6
GREAT PASTA-BILITIES

Remember when macaroni was only paired with cheese? When "spaghetti" was the only pasta you ever heard of? Times have changed. What was once just "noodles" has turned into a national love affair with pasta. This pasta passion has catapulted the per capita consumption to 14 *pounds* of pasta per year.

A staple of Italian and Chinese cooking, pasta was once shunned by dieters as "fattening". In reality, pasta is a gift to good health. According to the National Pasta Association, 4 ounces of plain pasta supplies 81 grams of complex carbohydrates, which provide sustaining energy without a traumatic surge in blood sugar levels. Plus, pasta is a great source of protein, contains no cholesterol, is low in calories and fat and provides iron, thiamine, riboflavin and niacin. With a profile like that, pasta is easy to love!

There's only one way to top our Easy Spaghetti Sauce *(recipe, page 127)* at only 79 calories per ½ cup serving—and that's with our Miniature Meatballs *(recipe, page 128)*. One taste of our Creamy Pasta Alfredo *(recipe, page 129)* will have you convinced it's too good to be true—but it's actually low in fat, calories and cholesterol. Other pasta-perfect dishes include Tuna Puttanesca on Rotelle *(recipe, page 130)* and Salmon and Pasta with Cilantro Sauce *(recipe, page 132)*.

As for "pasta salads," the phrase used to conjure up visions of mayonnaise-drenched macaroni. But that was before the culinary innovations of the '80's. Our elegant Lasagna Salad *(recipe, page 137)* is stuffed with low-fat cottage cheese, fresh spinach and savory basil. Or try Vermicelli-Stuffed Tomatoes with Basil *(recipe, page 141)* or a refreshing Pasta Peach Salad *(recipe, page 139)*.

Read on—the pasta-bilities are virtually limitless.

Cold Linguine with Tuna Sauce (recipe, page 131)

PASTA
WITH SAUCES

Easy Spaghetti Sauce (recipe, page 127),
Miniature Meatballs (recipe, page 128)

EASY SPAGHETTI SAUCE

Try adding your own special touches to this basic red sauce, such as mushrooms, diced prosciutto, Italian sausage or chopped vegetables.

Makes 3½ cups.

Nutrient Value Per ½ Cup Serving:
79 calories, 1 g protein, 4 g fat,
10 g carbohydrate, 425 mg sodium,
0 mg cholesterol.

1	medium-size onion
1	carrot
1	stalk celery
2	cloves garlic
2	tablespoons olive oil
1	can (28 ounces) whole tomatoes in purée
1	cup water

¾	teaspoon salt
½	teaspoon freshly ground pepper
½	teaspoon leaf basil, crumbled
½	teaspoon leaf oregano, crumbled
	Bay leaf
	Chopped parsley (optional)

1. Coarsely chop the onion. Coarsely chop together the carrot and the celery. Place the onion in the container of an electric blender and finely chop it. Scrape the onion out of the blender and set it aside. Repeat with the garlic, then with the carrot and celery together.
2. Heat the oil in a large skillet. Add the onion and sauté until it is softened but not brown, for 4 to 5 minutes. Add the garlic and sauté for 1 minute. Add the carrot and celery and sauté until they are softened, for 1 to 2 minutes.
3. To the skillet, add the tomatoes with their purée, the water, salt, pepper, basil, oregano and bay leaf. Bring the mixture to boiling. Reduce the heat and simmer, uncovered, for 10 minutes.

4. Place a food mill or fine sieve over a bowl. Pour the tomato mixture into the food mill and force the mixture through with the back of a wooden spoon. Discard any solids left in the mill.
5. Return the sauce to the skillet. Simmer for 10 to 15 minutes or until the sauce is the desired consistency. Remove the bay leaf. Just before serving, stir in chopped parsley, if you wish.

CookSmart

The Road to Perfect Pasta

● Bring a large pot of water to boiling — at least one quart of water for every ¼ pound of pasta. Pasta needs room to expand and cook evenly.

● You can add a pinch of salt to the water, if you wish, but it is not necessary. A tangy sauce will compensate for pasta cooked without salt.

● Stir the pasta often, using a wooden fork to avoid breaking or mashing the pasta.

● If the pasta is to be used in a dish requiring further cooking (such as lasagna), cook it only until it is just tender, but still firm — al dente.

● The best way to test pasta for doneness is to remove a strand and bite into it. The pasta should be tender, but with enough firmness to be felt between the teeth.

● Add a cup of cold water to the pot to stop the cooking and drain the pot immediately.

● Rinse the pasta with cold water only if you will be serving it cold. How much to cook:
Prepare ⅛ pound of pasta per person for an appetizer portion, ¼ to ⅓ pound for a main-dish serving.

MINIATURE MEATBALLS

These savory meatballs can be made ahead, then simmered with the Easy Spaghetti Sauce for 10 minutes before serving.

Makes 24 meatballs (4 to 6 meatballs per serving).

Nutrient Value Per Meatball:
59 calories, 4 g protein, 4 g fat, 1 g carbohydrate, 130 mg sodium, 23 mg cholesterol.

½ **pound sweet Italian sausage**
½ **pound ground beef**
1 **clove garlic, finely chopped**
½ **cup finely chopped parsley**
1 **egg, slightly beaten**
1 **cup fresh bread crumbs**
½ **teaspoon salt**
¼ **teaspoon freshly ground pepper**
½ **cup milk**
1 **tablespoon oil, or more as needed**
Easy Spaghetti Sauce (optional; recipe, page 127)

1. Remove the casings from the sausage and discard them. Crumble the sausage and combine it with the beef, garlic, parsley, egg, bread crumbs, salt and pepper in a large bowl. Pour the milk over the mixture and toss lightly with a wooden spoon or clean hands until the ingredients are thoroughly mixed. Do not overmix or the meatballs will become "tough."
2. Break off walnut-size pieces of the meat mixture and roll them between the palms of your hands to form 24 small meatballs. Place the meatballs on a platter or baking sheet lined with wax paper.

3. Heat the oil in a large nonstick skillet. Working in two batches, brown the meatballs in the hot oil for about 10 minutes per batch. (Be careful not to crowd the skillet or the meatballs will steam rather than brown.) Remove the meatballs to paper toweling to drain.
4. If you wish, add the meatballs to Easy Spaghetti Sauce in a large skillet and simmer for 10 minutes to blend the flavors.

CookSmart

The Pasta Profile

For a boost of complex carbohydrates with a low-calorie profile, pasta is a tough act to top. At only 200 calories per cup, pasta should be combined with other low-calorie, lowfat ingredients, such as fresh vegetables, fish, poultry or lean meats to maximize its healthy potential.

CREAMY PASTA ALFREDO

Yearning for an elegant Alfredo sauce but holding out because of the calorie overload? Our sauce has about 155 fewer calories than a traditional sauce — so indulge!

Makes 4 servings.

Nutrient Value Per Serving:
307 calories, 20 g protein, 2 g fat,
52 g carbohydrate, 499 mg sodium,
4 mg cholesterol.

HEALTH

Pasta Perfect

According to the National Pasta Association, 4 ounces of dry pasta — an average main-dish portion — supplies 81 grams of complex carbohydrates, which are slowly digested nutrients that provide sustaining energy without a traumatic surge in blood sugar levels. That's good news if you're watching your weight. A meal of pasta will leave you feeling satisfied and well fed, less tempted to nibble. And pasta is an important source of protein, especially when combined with small quantities of lean meat, fish, poultry or dairy products.

Pasta has no cholesterol and is low in calories and fat. It also provides several important nutrients: iron, thiamine, riboflavin and niacin.

Not bad for something most of us would eat just because it tastes so good!

HOTLINE

1½ cups 1% lowfat cottage
   cheese
2 cloves garlic, halved
½ cup skim milk
2 tablespoons all-purpose flour
3 teaspoons fresh lemon juice
1 teaspoon leaf basil, crumbled

½ teaspoon dry mustard
½ teaspoon freshly ground pepper
¼ teaspoon salt
8 ounces rotelle pasta
1 medium-size ripe tomato,
   halved, seeded and coarsely
   chopped, for garnish

1. Place the cottage cheese, garlic and milk in the container of a food processor or an electric blender. Cover and whirl, scraping down the sides of the container, for 3 to 5 minutes or until the mixture has no lumps. Add the flour, lemon juice, basil, mustard, pepper and salt. Cover and whirl to blend the ingredients well.* Pour the cream sauce into a medium-size saucepan and set aside.
2. Cook the rotelle in a large saucepan of boiling water, following the package directions, until it is *al dente,* firm but tender. Drain the rotelle and place it in a large serving bowl.

3. Heat the cream sauce over medium-low heat to thicken it slightly. Stir the sauce often until it just begins to bubble, for 1 to 2 minutes; do not allow the sauce to come to a full boil. Remove the saucepan from the heat.
4. Pour the cream sauce over the hot pasta in the bowl and toss gently to coat the pasta. Garnish with the tomato and serve immediately.

*****Note:** *The sauce can be made several hours in advance and refrigerated until ready to use.*

LINGUINE, TOMATOES AND TUNA

Need a quick dish to serve unexpected guests? This recipe takes only minutes to prepare.

Makes 4 servings.

Nutrient Value Per Serving:
371 calories, 30 g protein, 17 g fat, 40 g carbohydrate, 410 mg sodium, 42 mg cholesterol.

10	ounces linguine
2	tablespoons olive oil
2	tablespoons finely chopped garlic
4	cups seeded, peeled, chopped tomatoes

14 ounces water-packed chunk albacore tuna
2 cups green peas, fresh or frozen

1. Cook the linguine in a large saucepan of boiling water until it is *al dente*, firm but tender.
2. While the linguine cooks, heat the oil in a medium-size saucepan. Add the garlic and sauté until it is translucent. Add the tomatoes, tuna and peas and cook for about 2 minutes.

3. Drain the linguine, add it to the saucepan and toss to combine the ingredients. Serve the linguine immediately.

TUNA PUTTANESCA ON ROTELLE

Black and green olives add a spicy tang to this tomato-based sauce. If you start the water boiling right away, this dish takes about 20 minutes to prepare.

Makes 4 servings.

Nutrient Value Per Serving:
418 calories, 19 g protein, 14 g fat, 52 g carbohydrate, 37 mg sodium, 8 mg cholesterol.

1 medium-size onion, chopped
1 clove garlic, finely chopped
2 tablespoons olive oil
1 can (16 ounces) tomatoes in tomato purée
¼ cup pitted black olives, chopped

¼ cup stuffed green olives, chopped
¼ teaspoon pepper
8 ounces rotelle pasta
1 can (6½ or 7 ounces) tuna, drained and coarsely flaked
2 tablespoons chopped parsley

1. Sauté the onion and garlic in the oil in a saucepan until tender but not browned. Break up the tomatoes in the tomato purée slightly and stir them into the saucepan with the olives and the pepper. Bring the mixture to boiling. Lower the heat, partially cover the saucepan and simmer for 15 minutes, stirring occasionally.

2. Meanwhile, cook the rotelle, following the package directions, until it is *al dente*, firm but tender. Drain the rotelle and keep it warm.
3. Stir the flaked tuna into the tomato mixture. Combine the tuna-tomato mixture with the rotelle in a large serving bowl and toss to mix thoroughly. Sprinkle with the parsley and serve immediately.

CookSmart

Pasta Pointers

● Which wheat is what? Dried, factory-produced pasta contains almost no fat, because it's basically wheat flour and water. In the U.S., even salt usually is omitted, but it's best to check labels.
● For the most protein and vitamins and the best cooking quality, look for pasta made from durum wheat, ground into semolina flour.
● If you're concerned about getting adequate amounts of protein, look for high-protein pasta. Fortified with soy flour and whey protein, it supplies about the same amount of protein as a comparable weight of cooked meat, one third more than regular pasta.

COLD LINGUINE WITH TUNA SAUCE

LOW-CHOLESTEROL

Only the pasta needs cooking in this zesty dish that gets better and better as it chills.

Makes 8 servings.

Nutrient Value Per Serving:
508 calories, 22 g protein, 26 g fat, 48 g carbohydrate, 412 mg sodium, 39 mg cholesterol.

1	**pound linguine**
2	**tablespoons olive oil**
1½	**cups plain lowfat yogurt**
½	**cup reduced-calorie mayonnaise**
3	**tablespoons fresh lemon juice**
2	**cans (6½ ounces each) water-packed chunk light tuna, drained**
1	**can (6 ounces) pitted black olives, drained**

1	**cup thinly sliced green onion**
½	**cup chopped fresh parsley**
1	**teaspoon leaf oregano, crumbled**
½	**teaspoon freshly ground pepper**
½	**teaspoon salt (optional)**
	Lemon wedges, for garnish
	Additional green onion slices, for garnish

1. Break the linguine in half and cook it in a large saucepan of boiling water, following the package directions, until it is *al dente*, firm but tender. Drain the linguine in a colander and rinse it under cold water. Drain the linguine again. Place the linguine in a large bowl and toss it with the oil.

2. Whisk together the yogurt, mayonnaise and lemon juice in a large bowl. Break up the tuna with a fork and fold it into the sauce. Slice 3 olives and reserve them for the garnish. Slice the remaining olives and add them to the tuna sauce along with the 1 cup of green onion, the parsley, oregano, pepper and, if you wish, salt. Stir the sauce well and spoon it over the linguine. Toss together until all the ingredients are well mixed. Cover the bowl and refrigerate the linguine for at least 1 hour or overnight. Just before serving, garnish the linguine with the reserved sliced olives, the lemon wedges and additional green onion.

Note: *You can serve any leftover linguini and sauce as an appetizer.*

CookSmart

Just My Type: Pasta Varieties

● Whole wheat pasta contains more dietary fiber, iron and niacin than regular pasta. Its texture when cooked is somewhat grainy.

● Vegetable pastas are subtly flavored with such ingredients as spinach, tomato and carrot, which give the pastas attractive coloring but not much of a nutritional boost.

● Although noodles have eggs added to the basic flour and water formula, their cholesterol content doesn't make them off-limits for the average healthy eater. Their tenderness and delicate flavor are particularly well suited to stews.

● Oriental noodles are made from such diverse ingredients as wheat, rice and mung beans. Most noodles can be prepared in a fashion similar to regular pasta, with the exception of cellophane noodles, which need no cooking — they simply are soaked in hot water and rinsed with cold water.

● Is fresh better? Good-quality dry pasta is preferable to mediocre fresh pasta. Fresh pasta often contains eggs and salt, neither of which is found in regular dry pasta.

SALMON AND PASTA WITH CILANTRO SAUCE

This recipe calls for radiatore pasta, but you can substitute any other short, shaped pasta.

LOW-FAT

LOW-SODIUM

LOW-CHOLESTEROL

Bake salmon at 400° for 20 minutes.

Makes 8 servings.

Nutrient Value Per Serving:
479 calories, 79 g protein, 8 g fat, 69 g carbohydrate, 89 mg sodium, 49 mg cholesterol.

Cilantro Sauce:
1   cup tightly packed cilantro leaves
1   small onion, quartered
2   cloves garlic
3   jalapeño peppers, halved and seeded (wear rubber gloves)
¼   cup fresh lemon juice (1 lemon)
2   green onions, sliced
1   tablespoon olive oil

Salmon and Pasta:
1½   pounds fillet of salmon
    Juice of ½ lemon
1½   pounds radiatore pasta
1½   cups buttermilk
2   green onions, trimmed and sliced
½   cup cilantro leaves

1. Prepare the Cilantro Sauce: Place the cilantro, onion, garlic, jalapeño peppers, lemon juice, green onion and oil in the container of a food processor. Cover and process until the mixture is puréed.
2. Transfer the sauce to a small bowl; you should have about 1 cup of sauce. Spread one third of the sauce over the salmon and refrigerate the salmon for about 1 hour, if time permits.
3. Preheat the oven to hot (400°).

4. Prepare the Salmon and Pasta: Place the salmon, skin side down, on a nonstick baking sheet. Bake the salmon in the preheated hot oven (400°) for about 20 minutes or until the fish flakes when lightly touched with a fork. Remove the salmon from the oven and sprinkle it with the lemon juice.
5. Meanwhile, cook the pasta in a large saucepan of boiling water until it is *al dente*, firm but tender. Drain the pasta and place it in a large bowl.
6. Flake the salmon into the bowl. Beat together the remaining sauce and the buttermilk in another bowl. Taste and add a little more lemon juice, if you wish.
7. Pour the sauce over the salmon and pasta. Add the green onion and the cilantro leaves. Toss gently to blend all the ingredients. Add a little more buttermilk if the pasta seems too dry. Serve the pasta warm or at room temperature.

SAFFRON CARROT SAUCE

LOW-CALORIE
LOW-CHOLESTEROL

Make this sauce double as a delicious cold soup by adding extra buttermilk and lemon juice.

Makes about 2½ cups.

Nutrient Value Per ¼ Cup (without optional buttermilk):
38 calories, 1 g protein, 2 g fat, 6 g carbohydrate, 109 mg sodium, 0 mg cholesterol.

1	**very large onion**
2	**carrots, peeled**
1	**tablespoon olive oil**
1	**large clove garlic, crushed**
1	**cup chicken broth**

1	**teaspoon saffron threads**
¼	**cup fresh lemon juice**
⅔	**cup buttermilk* (optional)**
	Salt and freshly ground black pepper, to taste

1. Chop the onion. Cut the carrots into ½-inch-thick slices.
2. Sauté the onion in the oil in a small saucepan for 5 minutes.
3. Add the carrots and the garlic and sauté for 1 minute more. Add the broth and the saffron. Bring the mixture to boiling over medium heat. Lower the heat, cover the saucepan and simmer for 5 minutes.
4. Place the carrot mixture in the container of an electric blender or a food processor. Cover and whirl until the mixture is puréed. Cool the mixture slightly. Add the lemon juice, buttermilk, if you wish, and the salt and black pepper. Cover and whirl until the sauce is blended.

*Note: *When buttermilk is added to hot mixtures, it sometimes curdles. Cool the carrot mixture slightly as directed, or mix 2 teaspoons of cornstarch into the buttermilk. Return the puréed carrot mixture to the saucepan, stir in the buttermilk and cook for 1 minute, stirring constantly.*

LIGHT PESTO SAUCE

LOW-SODIUM
LOW-CHOLESTEROL

Presto, pesto! A lusciously light version of pesto sauce that you whip up in your food processor or electric blender.

Makes about 1½ cups.

Nutrient Value Per ¼ Cup:
164 calories, 3 g protein, 16 g fat, 7 g carbohydrate, 86 mg sodium, 0 mg cholesterol.

4	**large cloves garlic**
2	**cups firmly packed fresh basil leaves**
½	**cup walnut pieces (2 ounces)**
½	**cup chicken broth**

¼	**cup olive oil**
	Salt and freshly ground black pepper, to taste

1. With the motor of a food processor or an electric blender running, drop the garlic cloves, one at a time, through the feed tube or lid opening. Turn off the motor.
2. Add the basil and the walnuts. Cover and process until they are chopped.
3. Add the broth and the oil. Cover and process until the sauce is smooth. Season with the salt and black pepper.

RIGATONI WITH VEAL MEATBALLS

The veal meatballs also are delicious served with a tomato sauce or a dilled cream sauce.

LOW-FAT
LOW-CHOLESTEROL

Broil meatballs for 10 minutes.

Makes 12 servings.

Nutrient Value Per Serving:
427 calories, 20 g protein, 9 g fat,
60 g carbohydrate, 151 mg sodium,
75 mg cholesterol.

2   pounds ground veal
1   cup fresh whole wheat bread
    crumbs (2 slices)
6   ounces mixed vegetable juice
⅓   cup chopped fresh parsley
3   tablespoons finely chopped
    onion
1   egg
1   small clove garlic, finely
    chopped

2   pounds rigatoni
    Light Pesto Sauce (recipe,
    page 133)
    Saffron Carrot Sauce (recipe,
    page 133)
⅓   cup grated Parmesan cheese
    Freshly ground black pepper,
    to taste

1. Preheat the broiler to high.
2. Combine the veal, bread crumbs, vegetable juice, parsley, onion, egg and garlic in a medium-size bowl and lightly blend together the ingredients.
3. Shape the veal mixture into 1-inch balls and place them, 1 inch apart, on the broiler pan.

4. Broil the meatballs for 10 minutes or until they are golden brown.
5. Meanwhile, cook the rigatoni in a large pot of boiling water until it is *al dente*, firm but tender. Drain the rigatoni and place it in individual bowls.
6. Top the rigatoni with the Light Pesto Sauce, Saffron Carrot Sauce and meatballs. Sprinkle it with the Parmesan cheese and season with the black pepper.

ZUCCHINI AND PASTA WITH BASIL TOMATO SAUCE

For a finishing touch, grate a little fresh Parmesan cheese onto each serving of this flavorful pasta.

Makes 6 servings.

Nutrient Value Per Serving:
354 calories, 12 g protein, 4 g fat,
69 g carbohydrate, 21 mg sodium,
0 mg cholesterol.

Basil Tomato Sauce:
3   cloves garlic
½   cup tightly packed fresh basil
       leaves OR: 3 tablespoons
       leaf basil, crumbled
¼   cup fresh parsley sprigs
2½ pounds ripe tomatoes

1   pound pasta shells
1   pound zucchini
1   tablespoon olive oil
       Freshly ground black pepper,
       to taste

1. Prepare the Basil Tomato Sauce: With the motor of a food processor running, drop the garlic cloves, one at a time, through the feed tube. Turn off the motor. Add the basil and the parsley. Cover and process until the herbs and the garlic are finely chopped.
2. Quarter the tomatoes and add them to the container of the food processor. Cover and process until the tomatoes are puréed. Transfer the sauce to a large bowl. (Alternatively, the garlic, herbs and tomatoes can be chopped with a chef's knife and stirred together in a large bowl.) Cover the bowl and refrigerate the sauce overnight so the flavors blend. Remove the sauce from the refrigerator 1 hour before serving time. Taste and adjust the seasonings, if necessary.
3. At serving time, cook the pasta shells in a large saucepan of boiling water, following the package directions, until they are *al dente*, firm but tender.

4. While the pasta shells are cooking, scrub, trim and shred the zucchini into a medium-size bowl.
5. Drain the pasta shells and place them in a large bowl. Add the oil, toss the pasta and season it with the black pepper. Add the zucchini and half the sauce. Toss to combine all the ingredients. Pass the remaining sauce at the table.

Note: *In the summer, when fresh tomatoes and basil are plentiful, this quickly-made sauce can be used in many dishes. Add it to plain lowfat yogurt for a dressing or a dip for crudités. Top just-sautéed fish, chicken or veal scaloppine with a large dollop of the sauce.*

PASTA
SALADS

Good Health Cookbook

LASAGNA SALAD

To make this salad in advance, cover the assembled rolls (minus the dressing) with a damp cloth towel, wrap them tightly with plastic wrap, and refrigerate them for up to 3 days.

Makes 4 servings.

Nutrient Value Per Serving:
270 calories, 25 g protein, 7 g fat,
25 g carbohydrate, 624 mg sodium,
21 mg cholesterol.

4   lasagna noodles, cooked
      and drained
1   teaspoon olive oil
2   cups lowfat cottage cheese
1   cup shredded lowfat
      mozzarella cheese
      (4 ounces)
16 fresh spinach leaves, well
      washed, patted dry and
      coarsely chopped

4   cloves garlic, finely chopped
12 fresh basil leaves OR:
      12 fresh parsley sprigs
      Freshly ground black pepper,
      to taste
      Fresh Tomato Dressing
      (recipe, page 88)

1. Place the noodles on a damp cloth towel. Brush each noodle gently with some of the oil.
2. Combine the cottage cheese, mozzarella cheese, spinach and garlic in a small bowl until they are well blended.
3. Gently spread the cheese mixture over the noodles. Place the basil or parsley over the cheese mixture. Season with the black pepper.

4. Gently fold one end of each noodle over its filling, and roll the noodle into a neat round package, enclosing the filling.
5. Serve the lasagna rolls with the Fresh Tomato Dressing.

CookSmart

Beat the Heat with Pasta Salads

For a cool summer meal, pasta salads are hard to beat. By combining cooked and cooled pasta with tuna or salmon, cold chicken, raw or blanched vegetables and any number of fresh sauces, you have a great-tasting, nutritious meal that can be made in advance and refrigerated for your convenience. There's such a wonderful variety of recipes available, you don't have to settle for the mayonnaise-drenched deli versions anymore.

CAPELLINI AND ZUCCHINI TORTA

This herbed vegetable pie bakes in the microwave in less than 30 minutes. Delicious hot or served at room temperature.

Microwave at full power for 17½ minutes.

Makes 6 servings.

Nutrient Value Per Serving:
164 calories, 8 g protein, 6 g fat, 21 g carbohydrate, 80 mg sodium, 53 mg cholesterol.

2   medium-size zucchini, trimmed and shredded (about ¾ pound)
½   teaspoon salt
1   large onion, chopped (1 cup)
2   cloves garlic, finely chopped
1   tablespoon olive oil
¼   pound dry capellini pasta
1   egg
1   egg white
½   cup lowfat ricotta cheese

2   tablespoons grated Parmesan cheese
½   cup chopped green onion
¼   cup snipped chives
3   tablespoons fresh lemon juice
     Freshly ground pepper, to taste
     Microwave Tomato Sauce (recipe, page 139)
     Chopped fresh basil, for garnish

1. Combine the zucchini with the salt in a colander and place the colander in the sink. Let the zucchini stand for 20 minutes, tossing once or twice, so the liquid drains off. Squeeze out as much additional liquid as possible from the zucchini.

2. Combine the onion, garlic and oil in a microwave-safe 9-inch pie plate. Microwave at full power for 2 minutes, stirring once. Add the zucchini to the plate. Cover the plate with microwave-safe plastic wrap. Microwave at full power for 30 seconds. Cool the mixture slightly.

3. Cook the capellini in a large saucepan of boiling water for 3 minutes or until it is still slightly underdone (the microwave will finish cooking the pasta). Drain the capellini and place it under cold running water to stop the cooking. Drain the capellini again and return it to the saucepan.

4. Add the onion-zucchini mixture, egg, egg white, ricotta and Parmesan cheeses, green onion, chives, lemon juice and pepper to the capellini. Mix the ingredients gently. Place the mixture in the pie plate.

5. Microwave the torta, uncovered, at full power, turning the dish one quarter turn every 4 minutes, for 15 minutes or until the torta is firm when gently pressed with your fingertip. Remove the pie plate from the microwave and let the torta stand for 10 minutes.

6. Cut the torta into 6 wedges. Top it with the Microwave Tomato Sauce, garnish with the basil and serve.

CookSmart

The ABZ's of Zucchini

Zucchini, a green-skinned, Italian squash, looks somewhat like a slender cucumber and ranges in length from 6 to 8 inches. The skin may be evenly dark and green or striped with white. Its flesh is creamy white, its texture tender and its flavor mild.

Originally developed in Italy, zucchini is a variety of summer squash. However, it is available year-round, with the peak season during the summer months. Purchase 1 pound for 2 to 3 servings. A 3½-ounce raw serving contains 17 calories.

Zucchini does not need to be peeled. Just wash, cut off the ends, then cut it into slices or strips or dice. Serve zucchini raw, cook it briefly in a small amount of water or sauté in butter or oil.

MICROWAVE TOMATO SAUCE

Make extra batches of this sauce in the summer and freeze them for wintertime use. The tomatoes can be peeled and seeded, if you wish.

Microwave at full power for 32 minutes.

Makes 4 cups.

Nutrient Value Per ½ Cup:
52 calories, 2 g protein, 2 g fat, 8 g carbohydrate, 14 mg sodium, 0 mg cholesterol.

1	tablespoon olive oil
1	large onion, chopped
2	cloves garlic, finely chopped
2½	pounds ripe tomatoes
½	small carrot, peeled and sliced

¼	cup chopped fresh parsley
2	teaspoons freshly squeezed lemon juice
	Salt and freshly ground black pepper, to taste

1. Place the oil, onion and garlic in a microwave-safe 9-inch dish. Microwave at full power for 2 minutes, stirring once.
2. Core and slice the tomatoes into eighths. Toss the tomatoes with the onion mixture. Add the carrot, parsley and lemon juice. Cover the dish with microwave-safe plastic wrap.
3. Microwave at full power for 15 minutes, rotating the dish every few minutes.

4. Carefully remove the plastic wrap from the dish. Transfer the tomato mixture to the container of a food processor, cover and purée the mixture. Return the mixture to the dish. Season with the salt and black pepper.
5. Microwave at full power, uncovered, for 15 minutes more, stirring the sauce and rotating the dish every few minutes, until the sauce thickens.

PASTA PEACH SALAD

An unusual combination that makes a wonderfully refreshing salad. If ripe peaches or nectarines are not available, use 5 apricots.

Makes 10 servings.

Nutrient Value Per Serving:
259 calories, 8 g protein, 5 g fat, 45 g carbohydrate, 69 mg sodium, 5 mg cholesterol.

1	pound ziti or other tubular pasta
4	ripe peaches OR: nectarines
2	cups fresh spinach leaves, well washed and patted dry
1	cup sliced celery
¼	cup chopped fresh basil OR: 3 tablespoons leaf basil, crumbled

	Grated zest (orange part of rind only) and juice of 1 orange
1	cup plain lowfat yogurt
¼	cup mayonnaise
3	cloves garlic, finely chopped
1	teaspoon ground cinnamon
1	teaspoon ground cumin
	Freshly ground black pepper, to taste

1. Cook the pasta in a large saucepan of boiling water, following the package directions, until it is *al dente*, firm but tender. Drain the pasta immediately and rinse it under cold water. Drain the pasta again and place it in a large bowl.
2. Halve, stone and thickly slice the peaches or nectarines. Cut the spinach into strips. Gently toss together the peaches, spinach, celery, basil and pasta.
3. Combine the orange zest and juice, the yogurt, mayonnaise, garlic, cinnamon and cumin in a small bowl. Pour the dressing over the pasta mixture and toss gently to combine the ingredients. Season with the black pepper. Cover the bowl and refrigerate the salad until serving time.

PASTA-STUFFED TOMATOES

The lemon and parsley add a piquant touch to this dish. Other small pasta, such as orzo, can be substituted for the tubettini.

Makes 6 servings.

Nutrient Value Per Serving:
144 calories, 3 g protein, 7 g fat,
18 g carbohydrate, 15 mg sodium,
0 mg cholesterol.

6   firm, ripe tomatoes
    Salt (optional)
2   cups cooked tubettini pasta
1   small carrot, chopped
6   radishes, chopped
1   small red onion, chopped
3   tablespoons olive oil

3   tablespoons lemon juice
1   tablespoon snipped chives
1   tablespoon chopped parsley
    Cracked pepper
    Grated lemon zest
       (yellow part of rind only),
       for garnish

1. Hollow out each tomato with a sharp paring knife, leaving a ¾-inch-thick shell. Enlarge the top opening. Cut off a small piece from the bottom of each tomato so it will not wobble when filled. Sprinkle the insides with salt, if you wish. Invert the tomatoes onto paper toweling to drain.
2. Place the pasta, carrot, radishes and onion in a medium-size bowl.

3. Beat together the oil, lemon juice, chives and parsley in a small bowl. Pour the dressing over the pasta mixture and toss to combine all the ingredients.
4. Spoon the pasta into the tomatoes. Sprinkle the tops with the pepper and garnish with the lemon zest.

VERMICELLI-STUFFED TOMATOES WITH BASIL

The vibrant flavor of fresh basil permeates these pasta-stuffed tomatoes.

Makes 12 servings.

Nutrient Value Per Serving:
240 calories, 7 g protein, 8 g fat,
36 g carbohydrate, 93 mg sodium,
4 mg cholesterol.

12	firm, ripe medium-size tomatoes
1	pound vermicelli
¼	cup olive oil
3	tablespoons fresh lemon juice
½	cup plain lowfat yogurt
½	cup reduced-calorie mayonnaise

1	cup fresh basil leaves, thinly sliced
¼	cup snipped fresh chives
	Salt and freshly ground pepper, to taste
12	whole basil leaves, for garnish

1. Cut the stem ends from the tomatoes and remove the seeds and pulp. Invert the tomatoes onto paper toweling to drain.
2. Meanwhile, cook the vermicelli in a large saucepan of lightly salted, boiling water until it is *al dente,* firm but tender. Drain the vermicelli and place it in a large bowl.

3. Toss the oil and the lemon juice with the vermicelli and let the mixture cool.
4. Add the yogurt, mayonnaise, sliced basil leaves, chives and salt and pepper to the bowl. Toss to mix all the ingredients.
5. Spoon the salad into the tomato shells. Garnish with the whole basil leaves.

CookSmart

In-A-Pinch Pasta

Need a quick-fix dinner for spur-of-the-moment company? Try corkscrew pasta combined with chopped ripe tomatoes, shredded fresh basil leaves and cooked sweet corn kernels. Dress with a light vinaigrette made of 1 part virgin olive oil to 2 parts vinegar. Toss gently to combine the ingredients and garnish each serving with cracked black pepper and a whole basil leaf or two. Add a loaf of Italian bread and a tossed green salad and voilá — dinner is served!

7

MEATS THAT MAKE THE GRADE

Recently, there's been a popular attitude that meat, particularly red meat, is bad for you. On the contrary, *all* meat is an excellent source of protein and red meat is one of the best sources of iron available. Moderation is the key: Keep serving sizes to no more than 4 ounces, select lean cuts of beef, pork and lamb, and include more poultry in your diet. With our smart cooking techniques and healthful recipes, you can put meat back on the menu.

Poultry is one of the best friends a healthy cook can have. A good source of protein, poultry has less fat and fewer calories than other meats, and provides vitamin A, thiamine, riboflavin, niacin, iron and phosphorous. Not a bad resumé for a main dish.

Cumin Chicken and Orange Salad *(recipe, page 147)* combines the flavors of ground cumin, fresh mint and orange juice at only 283 calories per serving. Aluminum-foil packets eliminate added fat in cooking, so our Oriental Chicken *(recipe, page 149)* is naturally moist *and* low-cal. As for the "big bird," you can trot out Turkey Enchilada Pie *(recipe, page 161)* for a hearty dish low in calories and cholesterol.

Bring out your barbecue and sizzle up our spicy Blackened Pork Chops *(recipe, page 167)* — at only 181 calories per serving! You only need to add a side of rice to Broiled Lamb Chops and Tomatoes with Arugula *(recipe, page 170)* for a deliciously light dinner. We also offer savory Marinated Flank Steak *(recipe, page 173)* and moist, tangy Apricot-Stuffed Pork Tenderloin *(recipe, page 177).*

These sensational, health-savvy recipes all rate an A + — so enjoy!

Lamb Chops Baked in Parchment Paper
(recipe, page 169)

POULTRY

*Peppery Grilled Chicken Breasts
(recipe, page 145)*

PEPPERY GRILLED CHICKEN BREASTS

Chicken marinates for an hour in a refreshing citrus mixture to create a tangy entrée.

Grill or broil for 8 to 10 minutes.

Makes 4 servings.

Nutrient Value Per Serving:
362 calories, 38 g protein, 20 g fat, 5 g carbohydrate, 115 mg sodium, 116 mg cholesterol.

HEALTH

Three Cheers for Chicken!

Every time you eat chicken you get a complete array of amino acids to fuel the growth of fresh, new skin cells. You also get a good supply of niacin, the B vitamin that helps all cells obtain the energy they need to stay healthy. A 3-ounce serving of chicken can provide half your daily requirement for niacin. With all its nutritional advantages, chicken also is low in calories. Choosing light over dark meat can cut calories even further.

HOTLINE

1   cup fresh orange juice
½   cup fresh lime juice
2   tablespoons safflower oil
1   teaspoon ground hot red pepper, or to taste

1   fresh or canned jalapeño pepper, seeded and finely chopped (wear rubber gloves)
4   boned, skinless chicken breast halves (about 4 to 6 ounces each)

1. Combine the orange and lime juices, oil, ground hot red pepper and jalapeño pepper in a shallow container. Add the chicken breasts and turn to coat them. Marinate the chicken at room temperature for 1 hour.
2. Build a charcoal fire or preheat the broiler.
3. Remove the chicken from the marinade. Reserve ½ cup of the marinade.

4. Grill or broil the chicken for 4 to 5 minutes per side or until just cooked through.
5. Meanwhile, boil the reserved marinade in a small saucepan over high heat until it thickens.
6. Divide the chicken among 4 individual dinner plates and pour a tablespoon of the sauce over each portion.

GRILLED BREAST OF CHICKEN WITH ROSEMARY VINAIGRETTE

This unusual salad is prepared by placing the still-warm meat on a bed of mixed greens and tomatoes, and topping it with tangy vinaigrette.

LOW-CALORIE

LOW-SODIUM

Grill or broil for 9 to 10 minutes.

Makes 6 servings.

1   cup safflower oil
4   to 5 cloves garlic, crushed
1   jalapeño pepper, halved,
      seeded and chopped
      (wear rubber gloves)
6   to 7 sprigs fresh cilantro
      Zest (yellow part of rind only)
      of 1 lemon
6   boned, skinless chicken
      breast halves (4 to
      6 ounces each)

Nutrient Value Per Serving:
266 calories, 35 g protein, 11 g fat,
6 g carbohydrate, 125 mg sodium,
82 mg cholesterol.

Assorted lettuces, washed,
   dried and torn into bite-
   size pieces, enough to
   yield 12 cups
2   firm, ripe tomatoes,
      for garnish
   Rosemary Vinaigrette
   (recipe, page 87)

1. Combine the oil, garlic, jalapeño pepper, cilantro and lemon zest in a bowl. Add the chicken breasts and toss to coat them. Cover the bowl and refrigerate the chicken for at least 12 hours.
2. Build a charcoal fire or preheat the broiler.
3. Remove the chicken breasts from the marinade and blot them with paper toweling to remove excess oil and herbs (this prevents grill flare-ups).

4. Grill or broil the chicken for 5 minutes. Turn and grill the second side for 4 to 5 minutes or until the meat is cooked through but still juicy.
5. While the chicken cooks, arrange the lettuce on a serving platter. Quarter the tomatoes and set them aside.
6. Slice the cooked chicken on an angle and place it on the lettuce. Garnish with the tomato wedges. Dress with the Rosemary Vinaigrette.

CookSmart

Go, You Chicken Fat!

If you broil, roast or poach chicken instead of sautéing or frying it, you'll cut calories as you cook. These methods don't require butter or oil, so they do not add extra fat, and they also let much of the fat in chicken drip off during cooking. Most of the fat in chicken is in the skin, so removing the skin helps to lower the fat content even further. To keep the interior moist, cook the chicken with the skin intact and remove it before serving.

CUMIN CHICKEN AND ORANGE SALAD

Ground cumin, fresh mint and orange juice add zip to the marinade and the dressing in this recipe.

Grill or broil for 8 minutes.

Makes 4 servings.

Nutrient Value Per Serving:
283 calories, 27 g protein, 14 g fat, 11 g carbohydrate, 178 mg sodium, 68 mg cholesterol.

4   boned, skinless chicken
      breast halves
6   teaspoons ground cumin
2   cups plain nonfat yogurt
      Freshly ground black pepper,
      to taste
1   tablespoon chopped fresh
      mint OR: fresh cilantro

5   tablespoons fresh orange
      juice
¼   cup olive oil
4   cups mixed salad greens
2   oranges, peeled and sectioned
4   mint sprigs OR: cilantro
      sprigs, for garnish

1. Place the chicken breasts between 2 sheets of wax paper and lightly pound them with a meat pounder or the back of a heavy skillet to make the meat an even thickness. Rub the chicken lightly with 2 teaspoons of the cumin.
2. For the marinade, combine 1¼ cups of the yogurt with 2 teaspoons of the cumin, the black pepper and the mint or cilantro. Marinate the chicken, refrigerated, for 6 hours.
3. Combine 2 tablespoons of the orange juice with the oil.
4. Build a charcoal fire or preheat the broiler.
5. Bring the chicken to room temperature and brush off the marinade.
6. Grill or broil the chicken, basting occasionally with the juice mixture, until the chicken is just cooked through, for about 4 minutes per side. Cool the chicken to room temperature. Then shred the chicken.

7. For the dressing, combine the remaining ¾ cup of yogurt and 2 teaspoons of cumin with black pepper and enough of the remaining 3 tablespoons of orange juice to make the mixture pourable.
8. To serve, toss the greens with enough of the dressing to coat them lightly. Mound the greens on 4 individual salad plates. Nestle the chicken and the orange sections on top. Sprinkle with black pepper. Garnish with the mint or cilantro sprigs.

CookSmart

Chicken Little

When shopping for poultry, look for small, young chickens and turkeys. Younger birds have less fat and fewer calories than larger, more mature ones.

SPICY CHICKEN BREASTS

Fresh hot green chili peppers, chili powder and ground hot red pepper pack this chicken dish with spicy flavor.

Makes 6 servings.

Nutrient Value Per Serving:
195 calories, 21 g protein, 14 g fat, 2 g carbohydrate, 76 mg sodium, 66 mg cholesterol.

1 fresh hot green chili pepper, seeded and finely chopped (wear rubber gloves)
1 medium-size clove garlic, finely chopped
1 teaspoon ground cumin
¼ teaspoon chili powder
⅛ teaspoon ground hot red pepper
1 teaspoon lime juice

6 boned, skinless chicken breast halves
3 tablespoons oil
   Paprika
1 tablespoon chopped cilantro, for garnish
1 lime, cut into thin slices, for garnish

1. Mix together the green chili pepper, garlic, cumin, chili powder, ground hot red pepper and lime juice in a small bowl. Rub the mixture into the chicken breasts. Marinate the chicken at room temperature for ½ hour or refrigerate it for 2 to 3 hours.

2. Heat the oil in the skillet. Add the chicken and sauté until it is lightly browned on both sides. Cover the skillet and cook slowly just until the chicken is cooked through, for about 7 minutes.

3. Place the chicken on 6 warmed individual dinner plates and sprinkle it with the paprika. Garnish the chicken with the cilantro and the lime.

HEALTH

To Skin or Not to Skin?

Chicken skin has only about 17% fat, a small amount compared to the flavor it offers. Interestingly, two thirds of the fat present is unsaturated fat, which is good news to those trying to keep down their cholesterol levels. For a lower calorie count, remove the skin from chicken.

HOTLINE

ORIENTAL CHICKEN

LOW-FAT
LOW-CALORIE

A delicious combination of chicken and vegetables that cooks quickly in an aluminum foil packet.

Bake at 500° for 12 minutes.

Makes 4 servings.

Nutrient Value Per Serving:
262 calories, 41 g protein, 6 g fat,
9 g carbohydrate, 887 mg sodium,
99 mg cholesterol.

Vegetable oil
1   **large sweet red pepper, cored, seeded and cut into thin slices**
¼ **pound snow peas, cleaned and strings removed**
½ **cup water chestnuts, sliced**
⅓ **cup chopped green onion**
4   **boned, skinless chicken breast halves (6 ounces each)**

3   **tablespoons soy sauce**
1   **tablespoon Oriental sesame oil***
½ **teaspoon grated, peeled fresh gingerroot**
1   **clove garlic, finely chopped**

1. Preheat the oven to very hot (500°).
2. Tear off four 14 x 12-inch sheets of regular weight aluminum foil. Lightly oil the center of the lower half of each sheet with the vegetable oil.
3. Place one eighth of the red pepper, snow peas, water chestnuts and green onion on the oiled portion of each sheet. Place a chicken breast on the vegetables. Sprinkle the remaining vegetables over the chicken, dividing them evenly among the 4 sheets.
4. Stir together the soy sauce, Oriental sesame oil, ginger and garlic in a small bowl. Spoon the mixture evenly over the chicken and vegetables.
5. Fold the upper half of each sheet over the ingredients, matching up the edges evenly to enclose the filling. Turn up the long double edge of the foil to create a ½-inch double fold, and fold over again. Fold the two shorter sides in the same way to make a completely sealed packet.

6. Place 2 baking sheets in the preheated very hot oven (500°) for about 2 minutes. Place the aluminum foil packets in a single layer on the hot baking sheets.
7. Bake the packets in the preheated very hot oven (500°) for 12 minutes. Place each packet on an individual dinner plate. Cut an X from corner to corner in the top of each packet. Carefully fold back the edges and serve immediately, with rice if you wish.

***Note:** Oriental sesame oil is richer in flavor and darker than regular sesame oil. It can be found in the Oriental food section of many supermarkets or in specialty food stores.*

CHICKEN WITH PEANUT SAUCE

This is a colorful stir-fried combination of chicken and vegetables with a subtly flavored peanut sauce.

Makes 4 servings.

Nutrient Value Per Serving:
272 calories, 31 g protein, 13 g fat, 7 g carbohydrate, 684 mg sodium, 66 mg cholesterol.

3 tablespoons peanut butter
2 tablespoons soy sauce
2 tablespoons water
2 teaspoons brown sugar
2 teaspoons Oriental sesame oil*
1 canned flat anchovy
½ teaspoon crushed red pepper flakes
1 tablespoon peanut oil
1 pound boned, skinless chicken breasts, cut into strips about 3 x ½ inches

1 clove garlic, finely chopped
1 teaspoon finely chopped, peeled fresh gingerroot
4 green onions (first 5 inches from root end), cut into 1-inch pieces
1 medium-size sweet red pepper, cored, seeded and cut into ¼-inch-wide strips

1. Combine the peanut butter, soy sauce, water, brown sugar, Oriental sesame oil, anchovy and red pepper flakes in the container of an electric blender or a food processor. Cover and whirl to mix all the ingredients well.
2. Heat the peanut oil in a large wok or nonstick skillet over high heat until hot. Add the chicken and stir-fry until it is browned, for about 4 minutes. Add the garlic, ginger, green onion and red pepper. Reduce the heat to medium-high and stir-fry for 3 minutes.

3. Add the peanut butter mixture to the wok and cook for 1 minute, stirring to coat the chicken strips. Serve the chicken immediately, over rice if you wish.

*__Note:__ *Oriental sesame oil is richer in flavor and darker than regular sesame oil. It can be found in the Oriental food section of many supermarkets or in specialty food stores.*

CookSmart

Wok Talk

This Chinese cooking pan is traditionally large and round bottomed. A wok can be used for stir- or deep-frying, braising or steaming a variety of foods. Clean your wok with hot water and a brush or a nylon scrubber. Dry it thoroughly, and rub the inside with oil to prevent rusting if your wok is made of carbon steel.

DIJON CHICKEN

A simple dish that practically prepares itself — but with a taste that's special enough to serve on any occasion.

Bake at 350° for 25 to 30 minutes.

Makes 4 servings.

Nutrient Value Per Serving:
198 calories, 35 g protein, 3 g fat,
7 g carbohydrate, 307 mg sodium,
86 mg cholesterol.

2 **whole chicken breasts
   (1 pound each) halved,
   skinned and bone left in**
4 **teaspoons Dijon-style
   mustard**

2 **slices whole wheat bread,
   torn into pieces***
1 **teaspoon leaf basil, crumbled**
½ **cup dry white wine
   Steamed asparagus**

1. Preheat the oven to moderate (350°).
2. Coat the top of each chicken breast half with a teaspoon of the mustard, spreading the mustard evenly.
3. Place the bread in the container of a food processor. Cover and whirl until the bread has turned into crumbs. Transfer the crumbs to a plate and toss them with the basil. Roll the tops of the chicken breasts in the crumb mixture.
4. Place the chicken breasts, crumb side up, in a shallow baking dish. Pour the wine into the dish around the chicken.

5. Bake the chicken in the preheated moderate oven (350°) for 25 to 30 minutes or until the crumbs are golden and the chicken is just cooked through. Serve the chicken with the asparagus.

***Note:** Fresh bread crumbs have a greater volume and higher moisture content than commercially prepared dry crumbs. Therefore, you will need a smaller amount of fresh bread crumbs than if you were using the dry.*

THREE HERB GRILLED CHICKEN

This dish allows you to grill chicken, artichokes and eggplant and still have them ready to serve simultaneously.

Grill for 38 minutes.

Makes 8 servings.

Nutrient Value Per Serving (without added salt):
277 calories, 27 g protein, 14 g fat, 13 g carbohydrate, 109 mg sodium, 77 mg cholesterol.

1   chicken (3 to 4 pounds), cut up
½   cup coarsely chopped fresh oregano OR: 2 tablespoons leaf oregano, crumbled
½   cup coarsely chopped fresh tarragon OR: 2 tablespoons leaf tarragon, crumbled
¼   cup coarsely chopped fresh thyme OR: 1 tablespoon leaf thyme, crumbled
1   tablespoon virgin olive oil
   Salt and freshly ground black pepper, to taste
2   large artichokes, trimmed
1   large eggplant, trimmed

1. Cook the chicken in boiling water in a large pot for 4 minutes or until the fat rises to the surface and the chicken turns white. Drain and cool the chicken.
2. Combine the oregano, tarragon and thyme in a small bowl.
3. Lightly rub the chicken all over with the oil. Loosen the skin from the chicken pieces and stuff equal amounts of the herb mixture under the skins of the pieces. Season with the salt and pepper. Cover the chicken with aluminum foil and marinate it at room temperature for 1 hour. (Or refrigerate the chicken overnight and remove it from the refrigerator 1 hour before cooking.)

4. Bring 2 cups of water to boiling in the bottom of a steamer. Place the artichokes over the water. Cover the steamer and steam the artichokes for 15 minutes or until they are crisply tender. Cool the artichokes, quarter them and remove the fuzzy choke.
5. Build a charcoal fire.
6. Slice the eggplant into ¼-inch-thick rounds. Lightly oil the grill rack.
7. Place the eggplant rounds on the grill rack and cook until they are browned on each side, for about 3 minutes per side. Remove the eggplant and season it lightly with the salt and black pepper. Cover the eggplant and keep it warm in a low oven.
8. Place the chicken on the grill rack and brown it on both sides. Close the grill, making sure the vents are open, and cook the chicken for 10 minutes. Open the grill and continue cooking for 20 minutes or until the juices run clear when a piece of dark meat is pierced with a fork.
9. About 6 minutes before the chicken is finished cooking, place the artichoke quarters on the grill over the hottest part of the fire. Cook the artichoke quarters for about 4 minutes on each side or just until they are warmed through and slightly golden.
10. To serve, arrange the chicken on a warmed large serving platter. Place the eggplant and the artichokes around the chicken, and serve.

LEMON AND ROSEMARY GRILLED CHICKEN

The lemon, rosemary and white wine marinade also is delicious with lamb chops.

Grill or broil for 25 minutes.

Makes 4 servings.

Nutrient Value Per Serving:
243 calories, 36 g protein, 9 g fat,
3 g carbohydrate, 107 mg sodium,
108 mg cholesterol.

Juice of 3 lemons
⅓ cup dry white wine
2 tablespoons chopped fresh rosemary OR: 2 teaspoons leaf rosemary, crumbled
1 teaspoon cracked pepper

2 cloves garlic, finely chopped
1 broiler-fryer chicken (about 3 pounds), cut up and skinned
1 lemon, thinly sliced, for garnish
Watercress, for garnish

1. Combine the lemon juice, wine, rosemary, pepper and garlic in a shallow container. Add the chicken and turn to coat it. Marinate the chicken in the refrigerator for at least 2 hours.
2. Build a charcoal fire or preheat the broiler.
3. Remove the chicken from the marinade and discard the marinade.

4. Grill or broil the chicken, turning, for 25 minutes or until it is cooked through.
5. Garnish the chicken with the lemon slices and the watercress.

CookSmart

Smart Design

The broiler pans that come as standard issue with most stoves have a slitted insert that fits into a larger pan. This sensible design allows the fat to drain away from the food as it broils. To save on clean-up time, line the bottom of the pan with heavy-duty aluminum foil.

POLLO ALLA VINAIGRETTE

A taste of Spain, made quickly and easily in one skillet. Try serving with saffron rice and sangria. And yes, this recipe does use an entire bulb of garlic.

Makes 4 servings.

Nutrient Value Per Serving:
251 calories, 20 g protein, 17 g fat,
4 g carbohydrate, 74 mg sodium,
77 mg cholesterol.

1   chicken (4 pounds), cut into
    serving pieces*
1   tablespoon olive oil
1   whole bulb (not clove) garlic,
    finely chopped

4   large yellow onions, sliced
1   bay leaf
½   cup red wine vinegar
½   cup water

1. Brown the chicken in the oil in a large skillet over medium-high heat, working in batches, if necessary, to avoid crowding in the skillet.
2. Add the garlic, onion, bay leaf, vinegar and water to the skillet. Bring the mixture to boiling over medium-high heat. Reduce the heat and cover the skillet. Simmer over low heat, stirring occasionally, for 25 minutes or until the chicken is cooked through. Drain the chicken and reserve the cooking liquid.

3. Place the chicken on a serving platter and serve with the reserved cooking liquid as gravy.

*Note: To eliminate even more calories, skin the chicken before cooking it and use a nonstick skillet.

CookSmart

Pickin' Chicken

● Grade A chicken is meatier and better looking than grade B or C chicken.
● The bird's diet affects its skin tone, which can vary from yellow to white. Both colors are acceptable.
● When you are preparing a bird for storage, remove clumps of fat that are under the skin and around the edge of the cavity.
● Avoid packages with bruised-looking chicken, as well as those with an "off" odor. Packages with an accumulation of liquid generally have been sitting for a while; avoid them.
● Chicken parts are just as economical as a whole chicken and certainly save preparation time. The percentage of edible meat per chicken part is 50 percent of the wings, 53 percent of the legs and thighs and 63 percent of the breasts. In comparison, 51 percent of a whole bird is edible (42 percent with the fat and skin eliminated).
● For every 4-ounce serving, buy 8 ounces of chicken with the bone in or 5 to 6 ounces of boned parts.

STEAMED BROCCOLI AND CHICKEN

By steaming the chicken and broccoli together, you eliminate the need for extra fats or oils. Try serving this main dish with rice, preceded by a first course of flavorful broth.

Makes 4 servings.

Nutrient Value Per Serving:
196 calories, 28 g protein, 5 g fat,
12 g carbohydrate, 651 mg sodium,
94 mg cholesterol.

1 **pound chicken thighs, boned and skinned**
2 **teaspoons grated, peeled fresh gingerroot OR: 1 teaspoon ground ginger**
2 **teaspoons cornstarch**

2 **tablespoons reduced-sodium soy sauce**
5 **cups fresh broccoli flowerets**
¼ **cup thin strips of sweet red pepper**

1. Place the chicken in the freezer for 15 minutes; this will make it easier to cut. Cut the chicken thighs in half along the grain, then slice them into ⅛-inch-thick strips across the grain.
2. Transfer the chicken slices to a 10-inch heatproof plate. Add the ginger, cornstarch and soy sauce. Toss until the chicken is evenly coated. Spread out the chicken into an even layer on the plate.
3. Arrange the broccoli flowerets around the side of the plate.
4. Bring 2 quarts of water to boiling over high heat in a 12-inch wok or steamer. Place the plate of chicken and broccoli in the steamer and cover. Steam for 6 to 7 minutes or until the chicken is cooked through and the broccoli is just tender.

5. Remove the steamer from the heat and carefully remove the plate from the steamer. Garnish with the red pepper strips.

Notes: *If you don't have a steamer or wok, use a large pan with a lid. Place a clean, empty tuna fish can in the bottom of the pan. Fill the pan with water to within ¼ inch of the top of the can. Put the food on a dish with a raised edge, to prevent water from touching the food, and place the dish on the can. Cover and steam the food as above. Always use kitchen mitts to protect your hands when placing the plate of food in the steamer or removing it.*

CookSmart

The Poultry Store

● Store fresh chicken in the coldest part of the refrigerator, for up to 2 days. There's no need to rewrap it if the packaging is in good condition.
● To freeze chicken, rinse it under cold running water and pat it dry. Rewrap the chicken and freeze it for up to 2 months.
● Whenever possible, thaw frozen chicken in the refrigerator for 24 hours. Short of time? Immerse well-wrapped chicken in a bowl of cold water for four hours and change the water hourly. Don't forget: You can defrost chicken in the microwave, following the manufacturer's directions.
● Always make sure that chicken is thoroughly cooked.

CHICKEN RICE PILAF

Try serving this delicious combination of chicken, rice and nuts with a tossed green salad and a glass of dry white wine.

Toast nuts at 350° for 5 to 10 minutes.

Makes 6 servings.

Nutrient Value Per Serving:
461 calories, 31 g protein, 13 g fat, 55 g carbohydrate, 642 mg sodium, 62 mg cholesterol.

2	chicken breasts, skinned and halved (2 pounds)
5	cups water
1	carrot, chopped
1	medium-size onion, chopped
½	cup blanched almonds

¼	cup pine nuts (pignoli)
1	tablespoon butter
2	cups uncooked rice
1½	teaspoons salt
¼	teaspoon freshly ground pepper
	Ground cinnamon

1. Preheat the oven to moderate (350°).
2. Place the chicken, water, carrot and onion in a large saucepan and bring the mixture to boiling. Reduce the heat and simmer until the chicken still is a little pink inside, for about 10 minutes. Cool the chicken in the cooking liquid. Then bone and cut the meat into bite-size pieces. Reserve the cooking liquid.
3. Toast the almonds and the pine nuts on separate baking sheets in the preheated moderate oven (350°), turning occasionally, for 5 to 10 minutes or until the nuts are browned.

4. Sauté the rice in the butter in a large saucepan over low heat for 1 minute, stirring to coat the rice. Add the almonds and the pine nuts. Add the chicken pieces, reserved cooking liquid, the salt and pepper. Bring the mixture to boiling over high heat. Fluff the mixture with a fork, reduce the heat and cover the saucepan.
5. Simmer the mixture until the rice is tender and the liquid is absorbed, for about 25 minutes. Let the pilaf stand for 5 minutes. Sprinkle it with the cinnamon and serve.

CookSmart

Flash in the Pan

Sautéing — cooking food in a small amount of fat — is a quick cooking method that browns food for an appealing appearance.

● Select a large, shallow-sided pan and add a bit of fat (butter, margarine or oil). Or use a combination of butter and oil; butter burns at a lower temperature than oil but adds flavor, so using a combination enables you to sauté at higher temperatures and lowers the saturated fat content. Nonstick pans reduce or eliminate the need for fat.

● Set the pan over medium to high heat. Let the fat get hot (but not smoking) before adding the foods to be sautéed. Make sure there is plenty of room in the pan so the liquid can evaporate; if the ingredients are too crowded, they will steam rather than sauté.

● Parboil beforehand fibrous vegetables or those in larger pieces, to tenderize them and reduce sautéing time.

● If the food seems to be browning too quickly, add a tablespoon or so of water and continue to cook until the water is evaporated. (Add the water carefully so you don't get spattered with hot fat.)

● Stir or shake the pan frequently to prevent food from sticking.

DILLED CHICKEN PILAF

A wonderfully satisfying dish of chicken, vegetables and rice topped with a dilled yogurt sauce. Sautéing the rice gives it a nutty flavor.

Makes 8 servings.

**Nutrient Value Per Serving
(using unsalted chicken stock):**
304 calories, 25 g protein, 11 g fat,
24 g carbohydrate, 310 mg sodium,
65 mg cholesterol.

1 cup chopped mushrooms
1 medium-size onion, chopped
1 cup uncooked long-grain
 white rice
2 tablespoons vegetable oil
½ cup finely chopped celery
½ cup finely chopped carrot
2 cups chicken stock
½ teaspoon salt
 Freshly ground black pepper,
 to taste

Dill Sauce:
2 tablespoons reduced-calorie
 margarine
¼ cup finely chopped onion
2 tablespoons unbleached
 all-purpose flour

1 cup chicken stock
2 tablespoons chopped fresh dill
 OR: 2 teaspoons dried
 dillweed
3 tablespoons plain lowfat
 yogurt
 Salt and freshly ground
 pepper, to taste
½ cup finely diced peeled tomato
¼ cup grated Parmesan cheese
2 cooked chicken breasts,
 skinned and sliced into
 ¼-inch pieces (about ¾ pound)
2 cooked chicken thighs,
 skinned and sliced into
 ¼-inch pieces (about ½ pound)
 Parsley sprigs, for garnish

1. Sauté the mushrooms, onion and rice in the oil in a deep saucepan over medium heat, stirring often, until the rice is golden.
2. Add the celery, carrot, the 2 cups of stock, the salt and black pepper. Bring the mixture to boiling, cover the saucepan and reduce the heat to low.
3. Simmer the rice for 20 minutes or until it is tender and the liquid is absorbed.
4. Prepare the Dill Sauce: Melt the margarine in a small pan. Add the onion and sauté until it is translucent.

5. Lower the heat and blend in the flour with a wire whisk. Cook the mixture over low heat, stirring, for 2 minutes. Add the stock and the dill. Increase the heat to medium. Bring the mixture to boiling, stirring constantly, and cook until the sauce thickens. Remove the saucepan from the heat and stir in the yogurt. Season with the salt and pepper.
6. Stir the tomato and the Parmesan cheese into the hot pilaf.
7. To serve, place the pilaf on 8 individual dinner plates. Arrange the chicken on top. Spoon the Dill Sauce over the chicken. Garnish with the parsley.

CHICKEN CHUNKS WITH TOMATOES AND OLIVES

A one-skillet wonder that's full of flavor. Serve over hot cooked rice or tossed with pasta.

LOW-CALORIE

Makes 4 servings.

Nutrient Value Per Serving:
226 calories, 24 g protein, 12 g fat,
6 g carbohydrate, 765 mg sodium,
94 mg cholesterol.

1 pound boned, skinless
   chicken thighs, cut into
   1½-inch chunks
½ teaspoon freshly ground
   black pepper
¼ teaspoon salt
1 tablespoon olive oil
1 clove garlic, finely chopped
½ teaspoon leaf thyme,
   crumbled

½ teaspoon leaf marjoram,
   crumbled
½ teaspoon leaf basil, crumbled
1 can (14 ounces) Italian
   tomatoes, undrained
¼ cup dry white wine
⅓ cup oil-cured black olives,
   pitted

1. Sprinkle the chicken with the black pepper and the salt.
2. Heat the oil in a large nonstick skillet over medium-high heat until it is hot. Add the chicken and sauté, stirring constantly, until the chicken is browned on all sides, for about 5 minutes. Add the garlic, thyme, marjoram and basil and sauté, stirring, for 30 seconds more.

3. Pour the tomatoes with their liquid and the wine into the skillet. Bring the mixture to boiling over medium-high heat. Boil rapidly, stirring occasionally, for about 5 minutes or until the sauce is thickened. Stir in the olives and cook the mixture for 1 minute more.
4. Serve the chicken mixture hot, with rice or pasta, if you wish.

CHICKEN BREASTS WITH MUSTARD SAUCE

An innovative, low-cal way to serve chicken. Not to mention it's a cinch to prepare!

LOW-FAT
LOW-CALORIE

Makes 4 servings.

Nutrient Value Per Serving:
257 calories, 41 g protein, 8 g fat,
2 g carbohydrate, 457 mg sodium,
114 mg cholesterol.

1½ pounds boned, skinless chicken
   breast halves, thawed if frozen
2 tablespoons butter or margarine
1 tablespoon lemon juice

2 teaspoons cornstarch
1 cup chicken broth
2 to 3 teaspoons Dijon-style
   mustard

1. Pat the chicken dry with paper toweling. Sauté the chicken in the butter in a large skillet over medium heat until lightly browned and cooked through, for about 5 minutes each side.
2. Sprinkle with the lemon juice and transfer to a serving platter; keep warm.

3. Dissolve the cornstarch in the chicken broth in a small cup. Pour into the skillet. Bring to boiling, scraping up any browned bits from the bottom; cook for 1 minute. Remove the pan from the heat. Whisk in the mustard. Spoon the sauce over the chicken.

CURRIED CORNISH GAME HENS

LOW-CALORIE

LOW-SODIUM

The spiced hens are roasted ahead of time to be served at room temperature or chilled. They also can be grilled and served hot.

Roast at 450° for 15 minutes, then at 350° for 35 minutes.

Makes 12 servings.

6 **Cornish game hens (about 1 pound each)**
2 **tablespoons curry powder**
1 **teaspoon ground cinnamon**
1 **teaspoon ground nutmeg**
½ **teaspoon ground hot red pepper (optional)**

Nutrient Value Per Serving:
267 calories, 28 g protein, 14 g fat, 7 g carbohydrate, 83 mg sodium, 88 mg cholesterol.

1 **small pineapple, peeled, cored and cut into spears, for garnish**
Fresh mint sprigs, for garnish

1. Preheat the oven to hot (450°). Trim the hens of visible fat, then rinse and dry them.
2. Combine the curry powder, cinnamon, nutmeg and, if you wish, ground hot red pepper in a small bowl. Rub the spice mixture under and on top of the skin of each hen (being careful not to tear the skin). Sprinkle the remaining mixture inside the cavities.
3. Truss each hen using a 6-inch bamboo skewer or cooking twine. Place the hens in a single layer on a rack in 1 or 2 roasting pans.
4. Roast the hens in the preheated hot oven (450°) for 15 minutes. Lower the oven temperature to 350° and bake the hens for 35 minutes more or until the juices run clear when an inner thigh is pierced with a fork. Let the hens cool to room temperature and garnish them with the pineapple and the mint. Or cover the hens and refrigerate them until serving time.

Note: *If you prefer, the hens can be grilled. To keep the hens flat on the grill, slit them along the breast bone but do not completely sever them (this is known as butterflying). Rub the hens with the spices, place them in plastic bags and pack the bags in a cooler or refrigerator until ready to grill. Grill the hens several inches above the hot coals.*

Meats that Make the Grade

TURKEY KEBABS

Chunks of turkey are marinated in a tangy lime and honey mixture, then threaded on skewers with slices of onion and green and red peppers. (Assemble the kebabs and refrigerate until needed.)

Grill or broil for 8 to 10 minutes.

Makes 8 servings.

Nutrient Value Per Serving:
278 calories, 41 g protein, 6 g fat, 14 g carbohydrate, 116 mg sodium, 105 mg cholesterol.

Lime and Honey Marinade:
¼ cup fresh lime juice
      OR: lemon juice
¼ cup honey
2 tablespoons vegetable oil
3 tablespoons chopped fresh
      oregano OR: 1 tablespoon leaf
      oregano, crumbled
2 cloves garlic, finely chopped
1 teaspoon freshly ground black
      pepper
½ teaspoon ground hot red pepper

3 pounds turkey breast or turkey
      tenderloin, cut into 1½-inch
      cubes
2 medium-size red onions
2 sweet green peppers
2 sweet red peppers

1. Prepare the Lime and Honey Marinade: Combine the lime or lemon juice, the honey, oil, oregano, garlic, black pepper and ground hot red pepper in a large bowl.
2. Add the turkey cubes to the marinade and toss to coat them. Let the turkey marinate while preparing the vegetables.
3. Build a charcoal fire or preheat the broiler.
4. Cut the onions into large chunks and separate them into layers. Halve, seed and cut the green and red peppers into 1- to 2-inch squares.

5. Remove the turkey from the marinade, reserving the marinade. Alternately thread pieces of the turkey, green and red peppers and the onion onto 16 skewers. Brush the skewered turkey and vegetables with the reserved marinade.
6. Grill or broil the kebabs for 4 to 5 minutes. Brush them with the marinade and turn. Grill or broil them for 4 to 5 minutes more or until the turkey is cooked and the vegetables are just tender.

CookSmart

Trot Out the Turkey

This "big bird" is a favorite with just about everyone. Like most poultry, it's economical and relatively low-calorie. So don't wait for Thanksgiving—trot out one of the many varieties of turkey available today.
● The roaster is the traditional bird and comes in sizes that range from about 10 pounds to 30 pounds. Big birds are the most economical in cost per serving; however, they take longer to roast.
● A fryer-roaster is a small, meaty turkey weighing from 4 to 9 pounds—perfect for smaller families.
● Boneless turkey roast is a plump roast weighing between 2 and 5 pounds. It provides a combination of white and dark meat and is ideal for sandwiches.
● Frozen, prestuffed turkey can go directly from the freezer to the oven with no thawing. It is available in a broad range of sizes.
● A frozen, self-basting turkey is injected with butter before being frozen and bastes itself as it cooks. Available in a wide range of sizes.
● Turkey parts—drumsticks, wings, thighs and breasts—and turkey cutlets are marketed just like chicken parts and cutlets. Legs and wings offer especially good eating at relatively low cost.
● Smoked turkey is a gourmet item, ready to slice and eat.

TURKEY ENCHILADA PIE

This spicy casserole can be assembled a day in advance, then baked just before serving. Add a tossed green salad and a cold drink to have a complete meal.

Bake at 350° for 30 minutes.

Makes 10 servings.

Nutrient Value Per Serving:
310 calories, 25 g protein, 14 g fat, 21 g carbohydrate, 371 mg sodium, 69 mg cholesterol.

Jalapeño Yogurt Sauce:
½   cup chicken broth
1½ cups plain lowfat yogurt
1   jalapeño pepper, seeded and
     diced (wear rubber gloves)

Salsa Verde:
8   tomatillos
1½ cups chicken broth
1   medium-size yellow onion,
     coarsely diced
½   cup fresh cilantro

Filling:
2   pounds ground turkey
1   cup chopped yellow onion
1   teaspoon ground cumin
¼   teaspoon freshly ground pepper
½   cup chopped fresh cilantro
10   corn tortillas, cut into strips
½   cup shredded mild Cheddar
     cheese (2 ounces)
½   cup shredded lowfat Monterey
     Jack cheese (2 ounces)

1. Preheat the oven to moderate (350°).
2. Prepare the Jalapeño Yogurt Sauce: Combine the broth, yogurt and jalapeño pepper in a small bowl until they are well blended.
3. Prepare the Salsa Verde: Peel, wash and dice the tomatillos. Place them in a small saucepan with the broth, onion and cilantro. Bring the mixture to boiling over medium heat. Lower the heat and simmer the mixture for 10 minutes. Drain the vegetables (save the broth for another use).
4. Prepare the Filling: Sauté the turkey, onion, cumin and pepper in a large nonstick skillet over medium heat until the meat is cooked and the onion is softened and looks wilted. Remove the skillet from the heat and blend in the cilantro.

5. Scatter one third of the tortilla strips over the bottom of a shallow casserole dish. Layer half the meat filling on top. Spoon half the Jalapeño Yogurt Sauce and half the Salsa Verde over the meat. Sprinkle half the Cheddar and Monterey Jack cheeses over the sauces. Repeat the layering. Top with the remaining third of the tortilla strips.
6. Bake the enchilada pie in the preheated moderate oven (350°) for 30 minutes or until it is bubbly and the cheeses have melted.

TEX-MEX PITA POCKETS

A hearty sandwich that really packs a punch — courtesy of the Lone Star state.

LOW-FAT
LOW-CALORIE
LOW-CHOLESTEROL
MICROWAVE

Warm bread at 350° for 10 minutes.

Makes 6 servings.

Nutrient Value Per Serving:
335 calories, 21 g protein, 7 g fat,
44 g carbohydrate, 864 mg sodium,
49 mg cholesterol.

6   small pita breads
½   cup plain lowfat yogurt
¼   cup thick and chunky salsa
¼   teaspoon ground cumin
¼   teaspoon ground chili powder
1   pound frozen ground turkey,
      thawed

1   medium-size onion, chopped
1   package (1¼ ounces) taco
      seasoning mix
1   cup water
      Shredded lettuce (about
      ¼ head)

1. Preheat the oven to moderate (350°).
2. Wrap the pita breads in aluminum foil.
3. Combine the yogurt, salsa, cumin and chili powder in a small bowl and refrigerate the mixture.
4. Cook the turkey and the onion in a medium-size skillet over medium-high heat, stirring to break up the large chunks, until the meat loses its pink color. Drain the fat. Stir the taco seasoning mix and the water into the turkey. Bring the mixture to boiling, lower the heat and simmer for 15 minutes.

5. Meanwhile, heat the pita breads in the preheated moderate oven (350°) for 10 minutes or until they are warm and pliable. Unwrap the breads. Split the top of each bread along the seam to make a pocket. Spread the inside of each pocket with some of the salsa mixture. Spoon about ½ cup of the turkey filling into each pocket. Sprinkle on the lettuce and top with more salsa mixture.

Microwave Instructions *(for a 650-watt variable power microwave oven)*

Ingredient Changes: Reduce the water to ½ cup.
Directions: Scatter the turkey evenly over the bottom of a microwave-safe 12 x 9-inch baking dish. Sprinkle the onion over the turkey and cover with paper toweling. Microwave at full power for 7 minutes, stirring to further break up the turkey after 4 minutes. Stir in the water and the taco seasoning mix. Cover again with paper toweling. Microwave at full power for 5 minutes. Spread the inside of each pita bread with the salsa mixture, then fill each pocket with the turkey mixture. Loosely wrap each filled pita bread in paper toweling and place them on a microwave-safe plate. Microwave at half power for 3 minutes. Top with the lettuce.

TURKEY AND GUACAMOLE HERO

An updated version of the classic turkey club sandwich, with a smooth, tangy guacamole adding a special touch.

Makes 6 servings.

Nutrient Value Per Serving:
242 calories, 13 g protein, 10 g fat, 25 g carbohydrate, 453 mg sodium, 29 mg cholesterol.

Guacamole:
- 1 medium-size ripe avocado
- 1 teaspoon fresh lemon juice
- ¼ cup chopped seeded tomato
- 1 tablespoon finely chopped pickled jalapeño pepper (optional; wear rubber gloves)
  Salt and freshly ground pepper, to taste

- 1 large hero roll (about 12 inches long)
- 6 slices lowfat bacon, cooked until crisp, drained and crumbled
- 4 large leaves Boston lettuce, washed and patted dry
- 6 ounces thinly sliced cooked turkey breast
- 1 small red onion, thinly sliced

1. Prepare the Guacamole: Mash the avocado with a fork in a small bowl. Add the lemon juice, tomato, jalapeño pepper, if you wish, and the salt and pepper. Mix until the ingredients are well blended but still chunky.
2. Split the bread roll lengthwise, but do not cut it all the way through. Hollow out both sides of the roll, leaving a ⅓-inch-thick shell. Open the roll.
3. Sprinkle the bacon pieces inside the roll. Place the lettuce on the bottom. Arrange the turkey and the onion over the lettuce. Top with an even layer of the Guacamole.
4. Gently close the roll and cut it into 6 wedges with a serrated knife.

OPEN-FACED TURKEY SANDWICH WITH CHUTNEY DRESSING

The secret to this sandwich success: delicious chutney that you whip up in your blender!

Makes 4 open-faced sandwich halves.

Nutrient Value Per Sandwich:
314 calories, 29 g protein, 10 g fat, 25 g carbohydrate, 304 mg sodium, 66 mg cholesterol.

- ¼ cup mayonnaise-type salad dressing OR: reduced-calorie mayonnaise
- 3 tablespoons golden raisins
- ½ teaspoon ground cumin
- ¼ teaspoon ground ginger
  Dash red pepper flakes
  Leaf lettuce

- 2 unseeded club (rectangular) hard rolls, split lengthwise and toasted
- 12 ounces thinly sliced cooked turkey breast, warmed or at room temperature
- 1 medium-size red onion, sliced and separated into rings
- 1 medium-size sweet red pepper, seeded and cut into rings

1. Combine the salad dressing, raisins, cumin, ginger and red pepper flakes in a blender or food processor. Cover; whirl until blended and raisins are chopped.
2. Arrange the lettuce on each roll half. Top with the turkey, then the dressing, the onion and red pepper.

Meats that Make the Grade **163**

TURKEY FAJITAS WITH SPICY CILANTRO SALSA

A south-of-the-border favorite, fajitas usually are made with seasoned beef. Here we offer a low-cal, spicy turkey version.

Broil turkey for 20 minutes.

Makes 6 servings.

Nutrient Value Per Fajita:
247 calories, 16 g protein, 11 g fat, 21 g carbohydrate, 317 mg sodium, 36 mg cholesterol.

1   pound boned whole turkey breast
¼   teaspoon freshly ground pepper
1   clove garlic, chopped
1   teaspoon chili powder
2   tablespoons lime juice
1   tablespoon chopped fresh cilantro
1½   tablespoons vegetable oil
¼   teaspoon salt

Spicy Cilantro Salsa:
1½   cups chopped ripe tomatoes (about ½ pound)
2   tablespoons chopped fresh cilantro
1   tablespoon chopped red onion
¼   teaspoon finely chopped garlic

1   to 2 tablespoons chopped pickled jalapeño pepper, seeded OR: 1 fresh jalapeño pepper, seeded and chopped (wear rubber gloves)
⅛   teaspoon salt

8   to 10 flour tortillas (7-inch)

Garnishes:
2   to 3 cups shredded lettuce
1   avocado, sliced
1   can (16 ounces) black beans OR: pinto beans
½   cup dairy sour cream
4   ounces shredded Monterey Jack cheese OR: mild Cheddar cheese

1. Place the turkey in a shallow pan and sprinkle it with the pepper, chopped garlic clove, chili powder, lime juice, the 1 tablespoon of cilantro, the oil and the ¼ teaspoon of salt. Turn the turkey to coat it. Cover the pan and marinate the turkey in the refrigerator for at least 3 hours or overnight.
2. Prepare the Spicy Cilantro Salsa: Combine the tomatoes, cilantro, onion, garlic, jalapeño pepper and salt in a small bowl. Let the salsa stand for at least 1 hour before serving.
3. To cook the turkey, preheat the broiler. Place the turkey on the broiler pan and broil it 6 inches from the source of the heat for about 10 minutes on each side. The turkey should be completely opaque throughout. Cut the turkey into thin strips.

4. While the turkey broils, wrap the tortillas in aluminum foil and warm them in the oven for about 8 minutes.
5. To serve, arrange all the garnishes, the salsa and tortillas on the table. Allow each person to make his or her own fajita by wrapping turkey slices, salsa and the desired garnishes in a warm tortilla. Have plenty of napkins on hand.

TURKEY WITH CREAMY GARLIC BEAN SAUCE

Roasted cloves of garlic and white cannellini beans are the base of this thick, creamy purée, served over chunks of broiled turkey.

Bake garlic at 300° for 45 minutes; broil turkey for 4 to 5 minutes.

Makes 4 servings.

10 garlic cloves, unpeeled
1   cup drained canned white kidney beans (cannellini beans)
½   teaspoon lemon juice
1   to 2 drops liquid red pepper seasoning

Nutrient Value Per Serving:
187 calories, 30 g protein, 2 g fat, 10 g carbohydrate, 258 mg sodium, 70 mg cholesterol.

1   pound boned, skinless turkey (or chicken) breast, cut into 16 cubes, each 1½ to 2 inches
Freshly ground pepper, to taste
Nonstick vegetable cooking spray

1. Preheat the oven to slow (300°). Wrap the garlic cloves in aluminum foil and set them on a baking sheet.
2. Bake the garlic in the preheated slow oven (300°) for 45 minutes or until the cloves are very soft. Remove the cloves from the oven. Increase the oven temperature to broil.
3. When the cloves are cool, squeeze the garlic out from the skins into a food processor. Add the white kidney beans, lemon juice and liquid red pepper seasoning. Cover and whirl until the mixture is smooth. Turn the garlic bean sauce into a bowl.
4. Sprinkle the turkey with the pepper and set the meat on the broiler pan sprayed with nonstick vegetable cooking spray.

5. Broil the turkey 5 inches from the source of the heat, without turning it, for 4 to 5 minutes or until it no longer is pink in the center. Arrange 4 cubes of meat on each of 4 individual dinner plates. Serve the garlic bean sauce at room temperature alongside the turkey. Garnish the plates with steamed julienne carrots, if you wish.

Note: *The sauce may be refrigerated, covered, for up to 1 day. Return the sauce to room temperature before using it.*

CookSmart

Talkin' Turkey

When buying turkeys under 12 pounds, allow ¾ to 1 pound per serving; when buying birds weighing more than 12 pounds, allow ½ to ¾ pound per serving. Remember, the bigger the bird, the more meat there will be in proportion to bone. Half of a 20-pound bird, for example, will be meatier than a 10-pound bird — and less expensive per serving.

PORK,
LAMB & BEEF

Blackened Pork Chops (recipe, page 167)

BLACKENED PORK CHOPS

LOW-CALORIE
LOW-SODIUM
LOW-CHOLESTEROL

These chops have a spicy black crust that contrasts beautifully with the smooth, white meat inside. Dried herbs actually are preferable to fresh in this recipe.

Grill for about 20 minutes.

Makes 8 servings.

8   **pork chops (6 ounces each)**
¼   **cup leaf basil, crumbled**
¼   **cup leaf oregano, crumbled**
2   **tablespoons leaf thyme, crumbled**

Nutrient Value Per Serving:
181 calories, 23 g protein, 8 g fat, 5 g carbohydrate, 56 mg sodium, 67 mg cholesterol.

2   **tablespoons paprika**
1   **tablespoon freshly ground black pepper**
1½ **teaspoons ground hot red pepper**

1. Build a very hot charcoal fire*. Place the grill rack 4 inches from the hot coals.
2. Trim the fat from the pork chops.
3. Combine the basil, oregano, thyme, paprika, black pepper and ground hot red pepper in a small plastic bag.
4. Place a pork chop in the bag and shake until the chop is coated all over with the herb mixture. Remove the chop and repeat with the remaining chops.
5. Sear the chops on both sides by placing them on the grill rack directly above the coals. Move the chops to the side of the grill. Continue cooking them for 4 to 5 minutes more on each side or until the chops are very dark on the outside, cooked and juicy on the inside.

*__*Note:__ Blackened pork chops may be prepared indoors, but the kitchen must be very well ventilated by an exhaust fan because the blackening process generates considerable smoke. Preheat the oven to moderate (375°). Pour 1 tablespoon of peanut oil into a heavy-bottomed skillet (such as a cast iron skillet) placed over high heat. Heat until the oil starts to smoke. Carefully put in as many pork chops as the skillet will hold. Cook the pork chops for 1 minute on each side and transfer them to a baking dish. Repeat the process with the remaining pork chops and additional oil, 1 tablespoon at a time. When all the chops are in the baking dish, bake them in the preheated moderate oven (375°) for 15 minutes.*

VEAL SCALOPPINE WITH LEMON AND CAPERS

To retain the moist interior of veal, it's important to avoid overcooking it.

Makes 4 servings.

Nutrient Value Per Serving (using unsalted broth):
300 calories, 24 g protein, 17 g fat, 13 g carbohydrate, 153 mg sodium, 81 mg cholesterol.

1   lemon
¼   cup unbleached all-purpose flour
½   teaspoon salt
½   teaspoon freshly ground black pepper
½   teaspoon ground hot red pepper
1   pound veal scaloppine, pounded ¼ inch thick

1   tablespoon olive oil
1   tablespoon corn oil
1   tablespoon finely chopped shallots
½   cup vermouth
¾   cup chicken broth
1   teaspoon margarine
1   tablespoon capers, drained
1   tablespoon chopped parsley, for garnish

1. Halve the lemon and reserve one half for garnish. Squeeze the juice from the other half.
2. Combine the flour, salt, black pepper and ground hot red pepper in a shallow plate. Dredge the veal in the flour mixture, shaking off the excess. Reserve 2 teaspoons of the flour mixture for thickening the sauce.
3. Heat the olive and corn oils in a large nonstick skillet over medium heat. Add the veal, part at a time, and sauté it for 3 minutes on one side. Turn it and sauté the second side. Remove the veal to a warmed serving platter.
4. Pour off any fat remaining in the pan. Add the shallots, vermouth and broth. Bring the sauce to boiling over medium heat, scraping up any browned bits from the bottom of the pan with a wooden spoon. Lower the heat and simmer the sauce for several minutes.

5. Blend the reserved 2 teaspoons of flour mixture into the margarine in a small cup. Stir the flour-margarine mixture into the sauce. Continue simmering the sauce over low heat, stirring occasionally, for 2 to 3 minutes more or until the sauce thickens slightly. Stir in the capers.
6. Pour the sauce over the veal. Garnish with the reserved lemon half, cut into 4 slices, and the parsley. Serve with rice pilaf or noodles, if you wish.

HEALTH

Parsley: A Garnish That's Great For Your Skin!

Don't ignore that little sprig of parsley garnishing your plate. Each sprig is loaded with nutrients, including the hard-to-get B vitamin folacin (or folic acid), which is important for both pregnant women and those on the pill, whose needs for folic acid are almost doubled. Folacin helps keep skin tone vibrant because it plays a key role in the formation and maturation of red blood cells. A pale, sallow complexion is one of the signs of folacin-deficiency anemia. A half cup of parsley delivers your entire daily need for folacin and offers a substantial helping of vitamin C to boot.

HOTLINE

LAMB CHOPS BAKED IN PARCHMENT PAPER

The assembled paper packets can be refrigerated until 30 minutes before serving time.

Bake at 350° for 20 minutes.

Makes 6 servings.

Nutrient Value Per Serving:
253 calories, 27 g protein, 12 g fat, 9 g carbohydrate, 223 mg sodium, 98 mg cholesterol.

12	lamb rib chops
6	cloves garlic
1	tablespoon chopped fresh rosemary OR: 1 teaspoon leaf rosemary, crumbled
	Freshly ground black pepper, to taste

3	cups cubed eggplant
3	cups cubed zucchini
3	ripe tomatoes
¾	cup crumbled feta cheese (about 3 ounces)

1. Preheat the oven to moderate (350°). Cut 6 ovals or hearts, 2 to 3 times as large as the lamb chops, from parchment paper or aluminum foil (not wax paper).
2. Trim the fat from the lamb chops.
3. Finely chop the garlic and combine it with the rosemary and the black pepper. Rub the herb mixture on both sides of each chop.
4. Arrange 2 chops on one half of each piece of parchment paper or aluminum foil. Scatter the eggplant and zucchini cubes over the chops. Halve the tomatoes and place a half on each pair of chops. Evenly distribute the feta cheese among the chops.
5. Seal the parchment or aluminum foil packets by crimping the edges. Place the packets on a baking sheet.
6. Bake the packets in the preheated moderate oven (350°) for 20 minutes or until they are puffed. Transfer the packets to 6 individual dinner plates. Provide each person with a steak knife to open his or her own packet.

CookSmart

Get a Leg Up on Lamb

Lamb is tender, lean meat with a delicate but distinctive flavor. It is the meat of young sheep under 1 year in age, usually 6 months. Mutton is the meat from mature sheep.

● Lamb is available fresh or frozen. Frozen lamb is usually imported from New Zealand. Fresh lamb is pink to light red in color with firm, fine textured flesh. Some cuts of lamb have a thin, papery skin, called "fell," surrounding the fat. If it has not been removed, pull it off steaks and chops before cooking; leave it on roasts to help hold their shape during cooking.

● Some cuts of lamb, such as the rib or loin chops, have given lamb an expensive reputation, but there are many cuts that are economical and are excellent to use in everyday meals. For example, buy cuts from the shoulder, such as a shoulder arm roast or shoulder steaks.

BROILED LAMB CHOPS AND TOMATOES WITH ARUGULA

By broiling the lamb you are eliminating much of the fat content because most of the fat drains away.

Broil lamb chops for 10 minutes for medium-rare; broil tomatoes for 7 to 10 minutes.

Makes 6 servings.

2   tablespoons plus 2 teaspoons
      fresh oregano OR:
      1 teaspoon leaf oregano,
      crumbled
6   1-inch-thick lamb chops
      (about 1½ pounds)
1   large clove garlic, finely
      chopped

Nutrient Value Per Serving:
135 calories, 17 g protein, 5 g fat, 6 g carbohydrate, 70 mg sodium, 46 mg cholesterol.

6   ripe tomatoes, halved
      horizontally
      Salt and freshly ground black
      pepper, to taste
8   cups arugula leaves, rinsed
1   teaspoon extra-virgin olive oil
      (optional)
1   teaspoon fresh lemon juice

1. If using fresh oregano, finely chop 2 tablespoons of the leaves. Place the lamb chops in a single layer in a nonaluminum dish and rub them with the garlic. Sprinkle them with the chopped fresh oregano. Cover the dish and refrigerate the chops for 2 to 6 hours.
2. Preheat the broiler and the broiler pan.
3. Place the tomatoes, cut side up, in one layer in a nonaluminum dish. Season them with the salt and black pepper.
4. Place the lamb chops on the preheated broiler pan and broil until they are cooked as you like them, for about 5 minutes per side for medium-rare chops. Remove the chops from the broiler and season them with the salt and black pepper.
5. If there is room under the broiler, place the tomatoes under it with the lamb chops and broil them until they look almost charred, for 7 to 10 minutes. If there isn't room under the broiler, remove the broiled lamb chops from the pan, cover them and keep them warm in a very low oven while you broil the tomatoes.

6. Just before the lamb and the tomatoes are cooked, steam the arugula over boiling water just until the greens wilt, for about 1 minute.
7. Transfer the arugula to a warmed serving platter and season it with the salt and black pepper. Arrange the chops on top of the arugula and garnish them with the tomatoes. Drizzle the oil and the lemon juice over the chops. Sprinkle with the remaining 2 teaspoons of fresh oregano or with the leaf oregano.

CURRY MARINADE

This lively marinade adds a touch of India to your meat—it's especially delicious with skewered lamb.

Makes 1 cup.

Nutrient Value Per Tablespoon:
45 calories, 0 g protein, 5 g fat,
1 g carbohydrate, 69 mg sodium,
0 mg cholesterol.

½ cup fresh lemon juice
    (2 lemons)
⅓ cup corn or olive oil
½ medium-size onion, grated
2 cloves garlic, mashed

1 tablespoon curry powder
1 teaspoon ground coriander
½ teaspoon ground ginger
½ teaspoon salt

Combine the lemon juice, corn or olive oil, onion, garlic, curry powder, coriander, ginger and salt in a screw-top jar. Cover the jar and shake to mix all the ingredients well. Refrigerate the marinade for up to 1 week. Shake the marinade again just before using it.

LAMB MARINADE

Allow the flavors of the ten ingredients to marry for a few minutes before using. This marinade also doubles as a baste during grilling.

Makes 2 cups.

Nutrient Value Per ¼ Cup:
126 calories, 0 g protein, 14 g fat,
2 g carbohydrate, 5 mg sodium,
0 mg cholesterol.

1 cup dry red wine
½ cup olive oil
2 tablespoons finely chopped
    parsley
2 tablespoons chopped chives
2 cloves garlic, crushed

½ teaspoon Worcestershire sauce
¼ teaspoon pepper
    Pinch each leaf marjoram,
    rosemary and thyme,
    crumbled

Combine the wine, olive oil, parsley, chives, garlic, Worcestershire sauce, pepper, marjoram, rosemary and thyme in a small bowl. Blend well.

LAMB-STUFFED ZUCCHINI

Ground lean lamb is flavored with onion and cinnamon and baked in zucchini boats with tomato sauce. Try serving with pilaf or rice.

Bake at 400° for 40 to 50 minutes.

Makes 4 servings.

Nutrient Value Per Serving:
251 calories, 18 g protein, 14 g fat, 19 g carbohydrate, 783 mg sodium, 40 mg cholesterol.

½ **pound coarsely ground lean lamb**
1 **medium-size onion, finely chopped**
¼ **teaspoon ground cinnamon**
⅓ **cup pine nuts (pignoli)**

Salt and freshly ground pepper, to taste
1 **tablespoon olive oil**
8 **small zucchini, trimmed**
2 **cups tomato sauce**
Water

1. Preheat the oven to hot (400°).
2. Sauté the meat with the onion, cinnamon, pine nuts, salt and pepper in a nonstick skillet over medium heat until the meat is lightly browned. Remove the meat mixture with a slotted spoon from the skillet.
3. Heat the oil in the same skillet over medium heat. Add the whole zucchini and cook, turning, until slightly soft, for about 12 minutes. Transfer the zucchini to a large baking dish. Make a lengthwise slit almost, but not quite, through to the bottom of each zucchini. Stuff the zucchini with the meat filling, spooning any remaining filling over the top. Pour the tomato sauce over the zucchini. Add just enough water to barely cover the zucchini. Cover the dish with aluminum foil.

4. Bake the stuffed zucchini in the preheated hot oven (400°) until the zucchini and meat filling are tender, for 40 to 50 minutes.

HEALTH

A Squash By Any Other Name

Summer squash, of which zucchini is perhaps the best known variety, offers a mere five calories per ounce while contributing vitamins A and C, along with iron, calcium, part of the B complex, niacin, riboflavin, and thiamine. Combining summer squash with cheese or milk, or with lean cuts of meat, naturally boosts the protein and calcium levels.

HOTLINE

MARINATED FLANK STEAK

Steak on the grill is always a treat—and this combination of marinade and marmalade is unbeatable.

Grill or broil for 8 to 10 minutes for medium-rare.

Makes 10 servings.

½ **cup soy sauce**
½ **cup water**
1 **tablespoon chopped garlic**
1 **tablespoon sesame oil**
2 **teaspoons chili powder**
2 **teaspoons grated, peeled, fresh gingerroot**

Nutrient Value Per Serving (including 1 tablespoon Red Pepper Marmalade): 291 calories, 26 g protein, 16 g fat, 11 g carbohydrate, 498 mg sodium, 70 mg cholesterol.

3 **pounds flank steak, trimmed of all visible fat**
   Red Pepper Marmalade (recipe, page 107)

1. Mix together the soy sauce, water, garlic, sesame oil, chili powder and ginger in a large, self-sealing plastic bag placed in a roasting pan. Add the steak and seal the bag. Turn the bag to distribute the marinade. Refrigerate the steak for 12 hours, turning the bag two or three times.
2. Build a charcoal fire or preheat the broiler.

3. Remove the steak from the marinade and discard the marinade. Pat the steak dry with paper toweling. Grill or broil the steak for 4 to 5 minutes per side for medium-rare, or until done as you like.
4. Slice the steak into thin pieces, cutting on an angle across the grain. Serve each portion with a tablespoon of the Red Pepper Marmalade.

CookSmart

Marinade Maxims

A marinade imparts flavor to meat and can also tenderize or moisturize tougher cuts of meat.
● Dry rub: To tenderize as well as flavor, season meats with spices and herbs.
● Oil-based sauce: While cooking, slow-roasted meats need moisture. Olive oil is best, but any oil-based sauce will help to retain internal juices by sealing the surface of the meat quickly.
● Acidic mixture: Wine-, vinegar- or citrus juice-based marinades act as a tenderizer by breaking down the tough fibers of meat. Marinate large cuts overnight, small cuts for about 1 hour.

STIR-FRIED PORK WITH FOUR PEPPERS

Sweet red, yellow and green peppers team up with smoky-flavored ancho chili peppers in this East-meets-West recipe.

Makes 4 servings.

Nutrient Value Per Serving:
257 calories, 25 g protein, 11 g fat,
18 g carbohydrate, 666 mg sodium,
55 mg cholesterol.

¾   **pound boneless pork tenderloin**
4   **teaspoons grated, peeled fresh gingerroot**
2   **cloves garlic, finely chopped Flowerets from 1 small head broccoli (about ¾ pound)**
¼   **cup reduced-sodium soy sauce, divided**
3   **tablespoons dry sherry**
2   **teaspoons cornstarch or potato starch**
1   **teaspoon sugar**

1   **sweet red pepper**
1   **sweet green pepper**
1   **sweet yellow pepper**
1   **dried ancho chili pepper, soaked**
½   **pound mushrooms**
1   **tablespoon peanut oil, divided**
½   **teaspoon crushed red pepper flakes**
¼   **teaspoon chili oil (optional)**
¼   **cup whole dry-roasted peanuts**

1. Trim any fat from the tenderloin. Place the tenderloin in the freezer for 15 minutes to make the meat easier to slice. Cut the tenderloin across the grain into ¼-inch slices. Cut the slices into strips.
2. Place the strips in a medium-size bowl and toss with 1 teaspoon of the ginger and half the garlic. Let the pork stand while preparing the vegetables.
3. If you like broccoli somewhat tender, simmer the flowerets in a saucepan of boiling water for 3 minutes or until partially cooked. Drain the broccoli and quickly plunge it into a bowl of ice and water to stop further cooking. Let the broccoli stand for 5 minutes. Then drain on paper toweling. (For very crunchy broccoli, this step may be omitted.)
4. Stir together 2 tablespoons of the soy sauce with the sherry, cornstarch or potato starch and the sugar in a small bowl to form a smooth paste.
5. Halve, seed and cut the red, green and yellow peppers into strips. Seed and cut the soaked ancho chili pepper into thin strips. Wipe and trim the mushrooms and cut them into quarters.

6. Heat a wok or large, heavy-bottomed skillet over high heat. Add 1½ teaspoons of the peanut oil and heat until hot. Add the remaining ginger and garlic and the red pepper flakes. Stir-fry for 30 seconds. Add the broccoli and stir-fry for 1 minute. Add the mushrooms and stir-fry for 1 minute. Add the remaining soy sauce and toss to coat the vegetables. Add the chili oil, if you wish, and toss again. Transfer the vegetables with a slotted spoon or spatula to a warmed large platter.
7. Wipe out the wok or skillet with paper toweling. Heat the remaining peanut oil over high heat. Add the pork and stir-fry for 2 minutes. Transfer the pork with a slotted spoon to the platter.
8. Add the red, green, yellow and ancho chili peppers to the wok and stir-fry for 1 minute or until heated through.
9. Stir the cornstarch mixture to reblend and add it to the wok. Cook, stirring constantly, for 1 to 2 minutes or until the sauce thickens.
10. Return the pork and the vegetables to the wok along with the peanuts. Toss until coated and just heated through.

CookSmart

Pepper Power

Ancho chili peppers are a variety of dried poblano peppers from the Puebla valley in Mexico. Garnet colored, they are moderately hot to hot. Before being used in cooking, they must be soaked in hot water until softened. After soaking them, remove their stems and seeds and chop them or cut them into strips. Wear rubber gloves and wash your hands thoroughly when done.

PEACH CHUTNEY GLAZE

LOW-FAT
LOW-CALORIE
LOW-CHOLESTEROL
MICROWAVE

Use this glaze on poultry, pork or lamb. Any leftover glaze can be refrigerated and used as a condiment.

Makes about 1 cup.

Nutrient Value Per ¼ Cup:
83 calories, 1 g protein, 0 g fat,
22 g carbohydrate, 138 mg sodium,
0 mg cholesterol.

½ pound ripe peaches, peeled,
   stoned and quartered
2 tablespoons raisins
¼ cup sugar
3 tablespoons cider vinegar
1 clove garlic, finely chopped

1 teaspoon grated, peeled fresh
   gingerroot
¼ teaspoon salt
   Dash liquid red pepper
   seasoning

1. Combine the peaches and the raisins in the container of a food processor. Cover and process until the mixture is chopped, but not puréed.
2. Transfer the peach mixture to a saucepan or a microwave-safe 1-quart bowl and add the sugar, vinegar, garlic, ginger, salt and liquid red pepper seasoning. Cover with a paper toweling.

3. Simmer the glaze over medium heat until the mixture thickens slightly, for 10 to 15 minutes. Or, microwave at full power for 3 to 5 minutes. Then microwave at half power for 8 to 10 minutes or until the mixture thickens slightly. Use as a baste during the last 10 minutes of grilling.

ORANGE SAUCE FOR PORK

LOW-FAT
LOW-CALORIE
LOW-CHOLESTEROL

A spicy accompaniment! Try this sauce on fresh ham, smoked ham or spare ribs.

Makes about 1½ cups.

Nutrient Value Per Tablespoon:
17 calories, 0 g protein, 0 g fat,
4 g carbohydrate, 23 mg sodium,
0 mg cholesterol.

3 oranges
3 small green chilies, seeded and
   finely chopped
¼ cup water OR: white wine

3 tablespoons vinegar
3 tablespoons sugar
¼ teaspoon salt
⅓ teaspoon leaf oregano, crumbled

Squeeze the juice from the oranges into a small bowl; use a sharp-edged spoon to remove the pulp and add to the juice. Add the chilies, water or wine, vinegar, sugar, salt and oregano, blending well. Let the sauce stand for 1 hour. Serve with pork.

FUNNY-FACE PIZZA

Watch for the smiles when you serve this happy meal — fun to look at, good to eat!

LOW-CALORIE
LOW-CHOLESTEROL

Bake at 425° for 12 to 15 minutes.

Makes 8 servings (one 12-inch pizza).

1 pound ground round
1 medium-size onion, chopped
1 clove garlic, finely chopped
1 cup sloppy joe sauce (from 14½- or 15½-ounce jar)
1 tube (10 ounces) refrigerated pizza dough
1 package (8 ounces) shredded mozzarella cheese

Nutrient Value Per Serving:
158 calories, 20 g protein, 15 g fat, 21 g carbohydrate, 495 mg sodium, 58 mg cholesterol.

2 tablespoons grated Parmesan cheese
½ medium-size sweet red pepper, thinly sliced and tossed with ½ teaspoon olive oil
2 black olives, halved
3 to 4 cherry tomatoes, halved
2 tablespoons finely chopped parsley

1. Preheat the oven to hot (425°). Place an oven rack in the lowest position.
2. Cook the meat, onion and garlic in a medium-size skillet, stirring with a wooden spoon to break up the chunks, until the meat is no longer pink. Drain the fat. Stir in the sloppy joe sauce. Set aside the mixture.
3. Prepare the pizza crust following the package directions for a thick crust pie.
4. Spread the meat filling over the entire surface of the dough. Sprinkle the mozzarella and Parmesan cheeses over the filling.

5. Place the red pepper strips at the top of the pizza to form the "hair." Place 2 ripe olive halves below the hair to form the eyes and one half olive below the eyes to form the nose.
6. Bake the pizza on the lowest rack in the preheated hot oven (425°) for 12 to 15 minutes. Arrange the cherry tomato halves to form the mouth and sprinkle the chopped parsley above the eyes to form the eyebrows. Serve immediately.

HEALTH

The No-Vice Slice

Good news! Pizza is not a junk food. It's a healthful balance of protein, fat and carbohydrates. And with the right toppings, you can give yourself an extra boost of nutrition. Try mushrooms, green and red peppers, broccoli, thinly sliced zucchini or, for the daring, eggplant, artichoke hearts, avocado, pineapple — your imagination is the only limit.

HOTLINE

APRICOT-STUFFED PORK TENDERLOIN

Chopped apricots and currants add moistness and a sweet tang to this hearty dish.

Bake at 400° for 40 to 50 minutes.

Makes 4 servings.

Nutrient Value Per Serving:
245 calories, 29 g protein, 6 g fat,
19 g carbohydrate, 285 mg sodium,
152 mg cholesterol.

¼ cup dried currants
¼ cup finely chopped dried
　 apricots
2 tablespoons bourbon
1 tablespoon water
1 pound boneless pork tenderloin
1 cup fresh pumpernickel bread
　 crumbs

¼ teaspoon salt
¼ teaspoon leaf rosemary,
　 crumbled
⅛ teaspoon leaf sage, crumbled
⅛ teaspoon pepper
1 egg, lightly beaten

1. Preheat the oven to hot (400°). Soak the currants and apricots in the bourbon and water in a small bowl; set aside.
2. Cut the pork tenderloin lengthwise down the center but not all the way through. Pound the meat between 2 sheets of wax paper until the pork is an even ¼-inch thickness.
3. Add the bread crumbs, salt, rosemary, sage, pepper and egg to the dried-fruit mixture and mix well. Spread the stuffing down the center of the pork, leaving a ½-inch border on the ends. Bring up the long sides of the tenderloin to enclose the filling, overlapping the long edges slightly. Push in the short ends as you roll. Secure the rolls with string every 2 inches. Arrange the rolls on a rack in a roasting pan.

4. Bake in the preheated hot oven (400°) for 40 to 50 minutes, or until an instant-read meat thermometer registers 160° when inserted in the meat. Let the rolls stand for 5 minutes. Slice thinly to serve.

PORK TORTILLAS

Serve up these spicy bundles with an orange, red onion and avocado salad for a fast feast.

Warm tortillas at 350° for 3 minutes.

Makes 6 servings.

Nutrient Value Per Serving:
303 calories, 22 g protein, 18 g fat, 14 g carbohydrate, 103 mg sodium, 69 mg cholesterol.

1   large firm, ripe tomato
1   whole jalapeño pepper
3   tablespoons chopped fresh cilantro
   Salt and freshly ground pepper, to taste

6   corn tortillas
1   pound roast pork, trimmed of all excess fat and shredded

1. Preheat the oven to moderate (350°).
2. Core, seed and finely chop the tomato. Wearing rubber gloves, halve the jalapeño pepper and remove the seeds and ribs. Finely chop the jalapeño.
3. Combine the tomato, jalapeño pepper, cilantro and salt and pepper in a small bowl, tossing gently until the ingredients are well blended. (The recipe can be made ahead of time to this point; cover the bowl and store in the refrigerator until serving time.)

4. Stack the tortillas and wrap them in aluminum foil.
5. Bake the tortillas in the preheated moderate oven (350°) for 3 minutes or until the tortillas are soft and warm.
6. Unwrap the tortillas and place them on a serving platter. Place a spoonful of the shredded pork in the center of each tortilla. Top with a spoonful of the tomato-coriander mixture. Roll up the tortillas and serve.

PROSCIUTTO AND PEAR SANDWICHES

A sandwich out of the ordinary—perfect for a special luncheon. If you don't like arugula's peppery flavor, substitute watercress.

Makes 6 servings.

Nutrient Value Per Serving:
293 calories, 14 g protein, 8 g fat, 42 g carbohydrate, 876 mg sodium, 30 mg cholesterol.

¼   cup lowfat cream cheese, softened
1   baguette (thin French bread) split lengthwise, but not cut all the way through

8   thin slices prosciutto OR: coppa salami*
2   firm, ripe pears
1   bunch arugula, rinsed and patted dry

1. Spread the cream cheese onto half the baguette. Layer the prosciutto or salami on top of the cream cheese.
2. Core the pears and cut them into thin wedges. Place the pears over the prosciutto and top with the whole arugula leaves.

3. Close the loaf, gently pressing down. Cut the sandwich into 6 portions with a serrated knife.

***Note:** Coppa salami is a coarse, country-style salami.*

HAM AND LENTIL LOAVES

The loaves freeze well and may be sliced before freezing for quick-thawing individual servings.

Bake at 350° for 1 hour.

Makes 2 loaves (6 servings each).

Nutrient Value Per Serving:
214 calories, 16 g protein, 4 g fat,
30 g carbohydrate, 612 mg sodium,
78 mg cholesterol.

1 **pound dried lentils, picked over and rinsed**
1 **pound smoked ham hocks**
1 **small carrot, trimmed and halved**
1 **celery stalk, halved**
1 **small handful celery leaves**
6 **cups water**
1 **large onion, halved**
4 **whole cloves**

1 **cup chopped onion (1 large onion)**
1 **cup chopped celery**
1 **tablespoon butter or margarine**
4 **slices whole wheat bread**
3 **eggs**
1 **cup shredded carrot**
2 **teaspoons salt**
¾ **teaspoon freshly ground pepper**

1. Combine the lentils, ham hocks, carrot halves, celery stalk, celery leaves and water in a large saucepan. Stud the onion halves with the cloves and add to the saucepan. Bring the mixture to boiling. Lower the heat, cover and simmer the mixture for 45 minutes. Uncover the saucepan and simmer for 15 minutes more or until the lentils and the ham are very tender. Let the mixture cool.
2. Meanwhile, sauté the chopped onion and the chopped celery in the butter or margarine in a large skillet until tender, for about 5 minutes. Cool the mixture slightly.
3. Preheat the oven to moderate (350°). Grease two 9 x 5 x 3-inch loaf pans very well. Line the long sides and the bottoms of the pans with aluminum foil cut large enough to make a 4-inch overhang on each side. Grease the foil very well.
4. Remove the cloves from the onion halves and return the halves to the lentil mixture. Cut the meat from the ham hocks and add to the lentil mixture.
5. Place the bread in the container of a food processor. Cover and process to make crumbs. Transfer the crumbs to a large bowl.

6. Working in batches, place the lentil mixture in the container of the food processor. Pulse with on-and-off motions to chop the vegetables and the ham. Add the mixture to the bread crumbs along with the eggs, sautéed onion mixture, shredded carrot, salt and pepper. Mix gently to combine all the ingredients.
7. Spoon the mixture into the prepared pans and smooth the tops. Fold the foil overhangs over the tops of the loaves.
8. Bake the loaves in the preheated moderate oven (350°) for 1 hour or until the loaves are firm and set around the edges. Cool the loaves in the pans on a wire rack for 10 minutes. Invert the loaves onto a plate and remove the foil. Serve the loaves hot, at room temperature or chilled.

8

HOOKED ON FISH

The health catch-of-the-day: seafood. Virtually all seafood has impressive nutritional benefits, in addition to being low-calorie. Lean species, such as cod, pollock and halibut, yield a mere 110 calories per quarter pound. But even their "fatty" brothers, lake trout, king salmon and mackerel, yield only twice that amount of calories. Interestingly enough, the higher-calorie fish contain the highest levels of Omega-3 fatty acids — the unsaturated fats thought to actually help *lower* the level of harmful cholesterol in the blood. Even shellfish, such as shrimp and lobster, supply beneficial amounts of Omega-3's.

Fish and shellfish also supply niacin, riboflavin, vitamins B_6 and B_{12}, as well as trace minerals including calcium, magnesium and potassium. Saltwater fish is the richest source of iodine available, and all fish, fresh or saltwater, are naturally low in sodium.

Poaching, steaming, baking, sautéing: these are some of the methods we use to cook fish healthfully. The results are moist, tender dishes that retain their nutritional benefits. Even our sauces are calorie-smart. Recipes include Poached Trout with Orange Garlic Sauce *(recipe, page 183)*, Sautéed Prawns with Garlic *(recipe, page 203)*, Sole with Plums and Apricots *(recipe, page 185)* and Cajun-inspired Jambalaya *(recipe, page 204)*.

And don't overlook our seafood salads. Colorful Shrimp and Rice Salad Valencia *(recipe, page 207)* gets its tang from oranges, capers and yogurt. For a taste of the Mediterranean, try Greek Tuna Salad *(recipe, page 209)* — it's low in calories as well as cholesterol.

With all this lively bait, you'll be hooked on fish too!

Stuffed Fillet of Sole with White Wine Sauce (recipe, page 197), Bulgur Salad Primavera (recipe, page 77)

THE FISH

Poached Trout with Orange Garlic Sauce
(recipe, page 183)

POACHED TROUT WITH ORANGE GARLIC SAUCE

The poaching liquid gently flavors the trout with orange, fennel and garlic. The creamy orange garlic sauce tops it off perfectly.

Makes 6 servings.

Nutrient Value Per Serving:
289 calories, 27 g protein, 5 g fat, 32 g carbohydrate, 505 mg sodium, 61 mg cholesterol.

20 large cloves garlic, peeled, plus 3 cloves, crushed
4   rainbow trout (8 to 10 ounces each), cleaned, heads on
10 cups Fish Stock (recipe, page 196) OR: chicken stock
2   cups dry white wine
1   medium-size onion, sliced
2   large sprigs fresh thyme OR: ¼ teaspoon leaf thyme, crumbled
2   bay leaves
1½ teaspoons fennel seeds
10 black peppercorns
1   large sprig parsley
    Zest (orange part of rind only) of 1 orange, shredded
    Salt and freshly ground black pepper, to taste
½   teaspoon vegetable oil
8   slices crusty white bread, cut into triangles and toasted
    Small handful of parsley sprigs OR: fennel fronds, for garnish

1. Steam the 20 whole garlic cloves over boiling water until they are tender, for about 15 minutes. Remove the garlic cloves from the steamer and place them in a food processor. Cover and whirl until they are puréed. Transfer the garlic purée to a small bowl.

2. Rinse the trout and pat them dry with paper toweling.

3. Place the fish or chicken stock, the wine, onion, thyme, bay leaves, 1 teaspoon of the fennel seeds, the peppercorns, the large sprig of parsley, half the orange zest and 2 cloves of the crushed garlic in a fish poacher. Season with the salt. Grease the poaching rack with the oil. Place the trout on the rack, head to tail. Lower the rack into the stock and bring the stock to boiling over medium heat. If the poaching liquid doesn't entirely cover the trout, moisten a cotton tea towel or a double thickness of cheesecloth in the fish stock and lay it on top of the trout. Baste the trout several times while they are poaching. Reduce the heat so the liquid barely simmers and cook until the trout are opaque throughout, for about 8 minutes.

4. While the trout are poaching, rub the toast with the remaining crushed garlic clove.

5. When the trout are cooked, remove the rack from the poaching liquid and place the rack over the sink or on a platter to catch the dripping liquid. Cover the fish loosely.

6. Strain 1½ cups of the poaching liquid into a medium-size saucepan and bring it to boiling over high heat. Cook until the liquid is reduced by about one third. Whisk in the garlic purée, the remaining ½ teaspoon of fennel seeds and the remaining orange zest. Season to taste with the salt and black pepper.

7. Transfer the trout to a heated serving platter. Garnish them with the garlic toast. Pour the sauce over and garnish the platter with the additional parsley sprigs or fennel fronds.

POACHED HALIBUT
WITH LEMON GARLIC BUTTER

An easy, elegant main dish. Serve it with rice, baby peas and a dry, white wine.

Makes 4 servings.

Nutrient Value Per Serving (using clam juice):
261 calories, 30 g protein, 14 g fat, 1 g carbohydrate, 196 mg sodium, 78 mg cholesterol.

4   halibut steaks (4 ounces each)
    OR: 4 steaks firm, white-fleshed fish, such as haddock or flounder
¼   cup (½ stick) unsalted butter
1   tablespoon fresh lemon juice
1   clove garlic, finely chopped
2   cups bottled clam juice
    OR: Fish Stock
    (recipe, page 196)
    Salt and freshly ground pepper, to taste

1. Rinse the fish steaks and pat them dry with paper toweling.
2. Melt the butter in a small saucepan over medium heat. Add the lemon juice and the garlic. Keep the lemon garlic butter warm over very low heat, stirring it occasionally.
3. Bring the clam juice or fish stock to boiling in a large, nonaluminum skillet over medium-high heat. Reduce the heat to medium and add the fish steaks. Season with the salt and pepper. Cover the skillet.

4. Cook the fish steaks for 5 minutes or just until they are opaque throughout. Do not overcook the fish or they will dry out.
5. Carefully transfer the fish steaks with a slotted spatula to the centers of 4 warmed individual dinner plates.
6. Drizzle equal amounts of the lemon garlic butter over the fish steaks and onto the plates. Serve immediately.

HEALTH

The A-B-Seas of Good Nutrition

Fish and shellfish are hard to beat for their nutritional and health benefits. Most fish are low in total fat and calorie content. Lean uncooked cod, pollock and halibut have only 100 calories per quarter pound. Even the more fatty varieties of fish, such as lake trout, king salmon and mackerel, have only twice that amount.

Contrary to what many health-conscious cooks may think, caloric content is not the only consideration when selecting fish, and higher-calorie fish should not be shunned perfunctorily. All fish and shellfish contain some amount of Omega-3 fatty acids, the unsaturated fats that are thought to help lower levels of cholesterol in the blood. But it is the fatty species of fish that generally contain the highest levels of Omega-3's, more than twice those of the lean varieties. Even fish or shellfish that contain higher levels of cholesterol — shrimp and lobster, for example — still supply beneficial amounts of this wonder substance.

The nutritional pluses continue: Fish and shellfish supply niacin, riboflavin, vitamins B_6 and B_{12}, and at least a half dozen trace minerals, including calcium, magnesium and potassium. Saltwater seafood also is the richest natural source of iodine. Yet all fish, whether fresh or saltwater, are low in sodium.

HOTLINE

SOLE WITH PLUMS AND APRICOTS

LOW-FAT
LOW-CALORIE
LOW-SODIUM

Ripe plums and apricots simmered in port wine create a vibrantly colored sauce that enhances the delicate flavor of the fish.

Makes 4 servings.

Nutrient Value Per Serving:
241 calories, 32 g protein, 8 g fat, 8 g carbohydrate, 140 mg sodium, 97 mg cholesterol.

4   sole fillets (about 6 ounces each) OR: 4 snapper or cod fillets
2   tablespoons margarine
1   large shallot, finely chopped
¼   pound ripe apricots, pitted and quartered
¼   pound ripe plums, pitted and quartered

1   tablespoon port wine
1   teaspoon sugar
    Salt and freshly ground white pepper, to taste
    Flat-leaf Italian parsley sprigs, for garnish

1. Rinse the fish fillets and pat them dry with paper toweling.
2. Melt 1 tablespoon of the margarine in a medium-size saucepan over medium heat. Add the shallot and cook for 2 to 3 minutes or until it begins to soften.
3. Add the apricots, plums and port. Stir the mixture and cover the saucepan. Cook the mixture, stirring occasionally, for 15 minutes or until the fruit is soft.
4. Transfer the fruit to the container of a food processor. Cover and purée until the mixture is very smooth. Return the sauce to the saucepan. Stir in the sugar and the salt and white pepper. Keep the sauce warm over low heat.

5. Melt the remaining tablespoon of margarine in a large skillet over medium heat. Add the fish in one layer and sauté them for 4 to 5 minutes or until they are opaque on one side. Carefully turn the fish with a spatula and sauté them for 2 to 3 minutes more or just until they are opaque throughout.
6. Ladle the sauce onto 4 warmed individual dinner plates, spreading it out. Place the fish on the sauce. Garnish with the Italian parsley.

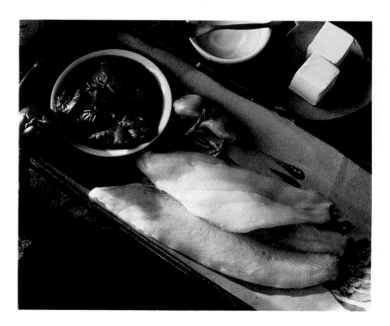

SHARK FILLETS WITH SAKE AND LEMON JUICE

Mako shark fillets (or any firm, white-fleshed fish) are lightly steamed and then delicately seasoned at the table.

Makes 4 servings.

Nutrient Value Per Serving:
231 calories, 36 g protein, 8 g fat,
1 g carbohydrate, 135 mg sodium,
87 mg cholesterol.

4   mako shark fillets (about
       6 ounces each) OR: 4 fillets
       firm, white-fleshed fish,
       such as sole, flounder or
       cod*
    Scant ½ teaspoon safflower oil
       OR: other flavorless vegetable
       oil

    Garlic chives and flowers,
       for garnish** (optional)
8   teaspoons sake
2   teaspoons fresh lemon juice
    Salt, to taste

1. Rinse the fish fillets and pat them dry with paper toweling. Rub the fish lightly all over with the oil.
2. Bring 2 cups of water to boiling in the bottom of a steamer or fish poacher. Place the fish in one layer on the steamer rack and cover the steamer or poacher. Adjust the heat so the liquid just simmers.
3. Cook the fish for 4 to 5 minutes, or just until they are opaque throughout. Remove the fish from the heat.
4. Place each fillet in the center of a warmed individual dinner plate. Garnish the plate with 3 garlic chives and a chive flower, if you wish.

5. At the table, pour 2 teaspoons of the sake, then ½ teaspoon of the lemon juice, over each portion. Let each person add the salt to his or her own portion.

*Note: *Since fish fillets vary in weight and thickness, adjust the cooking time accordingly.*
**Note: *Large garlic chives are grown easily in home gardens and sometimes can be found in Oriental specialty food stores. If they are not available, substitute regular chives.*

CookSmart

The Sauce Low-Down

Even if you're trying to cut down your fat intake, it's not necessary to shun sauces altogether. The key is to use the right ingredients.

● Use a lot of butter, cream or oil and you'll sink the sauceboat. Avoid them and you'll avoid excess fat.

● Puréed vegetables are a great choice to thicken sauces without adding fat — and they add flavor as well. Simmer carrots, parsnips or celery in broth for an extra flavor boost. Purée the vegetables in a food processor or an electric blender.

● Yogurt and buttermilk can substitute for heavy cream and sour cream in most sauces. To make cold sauces, mix them with chopped herbs and finely chopped tomatoes and cucumbers. Use these tangy cream sauces with poached chicken or fish, as well as with steamed vegetables.

● Freshly squeezed lemon and lime juices, used alone or with chopped fresh mint, chives, parsley or dill, add low-calorie pizzazz to steamed fish, grilled chicken and vegetables.

● For a bright spinach sauce, steam or microwave fresh spinach with chopped onion, shallots or leeks just until the spinach wilts. Purée the spinach and season it to taste with lemon juice and chopped fresh dill.

HERBED FISH FILLETS

LOW-CALORIE

Although this simple dish calls for fresh oregano, you can substitute fresh basil or dill, if you wish.

Bake at 450° for 10 to 15 minutes.

Makes 6 servings.

Nutrient Value Per Serving (without rice): 207 calories, 29 g protein, 9 g fat, 1 g carbohydrate, 201 mg sodium, 93 mg cholesterol.

1 tablespoon margarine
  Juice of 1 lemon
1 tablespoon chopped fresh oregano OR: 1 teaspoon leaf oregano, crumbled
1 very small clove garlic, crushed (optional)

  Salt, to taste (optional)
2 pounds fish fillets, such as flounder, sole, trout or catfish
  Cooked rice

HEALTH

What a Catch!

Flounder, a veritable gift from the sea, is a saltwater flatfish that is related to sole, fluke, halibut and turbot. It is sold fresh or frozen in fillets, and fresh in whole, small sizes. Flounder has a delicate, fine-textured white flesh and is an excellent source of protein with only a small amount of fat.

HOTLINE

1. Preheat the oven to hot (450°).
2. Melt the margarine in the oven in a baking dish large enough to hold the fish fillets in one layer. Stir in the lemon juice, oregano and, if you wish, garlic and salt.
3. Arrange the fish fillets in the butter mixture and turn to coat them on both sides.

4. Bake the fish in the preheated hot oven (450°), basting frequently with the pan liquid, for 10 to 15 minutes or just until the fish flake easily when lightly touched with a fork. Serve the fish and pan liquid with the cooked rice.

POACHED SOLE WITH ORANGES

LOW-FAT
LOW-CALORIE

White wine makes a delicious poaching liquid for fish. Grapes and oranges give this dish an elegant twist.

Makes 6 servings.

Nutrient Value Per Serving: 194 calories, 26 g protein, 3 g fat, 14 g carbohydrate, 690 mg sodium, 81 mg cholesterol.

2 packages (1 pound each) frozen sole, flounder or other white fish fillets
1 cup dry white wine
2 tablespoons lemon juice
1½ teaspoons salt

½ teaspoon white pepper
2 large oranges
1½ tablespoons cornstarch
1 tablespoon butter or margarine
1 cup seedless green grapes

1. Cut the fish into 6 pieces and place the pieces in a large skillet. Add the wine, lemon juice, salt and pepper. Cover the skillet. Bring the liquid to boiling; lower the heat and simmer for 8 minutes, or just until the fish flakes easily when lightly touched with a fork.
2. Carefully remove the fish to a hot platter. Cover the platter and keep it warm.
3. Pare and section the oranges over a small bowl to catch the juices.

4. Pour the poaching liquid from the skillet into a small saucepan. Combine the cornstarch with the juice from the oranges in a 1-cup measure. Stir the cornstarch mixture into the poaching liquid. Cook over low heat, stirring constantly, for 1 minute, or until the sauce thickens and bubbles. Add the butter or margarine, the orange segments and grapes. Heat the sauce and spoon over the fish.

BAKED TUNA WITH PEPPERCORNS

This remarkably light and easy dish blends the mild heat of black pepper with the rich-tasting, lean meat of tuna. If you like tuna completely cooked, add 2 to 3 minutes to the cooking time.

Bake at 300° for 45 minutes.

Makes 4 servings.

Nutrient Value Per Serving (without added salt):
200 calories, 28 g protein, 6 g fat, 8 g carbohydrate, 47 mg sodium, 43 mg cholesterol.

1   **pound tuna loin (cross-section in one piece)**
    Salt, to taste
1   **tablespoon black peppercorns, coarsely ground**

1   **pound onions, thinly sliced**
¼   **cup dry white wine**
2   **tablespoons finely chopped chives, for garnish**

1. Preheat the oven to slow (300°).
2. Rinse and pat the tuna dry. Season it lightly with the salt all over, then press the pepper into it, covering the tuna on all surfaces.
3. Place the onion and the wine in a large, ovenproof, heavy-bottomed skillet over medium-high heat. Toss to mix the ingredients. Cook the mixture, covered, for 5 minutes or until the onion softens very slightly. Season the mixture to taste with additional salt and pepper and remove the skillet from the heat.

4. Place the tuna on top of the onion mixture.
5. Bake the tuna in the preheated slow oven (300°) for 20 minutes. Turn over the tuna. Bake it for 25 minutes more or until it is almost opaque throughout. Remove the tuna from the oven and garnish it with the chives. Serve the tuna immediately, if you like tuna pale pink in the center. Or let the tuna sit for 10 minutes, if you like tuna cooked through.

CookSmart

The Fresh Test

All fresh fish should smell sweet and clean.
- Whole fish: Look for bright, glossy, smooth skin with few scales missing; bright, bulging eyes with dark corneas (contact with ice may cause clouding); and moist, vivid red gills. Avoid fish with rib bones separating from the flesh.
- Fish fillets and steaks: They should look translucent, lustrous and moist. Avoid fish that is discolored, brown around the edges, separating or sitting in liquid.
- Clams and mussels: An open-and-shut case — a quick tap should close them up.
- Oysters: These shellfish often are open, even when fresh. Oysters have 2 shells, 1 flat and 1 rounded. They should be kept with the rounded shell down to preserve the flavorful juices.

GRILLED SWORDFISH

Swordfish can be cooked like beef—rare to well done. The cooking time given here will yield a succulent, medium-rare interior. Reduce the time if the steaks are less than 1 inch thick.

Grill or broil for 8 minutes.

Makes 6 servings.

Nutrient Value Per Serving:
324 calories, 38 g protein, 14 g fat,
72 g carbohydrate, 174 mg sodium,
0 mg cholesterol.

3   tablespoons olive oil
    Juice of 2 lemons
    Juice of 1 orange
4   cloves garlic, finely chopped
⅓   cup chopped fresh basil
    OR: 2 tablespoons leaf
    basil, crumbled
1   teaspoon cracked pepper
6   swordfish steaks (about
    7 ounces each)

3   large ripe tomatoes
1   large red onion
1   recipe Very Green Sauce
    (recipe, page 91)
    Lemon wedges, for garnish
    Freshly ground pepper,
    to taste

1. Combine the oil, lemon and orange juices, garlic, basil and cracked pepper in a shallow dish. Add the fish steaks and turn to coat both sides. Cover the fish and refrigerate them for several hours, turning once or twice, if possible. Remove the fish from the refrigerator 20 minutes before grilling.
2. Build a charcoal fire or preheat the broiler. Place the grill rack or broiler pan 6 inches from the source of the heat.
3. Remove the fish steaks from the marinade, reserving the marinade for basting during the cooking.
4. Grill or broil the fish for 4 minutes. Brush the fish with the marinade and turn them over. Grill them for 4 minutes more or until the interior of each fish steak is slightly pink. (The medium-rare fish will be moist and tender.) Brush them once more with the marinade.

5. While the fish cooks, cut the tomatoes and the onion into ¼-inch-thick slices. Place 2 tomato slices on each of 6 individual dinner plates and tuck an onion slice between the tomato slices.
6. Place 1 tablespoon of the Very Green Sauce on each plate. Top it with a fish steak, then 1 or 2 more tablespoons of the sauce. Garnish with the lemon wedges and season with the pepper.

GRILLED SALMON WITH KIWI BARBECUE SAUCE

Although the grilling is done quickly, the kiwi sauce needs to be prepared 2 days in advance.

Grill or broil for 8 to 12 minutes.

Makes 6 servings.

Nutrient Value Per Serving:
254 calories, 23 g protein, 16 g fat,
3 g carbohydrate, 126 mg sodium,
62 mg cholesterol.

Shallot Marinade:
1 cup safflower oil
¼ cup finely chopped shallots,
   OR: ¼ cup finely chopped
   green onion
¼ cup cracked black
   peppercorns
   Juice of 1 lemon

1½ pounds salmon steaks
   Kiwi Barbecue Sauce (recipe,
   page 191)
3 kiwifruit, peeled and sliced
   crosswise into quarters,
   for garnish

1. Prepare the Shallot Marinade: Blend together the oil, shallots or green onion, the black peppercorns and lemon juice in a shallow container. Add the salmon steaks and spoon the marinade over them. Refrigerate the salmon for 1 hour, turning them once or twice.
2. Build a charcoal fire or preheat the broiler.
3. Remove the salmon from the marinade and blot them with paper toweling to remove excess oil.

4. Rewarm the Kiwi Barbecue Sauce, if necessary. Baste each side of the salmon with 1 teaspoon of the sauce.
5. Grill or broil the salmon for 4 to 6 minutes per side or just until they flake when lightly touched with a fork. (Do not overcook the fish, or they will be dry.) Remove the salmon and place them on a warmed serving platter or 6 individual dinner plates. Garnish each portion with 2 slices of the kiwifruit. Pass the remaining barbecue sauce.

KIWI BARBECUE SAUCE

This deliciously different barbecue sauce must be prepared 2 days before being used so the flavors can combine thoroughly.

Makes about 3 cups.

Nutrient Value Per ¼ Cup:
63 calories, 1 g protein, 0 g fat,
15 g carbohydrate, 454 mg sodium,
0 mg cholesterol.

HEALTH

Kiwis: Nutritional Knock-Outs

Kiwifruit—those small, green, egg-shaped things that look like they need a shave—turn out to be nutritional blockbusters. Two average-size kiwis have more potassium than a 6-inch banana, more dietary fiber than a ⅔-cup serving of bran flakes, nearly twice as much vitamin C as an orange and twice the vitamin E of an avocado—all for only 90 calories. Kiwifruit is ripe when slightly soft to the touch. To serve kiwi, cut it into wedges or halves and eat it with a spoon like a melon; or peel and slice it to add to salads, sandwiches and desserts.

HOTLINE

1   cup low-sugar, low-salt catsup
1   cup prepared chili sauce
½   cup flat beer
¼   cup firmly packed dark brown sugar
2   tablespoons red wine vinegar
2   teaspoons dry mustard powder

1   teaspoon coarsely cracked black pepper
    Dash liquid red pepper seasoning
2   kiwifruit
2   teaspoons cider vinegar

1. Prepare the Kiwi Barbecue Sauce 2 days ahead of time. Combine the catsup, chili sauce, beer, brown sugar, red wine vinegar, mustard powder, black pepper and liquid red pepper seasoning in a medium-size saucepan. Bring the mixture to boiling over medium-low heat. Lower the heat and simmer for 30 minutes, stirring frequently. Cool the mixture to room temperature. Cover and refrigerate the sauce for 2 days.

2. When ready to complete the barbecue sauce, peel the kiwis and place them in the container of an electric blender or a food processor. Cover and whirl until the fruit is puréed.
3. Bring the catsup mixture to simmering in a small saucepan over low heat and simmer it for 10 minutes. Add the puréed kiwi and the cider vinegar and simmer the sauce for 5 minutes more.

POACHED SALMON

Salmon, asparagus and sweet pepper diamonds are simmered together in a seasoned stock. Chicken stock may be substituted for the fish stock, if you wish.

Makes 4 servings.

Nutrient Value Per Serving:
202 calories, 30 g protein, 12 g fat,
5 g carbohydrate, 355 mg sodium,
118 mg cholesterol.

4   **fresh salmon fillets (6 to 7 ounces each)**
2   **teaspoons Seafood Seasoning (recipe, page 205)**
1   **sweet red pepper, cut into ¾-inch diamonds**
1   **sweet green pepper, cut into ¾-inch diamonds**

8   **spears of asparagus, cut into 1½-inch pieces**
1   **small red onion, sliced**
3   **cups Fish Stock (recipe, page 196) OR: chicken stock**

1. Season the salmon with the Seafood Seasoning and put them in a skillet in a single layer. Put the red and green peppers, asparagus and onion around the salmon. Add the fish stock or chicken stock. Cover the skillet and bring the mixture to a simmer. Simmer until the salmon is almost done, for about 5 minutes.

2. Transfer the salmon to 4 individual soup bowls. Spoon an equal amount of the vegetables around each fillet. Ladle some of the cooking liquid into each bowl and serve.

CookSmart

Poaching Calories

To poach means to cook in barely simmering liquid. This can be done in a skillet or wok on top of the stove, or in a fish poacher either on top of the stove or in the oven. Fish poachers are long narrow pans equipped with a rack used to suspend the food in the poaching liquid. To poach, lightly oil the rack and then place the fish (or other food) on it and lower the rack into the cooking liquid. This method of cooking preserves the natural moistness of fish (or poultry) and adds absolutely no fat.

SESAME SALMON

The flavors of the Orient grace this marinade with its blend of soy sauce, pepper, honey and sesame oil.

Makes 6 servings.

Nutrient Value Per Serving:
231 calories, 21 g protein, 14 g fat, 4 g carbohydrate, 861 mg sodium, 62 mg cholesterol.

½ cup light soy sauce
1 hot green chili pepper, seeded and finely chopped (wear rubber gloves)
1 clove garlic, crushed
1 teaspoon honey
2 teaspoons vinegar
2 tablespoons sesame oil

6 fresh salmon fillets (about 4 ounces each)
3 tablespoons toasted sesame seeds,* for garnish
2 green onions (green part only), thinly sliced, for garnish

1. Combine the soy sauce, chili pepper, garlic, honey, vinegar and 1 tablespoon of the oil in a bowl. Add the salmon fillets and turn to coat them with the marinade. Marinate the salmon for 2 hours. Remove the fish from the marinade and pat them dry.
2. Heat the remaining 1 tablespoon of oil in a nonstick skillet over medium-high heat. Add the salmon and sauté, turning once, just until the fish are cooked through, for about 3 minutes on each side.

3. Garnish the salmon with the toasted sesame seeds and the green onion.

*Note: *To toast sesame seeds, place them in a skillet over medium-low heat. Toast the seeds, stirring, until they turn golden, for about 1 minute.*

CHILLED SALMON WITH DILL SAUCE

Poached salmon is delightfully enhanced by this creamy dill sauce.
(Leftover sauce is great in tuna salad, too.)

Makes 4 servings.

Nutrient Value Per Serving:
354 calories, 35 g protein, 22 g fat,
2 g carbohydrate, 235 mg sodium,
103 mg cholesterol.

1   **cup water**
½   **cup dry white wine**
½   **small onion, thinly sliced**
10 **whole peppercorns**
1   **3-inch sprig fresh thyme**
      OR: pinch leaf thyme,
      crumbled
4   **salmon steaks or fillets**
      (6 ounces each)

Dill Sauce:
¼   **cup mayonnaise**
¼   **cup plain lowfat yogurt**
1   **tablespoon lemon juice**
2   **tablespoons chopped fresh dill**
1   **tablespoon chopped fresh**
      parsley
¼   **teaspoon freshly ground**
      white pepper
⅛   **teaspoon salt**

1. Combine the water, wine, onion, peppercorns and thyme in a nonaluminum skillet just large enough to hold the salmon in one layer. Bring the wine mixture to boiling. Reduce the heat, cover the skillet and simmer the liquid for 5 minutes.
2. Add the salmon to the skillet. Cover the skillet and simmer the salmon for 8 to 10 minutes or until the fish just flake when lightly touched with a fork. The fish should be slightly undercooked since they will continue to cook after the heat is turned off. The flesh should have just turned opaque in the center. Let the fish cool to room temperature in the poaching liquid. Cover the skillet and refrigerate the salmon in the poaching liquid for up to 24 hours.

3. Prepare the Dill Sauce: Stir together the mayonnaise, yogurt, lemon juice, dill, parsley, white pepper and salt in a small bowl. Cover the bowl and refrigerate the sauce.
4. To serve, remove the salmon from the liquid and place each steak on an individual dinner plate. Serve with the sauce on the side.

CookSmart

The Pepper Pot

Did you know that black and white peppercorns grow on the same vine? The differences between these types are the stage of harvesting and method of processing the berries.
Black peppercorns are berries picked when they are considered almost ripe (orange-red in color), then dried in the sun. They become hard and turn black, with a shriveled appearance. White peppercorns are produced from the fully-ripened berries. White pepper is less pungent than black pepper. Use it in light-colored foods where black pepper may detract from the appearance of the dish.

SPICY SNAPPER

Crabmeat topping adds a touch of luxury to the broiled fish in this recipe. If Gulf snapper is not available, substitute flounder, scrod or redfish. (To lower the cholesterol level, omit the crabmeat.)

Broil fillets for 7 minutes.

Makes 4 servings.

Nutrient Value Per Serving:
186 calories, 28 g protein, 12 g fat,
7 g carbohydrate, 461 mg sodium,
120 mg cholesterol.

2	teaspoons margarine
½	pound mushrooms, sliced
2	tablespoons chopped green onion
1	tablespoon lemon juice
1	teaspoon Worcestershire sauce
2	tablespoons gumbo stock* OR: Fish Stock (recipe, page 196)
¼	tablespoon ground hot red pepper
¼	teaspoon salt

1	tablespoon dry vermouth
4	snapper fillets (6 ounces each) OR: flounder, scrod or redfish fillets
½	pound lump crabmeat (optional)
	Chopped parsley, for garnish
1	lemon, quartered, for garnish

1. Heat 1 teaspoon of the margarine in a skillet over medium-high heat. Add the mushrooms, green onion, lemon juice, Worcestershire sauce, gumbo or fish stock, ground hot red pepper, salt and vermouth. Reduce the heat and simmer the mixture until the mushrooms are cooked and the liquid is reduced by about one quarter, for about 10 minutes.
2. Preheat the broiler.
3. Broil the fish, turning once, until they flake easily when lightly touched with a fork, for about 7 minutes.

4. If you wish, heat the remaining 1 teaspoon of margarine in a small frying pan, add the crabmeat and warm it over low heat.
5. Transfer the fillets to 4 warmed individual dinner plates. Top the fish with the mushroom sauce and, if you wish, the crabmeat. Garnish with the parsley and the lemon.

Note: *Prepared gumbo stock is available in specialty food stores and some Southern supermarkets.*

CookSmart

Seeing Red

Red pepper isn't related to peppercorns at all. In fact, red pepper is made from a variety of small red chili peppers that are dried and ground. The final product is called either ground hot red pepper or cayenne.

FISH STOCK

Fish stock can be used as a poaching liquid for any kind of seafood or as a base for a fish or shellfish soup. You can use almost any kind of fish except strong-tasting, oily varieties, such as bluefish or mackerel.

Makes about 1 quart.

Nutrient Value Per Serving:
Analysis varies greatly, depending on the type of fish bones used to make the stock.

2	pounds fish bones		1	rib celery
1½	quarts water		2	bay leaves
1	small onion		1	teaspoon black peppercorns
1	sprig parsley			

Simmer the fish bones, water, onion, parsley, celery, bay leaves and black peppercorns in a saucepan over low heat for about 30 minutes. Strain the stock and discard the solids.

BASTE FOR FISH STEAKS

A tangy marinade that takes no time to prepare and enhances the taste of any firm-fleshed fish.

Makes 1 cup.

Nutrient Value Per Tablespoon:
66 calories, 1 g protein, 7 g fat, 1 g carbohydrate, 359 mg sodium, 0 mg cholesterol.

½	cup vegetable oil		2	teaspoons Dijon-style mustard
⅓	cup soy sauce		1	teaspoon grated lemon rind
¼	cup lemon juice		1	clove garlic, finely chopped

Combine the oil, soy sauce, lemon juice, mustard, lemon rind and garlic in a small bowl, blending the ingredients well. Pour the baste over fish steaks in a glass baking dish. Cover the dish and marinate the fish in the refrigerator for 3 hours before grilling.

STUFFED FILLET OF SOLE WITH WHITE WINE SAUCE

LOW-CALORIE

A veritable garden of vegetables and herbs makes a fabulous stuffing for fillet of sole.

Bake at 375° for 12 to 15 minutes.

Makes 6 servings.

Nutrient Value Per Serving:
261 calories, 34 g protein, 9 g fat,
8 g carbohydrate, 502 mg sodium,
92 mg cholesterol.

3	tablespoons finely chopped carrot (1 medium-size carrot)
¼	cup finely chopped celery
3	tablespoons olive oil
½	cup finely chopped onion (1 medium-size onion)
½	cup finely chopped zucchini
⅓	cup finely chopped sweet red pepper
1½	teaspoons finely chopped garlic (2 cloves)
1½	teaspoons finely chopped fresh basil
½	teaspoon poultry seasoning
⅛	teaspoon freshly ground white pepper
⅔	cup chicken broth
⅔	cup clam broth OR: Fish Stock (recipe, page 196)
2	tablespoons plus ¼ cup dry white wine
¼	pound lump crabmeat, picked over
⅓	cup seasoned bread crumbs
6	sole fillets (about 2 pounds) OR: flounder fillets Paprika
2	tablespoons cornstarch
1	teaspoon lemon juice

1. Sauté the carrot and the celery in the oil in a large skillet over medium heat for 3 minutes. Add the onion, zucchini, red pepper, garlic, basil, poultry seasoning and white pepper. Cook, stirring the mixture occasionally, until the vegetables are tender, for about 7 minutes.
2. Add ⅓ cup of the chicken broth, ⅓ cup of the clam broth or fish stock and the 2 tablespoons of wine to the skillet. Stir in the crabmeat and the bread crumbs and cook for 3 minutes more. Let the stuffing cool to room temperature.
3. Preheat the oven to moderate (375°). Lightly grease a 9 x 9 x 2-inch baking pan. Set the pan aside.
4. Lay the fillets, skinned side down, on a flat surface. Spoon the stuffing onto the fillets and roll them up. Place the fillets, seam side down, in the prepared pan. Sprinkle them with the paprika.

5. Bake the fillets in the preheated moderate oven (375°) for 12 to 15 minutes or until the fish flake when lightly touched with a fork. Transfer the fillets with a slotted spatula to a serving platter.
6. Dissolve the cornstarch in the remaining ¼ cup of wine in a small saucepan. Stir in the remaining chicken broth and clam broth. Stir in the lemon juice. Stir in the juices from the baking pan. Bring the sauce to boiling, stirring, over medium heat and boil for 1 minute. Pour the sauce over the fillets and serve.

TURKISH FISH IN PARCHMENT

Fish and vegetables wrapped in parchment paper (paper specially treated for baking) are cooked to moist perfection.

Bake at 450° for 13 minutes.

Makes 4 servings.

Nutrient Value Per Serving:
287 calories, 26 g protein, 13 g fat,
16 g carbohydrate, 392 mg sodium,
84 mg cholesterol.

2   **small russet potatoes (about 4 ounces each), peeled and cut into ¼-inch cubes**
1   **pound cod, boned OR: 1 pound other firm-fleshed white fish, such as haddock, halibut, grouper or snapper OR: 1 pound swordfish**
    Salt and coarsely ground black pepper, to taste
½   **pound ripe tomatoes, cut into 1 x ½-inch pieces**
1   **large onion, diced**

1   **medium-size sweet green pepper, halved, seeded and finely diced**
¼   **cup fresh oregano, coarsely chopped OR: 1 teaspoon leaf oregano, crumbled**
4   **teaspoons olive oil plus additional oil for lightly greasing the paper**
¼   **pound feta cheese, at room temperature, crumbled into pea-size pieces**

1. Preheat the oven to hot (450°). Cut four 12 x 15-inch pieces of parchment paper.

2. Bring 8 cups of water to boiling in a large saucepan, adding salt, if you wish. Add the potatoes and return to boiling. Continue cooking for 1 minute more or until the potatoes are slightly tender but still crisp. Drain the potatoes and let them cool until tepid.

3. Rinse the fish and pat it dry. Cut it crosswise into 4 equal-size pieces. Season it with the salt and black pepper.

4. Place one piece of fish on the bottom third of each piece of parchment paper. Top each portion with one quarter each of the tomatoes, onion, green pepper and potatoes. Sprinkle with the oregano, salt and black pepper and drizzle 1 teaspoon of the oil over each portion.

5. To form each parchment packet, lightly brush the edges of the parchment paper with oil. Fold over the top half of the paper to meet the bottom half, as if you were closing a book. Make a narrow fold all the way around the edges of the paper, then make a second fold around the edges, crimping it as you go, to close the paper around the fish and vegetables. Place the packets on 2 baking sheets.

6. Bake the packets in the preheated hot oven (450°) for 13 minutes or until the paper is puffed and golden brown all over. Place each packet on an individual dinner plate. Supply each person with a sharp knife to cut open his or her own packet. Serve the feta cheese separately, to be sprinkled on top of the vegetables.

THE SHELLFISH

Stir-Fried Clams in Black Bean Sauce
(recipe, page 201)

STIR-FRIED CLAMS IN BLACK BEAN SAUCE

LOW-FAT
LOW-CALORIE
LOW-CHOLESTEROL

What could be easier—Littleneck clams are cooked right in the spicy bean sauce!

Makes 4 servings.

Nutrient Value Per Serving:
71 calories, 10 g protein, 1 g fat,
5 g carbohydrate, 369 mg sodium,
23 mg cholesterol.

2 tablespoons fermented black beans
2 large cloves garlic, chopped
2 tablespoons finely chopped, peeled fresh gingerroot
2 teaspoons reduced-sodium soy sauce
2 tablespoons mirin (Japanese sweet cooking wine)

1 teaspoon chili paste with soy bean
4 pounds Littleneck or other similar small clams, scrubbed
2 green onions, trimmed and diagonally sliced, for garnish

1. Mash together the black beans, garlic and ginger in a small bowl. Add the soy sauce, mirin and chili paste. Mix all the ingredients well.

2. Place the clams in a large, heavy-bottomed saucepan or a wok. Cover the saucepan and place it over medium-high heat.

3. When the clams begin to open, stir in the bean mixture. Cover the saucepan and continue cooking, stirring occasionally, until all the clams open. Discard any clams that do not open.

4. Transfer the clams and sauce to a large serving platter or bowl. Garnish them with the green onion.

CookSmart

Clamming Up

Clams are categorized as soft shell or hard shell.

● Soft shell clams have long necks, or siphons, protruding from their thin and brittle shells. Small, tender varieties are excellent steamed, and are rarely eaten raw. Larger types, such as the massive Geoduck, should be chopped and cooked.

● Hard shell clams range in size from the small Littleneck and slightly bigger Cherrystone to the still larger Quahog, or Chowder, clam. Size determines the tenderness and method of preparation. Littleneck clams usually are served raw. Cherrystones, sometimes served raw, more often are steamed or baked. As their name implies, Chowder clams usually are chopped and added to chowders, soups and other cooked dishes. *Note:* When eating shellfish raw, be sure of the source and the freshness of the fish.

CURRIED SHRIMP BAGUETTE

Butterflying the shrimp ensures even broiling—and makes the sandwich easier to construct.

Broil for 3 to 4 minutes.

Makes 6 servings.

Nutrient Value Per Serving:
290 calories, 18 g protein, 8 g fat, 35 g carbohydrate, 570 mg sodium, 101 mg cholesterol.

½ cup reduced-calorie mayonnaise OR: ¼ cup plain lowfat yogurt and ¼ cup mayonnaise
1 tablespoon curry powder
1 pound shrimp, peeled and deveined
1 baguette (thin French bread), split lengthwise

1 sweet red pepper, halved, seeded and cut into julienne sticks
2 green onions (green part only), cut into julienne sticks
   Fresh cilantro, for garnish

1. Preheat the broiler.
2. Combine the mayonnaise with the curry powder in a small bowl and mix until they are well blended. Set aside.
3. Split the shrimp almost, but not completely, in half lengthwise, using scissors and cutting along the inside from the tail to the head; this is known as butterflying. Place the shrimp on an oiled broiler pan.

4. Broil the shrimp, turning them once halfway through the broiling time, until they are pink and just opaque, for 3 to 4 minutes.
5. Spread a thin layer of the curried mayonnaise on the baguette. Top with the shrimp, red pepper and green onion. Close the loaf, gently pressing it down. Cut the loaf into 6 portions with a serrated knife and garnish with the cilantro.

GREEK-STYLE SHRIMP WITH PASTA

If you shell and devein the shrimp beforehand, this dish is a deliciously quick toss-together.

Makes 4 servings.

Nutrient Value Per Serving:
339 calories, 29 g protein, 13 g fat, 28 g carbohydrate, 897 mg sodium, 195 mg cholesterol.

1 clove garlic, finely chopped
1 tablespoon olive oil
1 can (16 ounces) stewed tomatoes
½ teaspoon leaf oregano, crumbled
1 pound fresh or frozen medium-size shrimp, shelled and deveined

4 ounces feta cheese, cut into ½-inch cubes
8 ounces hot cooked rotelle OR: fusilli pasta

1. Sauté the garlic in the oil in a large skillet over low heat for 1 minute. Stir in the tomatoes and the oregano and cook for 3 minutes.
2. Stir in the shrimp and the feta cheese. Cook for 2 to 3 minutes, or just until the shrimp is pink and cooked through.

3. Gently toss the shrimp mixture with the cooked pasta in a large serving bowl, and serve immediately.

SAUTÉED PRAWNS WITH GARLIC

Prawns or shrimp sautéed this way are bright pink and redolent with garlic. Cooking the prawns with their shells on intensifies the flavor.

Makes 6 servings.

Nutrient Value Per Serving:
275 calories, 32 g protein, 15 g fat,
3 g carbohydrate, 228 mg sodium,
233 mg cholesterol.

⅓ cup olive oil
10 cloves garlic, coarsely
    chopped
2½ pounds large Alaska spot
    prawns (about 31 to 35
    prawns), shells left on
    OR: 2½ pounds large
    shrimp, shells left on

1 lemon, cut into 6 wedges,
    for garnish

1. Heat the oil in a large skillet over medium-high heat until it is hot but not smoking.
2. Add the garlic. Cook, stirring constantly, for 2 to 3 minutes or until the garlic begins to turn translucent but does not brown.
3. Add the prawns or shrimp and toss to coat them with the oil. Continue cooking, stirring occasionally, for 5 minutes more or just until the prawns are pink but still supple. Do not overcook the prawns or they will lose their succulence and tenderness.

4. Remove the skillet from the heat. Transfer the prawns to a large serving platter, piling them in a mound. Pour all the cooking juices over the prawns and garnish the platter with the lemon wedges. Serve the prawns immediately.

CookSmart

Peelin' Out!

To peel a clove of garlic quickly and easily: With the palm of your hand, crush the entire head of garlic so that the cloves fall apart. Select one clove and place the flat side of a large knife over it; hit the knife gently with your hand. The clove skin will come off immediately. *Note:* To get the smell of garlic off your hands, rub them in used coffee grounds.

JAMBALAYA

Jambalaya, a spicy stew of rice, seafood and vegetables, is a typical Cajun dish. Traditional jambalaya recipes often call for smoked ham or sausage.

Makes 4 servings.

Nutrient Value Per Serving:
322 calories, 21 g protein, 11 g fat, 28 g carbohydrate, 588 mg sodium, 173 mg cholesterol.

½ **pound small shrimp**
½ **pound catfish fillet**
1 **medium-size yellow onion**
1 **medium-size sweet green pepper**
½ **pound mushrooms**
2 **tablespoons safflower oil**
1 **teaspoon chopped garlic**
½ **teaspoon salt**
½ **teaspoon ground hot red pepper**

2 **tablespoons tomato paste**
½ **teaspoon chopped fresh basil OR: pinch leaf basil, crumbled**
½ **teaspoon chopped fresh oregano OR: pinch leaf oregano, crumbled**
2 **tablespoons chopped green onion**
1 **pint shucked oysters**
2 **cups cooked rice**

1. Peel and devein the shrimp. Cut the catfish into 1-inch pieces. Thinly slice the onion, green pepper and mushrooms.
2. Heat 1 tablespoon of the oil in a large skillet. Add the onion, green pepper, mushrooms, garlic, salt and ground hot red pepper. Sauté the mixture over medium heat until the onion is soft, for about 5 minutes. Add the tomato paste, basil, oregano and enough water to give the mixture a sauce-like consistency. Reduce the heat to low and simmer the sauce for 15 minutes.

3. Heat the remaining tablespoon of oil in a second large skillet over medium-high heat. Add the catfish, shrimp and green onion to the skillet and sauté. When the seafood is not quite cooked through, add the oysters and the sauce. Continue cooking the jambalaya just until the seafood is cooked through. Stir in the cooked rice and serve immediately.

HEALTH

"Heavy Metal" Oysters

Oysters are rich in zinc, copper and iron. Here's the breakdown.

● Over half your RDA of zinc is supplied by 7 medium-size oysters, for a mere 66 calories. Zinc plays a three-part role in skin health: It transports vitamin A to skin tissue, aids in the disposal of beauty-robbing carbon dioxide from the dermis, and facilitates protein synthesis that is essential for skin-cell renewal. When you don't get enough zinc, in fact, an eczema-like condition may erupt on your face, making skin scaly and reddish-looking.

● Eating oysters also provides you with one of the chief sources of copper, which is instrumental in the formation of healthy red blood cells that nourish skin.

● The typical appetizer portion of oysters delivers one third of your RDA for iron.

● Be sure to purchase oysters that are truly fresh, from a reputable source. To be on the safe side, eat fully cooked oysters.

HOTLINE

SESAME SAUCE

*A blender or food processor makes easy work of this versatile sauce —
try it on fish, vegetables or salads.*

Makes 1½ cups.

Nutrient Value Per Tablespoon:
31 calories, 1 g protein, 3 g fat,
2 g carbohydrate, 51 mg sodium,
0 mg cholesterol.

1   **clove garlic**
½   **teaspoon salt**
½   **cup tahini (sesame paste)**

½   **cup cold water**
½   **cup fresh lemon juice**
     (4 lemons)

Place the garlic, salt, tahini, cold water
and lemon juice in the container of an
electric blender or a food processor.
Cover and blend until the sauce is
smooth, for about 1 minute.

SEAFOOD SEASONING

*Sprinkle this spicy blend of seasonings on any of your favorite fish or
shellfish.*

Makes about ¾ cup.

Nutrient Value Per ½ Teaspoon:
1 calorie, 0 g protein, 0 g fat,
0 g carbohydrate, 31 mg sodium,
0 mg cholesterol.

2   **tablespoons powdered garlic**
2   **tablespoons freshly ground
     black pepper**
1   **tablespoon ground hot red
     pepper**
1   **tablespoon leaf thyme,
     crumbled**

1   **tablespoon leaf oregano,
     crumbled**
2½ **tablespoons paprika**
1½ **tablespoons granulated or
     powdered onion**

Combine the garlic, black pepper,
ground hot red pepper, thyme, oregano,
paprika and onion in a small bowl until
they are well blended. Store the
seasoning in an airtight container.

SEAFOOD SALADS

Shrimp and Rice Salad Valencia
(recipe, page 207)

SHRIMP AND RICE SALAD VALENCIA

LOW-CALORIE

Green beans can be substituted for the asparagus in this colorful salad enhanced with orange, capers and yogurt.

Makes 6 servings.

Nutrient Value Per Serving:
311 calories, 19 g protein, 11 g fat, 35 g carbohydrate, 187 mg sodium, 95 mg cholesterol.

1   pound shrimp, unpeeled
1   pound thin asparagus
2   navel oranges
¾   cup plain lowfat yogurt
¼   cup olive oil
2   cloves garlic, finely chopped
2   tablespoons drained capers
1   tablespoon chopped fresh tarragon or mint OR:
    1 teaspoon leaf tarragon or mint, crumbled
3   cups cooked rice (1 cup uncooked)
¼   cup sliced green onion

1. Add the shrimp to a large saucepan of boiling water. Return the water to boiling. Lower the heat and simmer for 3 minutes or just until the shrimp are pink and opaque. Immediately drain the shrimp and let them stand until cool enough to handle. Peel and devein the shrimp.

2. Trim the asparagus spears and cut them into 3-inch pieces. Cook the asparagus in boiling water for 3 minutes or until they are barely tender. Drain the asparagus and immediately plunge the spears into a large bowl of ice and water to stop the cooking. Let them stand for 5 minutes. Drain the asparagus again.

3. Grate the zest (orange part of the rind only) from one of the oranges into a small bowl. Squeeze the juice. Combine the orange zest and juice with the yogurt, oil, garlic, capers and tarragon or mint in a small bowl. Stir until the mixture is blended.

4. To section the second orange, peel off the skin and white pith just deeply enough to expose the flesh. Working over a bowl to catch the juices, make V-shaped cuts between the orange sections to remove the sections from the membranes.

5. Combine the shrimp, asparagus, orange sections, rice and green onion in a large bowl. Add the dressing and toss gently to combine all the ingredients. Cover the bowl and refrigerate the salad for 30 minutes or until it is lightly chilled.

SALMON AND WHITE BEAN SALAD

Like many bean salads, the flavor of this salad is enhanced by overnight marinating.

LOW-CALORIE

LOW-CHOLESTEROL

Makes 6 servings.

Nutrient Value Per Serving:
243 calories, 12 g protein, 14 g fat,
19 g carbohydrate, 279 mg sodium,
13 mg cholesterol.

1 cup fresh parsley leaves, washed, patted dry and finely chopped
10 green onions, trimmed and thinly sliced (including green tops)
1 can (7¾ ounces) water-packed red sockeye salmon, drained and flaked
 OR: 1½ pounds poached, fresh salmon fillets
1 can (15 ounces) white beans (cannellini), drained
4 cloves garlic, finely chopped

3 tablespoons drained capers
2 tablespoons fresh lemon juice
5 tablespoons red wine vinegar
5 tablespoons olive oil
 Salt and freshly ground pepper, to taste
 Bibb lettuce leaves
6 lemon wedges, for garnish
18 thick tomato slices, for garnish
6 to 12 green onions, for garnish

1. Combine the parsley, sliced green onion, salmon, white beans, garlic, capers, lemon juice, vinegar and oil in a large bowl. Toss gently to blend all the ingredients. Taste and add the salt and pepper. Cover the bowl and refrigerate the salad overnight.

2. To serve, bring the salad to room temperature. Toss and adjust the seasonings, if necessary. Serve the salad on 6 individual salad plates lined with the lettuce leaves. Garnish each portion with a lemon wedge, 3 tomato slices and a green onion or two.

GREEK TUNA SALAD

Marinating the tuna with garlic and herbs brings out its flavor. To cut down on calories, reduce the oil in the dressing to 2 tablespoons.

Makes 4 servings.

Nutrient Value Per Serving:
322 calories, 25 g protein, 20 g fat, 11 g carbohydrate, 446 mg sodium, 35 mg cholesterol.

1   can (12½ ounces) water-packed chunk light tuna
1   small red onion, quartered and thinly sliced
1   clove garlic, crushed but left whole
1   tablespoon drained capers
⅓   cup extra-virgin olive oil
¼   cup red wine vinegar
1   tablespoon chopped fresh basil OR: 1 teaspoon leaf basil, crumbled

1   teaspoon chopped fresh oregano OR: ½ teaspoon leaf oregano, crumbled
1   package (9 ounces) frozen artichoke hearts
1   cup sliced celery
1   cup sliced carrot
½   cup sliced sweet green pepper
     Lettuce leaves
     Black olives, for garnish

1. Drain the tuna, place it in a medium-size bowl and break it into large chunks with a fork. Add the onion, garlic and capers to the bowl.
2. Whisk together the oil, vinegar, basil and oregano in a small bowl until they are blended. Pour half the dressing over the tuna mixture and toss gently to blend. Cover the tuna mixture and let it stand at room temperature for 30 minutes, or refrigerate it for several hours, tossing gently once or twice.

3. Meanwhile, cook and drain the artichoke hearts, following the package directions. Cut each heart in half. Place the artichoke hearts, celery, carrot and green pepper in a small bowl. Add the remaining dressing to the vegetables and toss to combine all the ingredients.
4. At serving time, remove and discard the garlic from the tuna. Line a large salad bowl or 4 individual salad plates with the lettuce leaves. Mound the tuna salad in the center of the leaves and arrange the vegetables around the tuna. Garnish the salad with the black olives.

CookSmart

Name That Tuna!

Do you know the different types of canned tuna? Tuna is available packed in water or oil, and as solid-pack (the fanciest and most expensive), chunk-style or flaked. Don't pay extra to buy a fancier type than you need. For many recipes, such as sandwich spreads and dips, flaked tuna (the least expensive) will work just fine. The oil drained from tuna can be used in a tossed seafood and vegetable salad. Or buy water-packed tuna to reduce calories.

MARINATED FISH SALAD

Use leftover cooked fish (one kind or a combination) or albacore tuna packed in water to prepare this colorful salad.

LOW-CALORIE

LOW-CHOLESTEROL

Makes 4 servings.

Nutrient Value Per Serving:
270 calories, 22 g protein, 15 g fat,
14 g carbohydrate, 175 mg sodium,
47 mg cholesterol.

Garlic Vinaigrette:
3 tablespoons fresh lemon juice
½ teaspoon Dijon-style mustard
¼ cup extra-virgin olive oil
   Salt and freshly ground pepper,
      to taste
2 cloves garlic, finely chopped

Salad:
2 cups cooked fish
¾ pound carrots (4 large carrots),
      peeled and finely grated
1 tablespoon drained capers
2 green onions, thinly sliced
½ cup fresh tarragon
      OR: 1 tablespoon leaf
      tarragon, crumbled
3 medium-size ripe plum
      tomatoes, sliced ½ inch thick

1. Prepare the Garlic Vinaigrette: Combine the lemon juice with the mustard in a small bowl. Slowly whisk in the oil until the mixture is well blended. Add the salt and pepper. Stir in the garlic.
2. Prepare the Salad: Gently flake the fish into bite-size pieces in a medium-size bowl. Pour half the vinaigrette over the fish and gently toss to mix. Cover the bowl and refrigerate the fish for 30 minutes or until just before serving time.

3. Place the carrot in a large bowl. Add the capers, green onion and tarragon and toss gently to mix them. Pour the remaining vinaigrette over the carrot mixture and toss until all the ingredients are well mixed.
4. Mound the carrot mixture on a serving platter and arrange the fish on top. Surround the salad with a ring of the tomato slices.

CookSmart

To Cook A Fish

There are any number of ways to cook fish. But fresh or frozen, keep in mind that fish cooks very quickly. People often overcook fish — robbing flavor from the finished dish. Fish should be cooked only until the flesh is firm and has lost its translucent appearance. The general rule of thumb: Cook fish 10 minutes for every 1 inch of thickness.

To test for doneness in fish, insert a fork into the thickest part of the fish or fillet and gently separate the flesh — it should flake easily. With whole fish, the flesh should separate easily from the backbone.

Most fresh or frozen fish can be baked, panfried, broiled, grilled, poached or steamed.

FISH AND FRUIT SALAD

A different and light way to serve fish, this is a delightful luncheon dish or first course.

Bake frozen fish at 450° for 30 minutes, fresh fish for 10 minutes.

Makes 6 servings.

1   **pound frozen or fresh cod fillets**
5   **teaspoons lemon juice**
1   **tablespoon butter**
¼   **teaspoon salt**
1   **can (17 ounces) fruit cocktail, drained**
¾   **cup diced celery**

Nutrient Value Per Serving:
207 calories, 15 g protein, 9 g fat, 17 g carbohydrate, 233 mg sodium, 50 mg cholesterol.

3   **tablespoons mayonnaise**
3   **tablespoons dairy sour cream**
1   **tablespoon thinly sliced green onion**
1   **small head iceberg lettuce, separated for lettuce cups**

1. If using frozen fish, unwrap the fish fillets and let them stand at room temperature for 20 minutes.
2. Preheat the oven to very hot (450°).
3. Place the frozen or fresh fish on a sheet of greased aluminum foil large enough to enclose the fillets. Sprinkle the fillets with 2 teaspoons of the lemon juice and dot them with the butter. Fold the foil over the fish, folding the edges together to form a tightly sealed package.
4. Bake the fish in the preheated very hot oven (450°) for about 30 minutes for frozen fillets, 10 minutes for fresh fillets, or until the fish flake easily when lightly touched with a fork.

5. Carefully unwrap the fillets, separate them into bite-size pieces and remove any bones. Season the fish with the salt. Place the fish on a plate, cover the plate and refrigerate the fish until chilled.
6. Combine the fruit cocktail with the celery in a medium-size bowl. Add the fish to the bowl and mix the ingredients together lightly. Combine the mayonnaise, sour cream, the remaining 3 teaspoons of lemon juice and the green onion in a small bowl. Gently fold the dressing into the fish mixture. Serve the salad in the lettuce cups.

9
THE SWEET TOOTH

While no one regards sweets as a cornerstone of good health, it makes sense to devote a chapter to desserts. By satisfying your sweet tooth with some tasty—but not devastating—treats, you're less likely to binge on the calorie heavyweights. The strategy for this chapter: increase your use of fruits and skim off or eliminate excess fats and sugars.

Fruit, naturally low in calories and high in vitamins and fiber, is the ideal base for many refreshing desserts: Minted Melon Balls *(recipe, page 216)*, elegant Spicy Wine-Poached Pears and Cherries *(recipe, page 219)*, luscious Ricotta-Filled Plums *(recipe, page 220)*.

Another way to give fat the cold shoulder is with our Pear Champagne Sorbet *(recipe, page 225)* or delectable Chocolate Granita *(recipe, page 227)*; both are make-ahead marvels that check in at less than 150 calories each and almost no fat!

And just when you thought you'd never see a low-calorie cake or cookie that's worth a dime, we suggest you sample Angel Food Cake with Berries *(recipe, page 229)*, Pumpkin Cheesecake *(recipe, page 235)* or Mocha Meringue Kisses *(recipe, page 230)*.

Terrific toppings add a smidgeon of calories and lots of taste over frozen yogurt, sponge cake or fruit. Two of our favorites: Strawberry Sauce with Cognac *(recipe, page 237)* and Fresh Mint Sauce *(recipe, page 239)*.

So don't feel guilty about indulging in something sweet—especially now!

Fresh Fruit in Lemon Juice and Port (recipe, page 223)

FRUITFUL PURSUITS

Mixed Berries with Light Ricotta Cream
(recipe, page 215)

MIXED BERRIES WITH LIGHT RICOTTA CREAM

LOW-FAT
LOW-CHOLESTEROL

The tart sweetness of fresh berries is complemented perfectly by this surprisingly rich, quick sauce.

Makes 8 servings.

Nutrient Value Per Serving:
155 calories, 7 g protein, 5 g fat,
23 g carbohydrate, 71 mg sodium,
17 mg cholesterol.

Mixed Berries:
1   pint raspberries, picked over
1   pint blackberries,
      boysenberries and/or
      blueberries, picked over
¼   cup sugar, preferably superfine

Light Ricotta Cream:
1   container (15 or 16 ounces)
      lowfat ricotta cheese
2   to 3 tablespoons lowfat milk
      OR: plain lowfat yogurt, if
      needed
3   tablespoons sugar, preferably
      superfine
1   teaspoon vanilla

1. Prepare the Mixed Berries: Combine the raspberries and the blackberries, boysenberries or blueberries with the sugar in a large glass serving bowl, tossing very gently to mix them. Cover the bowl and refrigerate the berries for 1 to 2 hours, gently stirring the fruit once or twice.

2. Prepare the Light Ricotta Cream: Place the ricotta cheese in the container of a food processor. Cover and pulse the machine on and off just until the cheese is smooth. (Or place the ricotta cheese in a mixing bowl and beat it with a wooden spoon.) If the ricotta cheese seems dry and grainy, add a little of the milk or yogurt until the cheese is creamy and smooth; do not overprocess the cheese. Add the sugar and the vanilla, blending just until the cream is smooth. Transfer the cream to a glass serving bowl. Cover the bowl and refrigerate the cream until needed.

3. To serve, spoon some of the berries and their syrup into each of 8 individual serving bowls or wine glasses. Top each portion with a dollop of the ricotta cream.

MINTED MELON BALLS

Any variety of melon (except watermelon) may be substituted for the cantaloupe in this recipe.

Makes 4 servings.

Nutrient Value Per Serving:
53 calories, 1 g protein, 0 g fat,
14 g carbohydrate, 11 mg sodium,
0 mg cholesterol.

1   large cantaloupe melon
     (1 pound), halved,
     seeded and cut into
     balls
2   tablespoons freshly squeezed
     lemon juice (1 lemon)
2   tablespoons freshly squeezed
     lime juice (2 limes)

1   tablespoon honey
1   tablespoon finely chopped
     fresh mint leaves
½   honeydew melon (1 pound),
     peeled and cut into thin
     slices
     Mint sprigs, for garnish

1. Put the melon balls in a bowl.
2. Combine the lemon and lime juices, honey and chopped mint in a cup and pour the mixture over the melon balls. Toss gently to combine the ingredients. Cover the bowl and refrigerate the melon balls for at least 1 hour.

3. To serve, arrange the honeydew slices, curved sides in, on each of 4 individual salad plates. Spoon the melon balls into the centers of the plates. Garnish with the mint sprigs.

HEALTH

A Melon for All Seasons: Cantaloupe

Although cantaloupe is in season only from May to November, it now can be found in many cities year-round. Cantaloupe is an excellent source of vitamins A and C, with only about 60 calories in half a 5-inch melon.

HOTLINE

GRILLED BANANAS AND PINEAPPLE WITH DRIED CHERRY SAUCE

Dried cherries add an intense flavor to sauces, desserts and baked products. They are available in specialty food stores and through mail-order catalogs.

Grill for 4 minutes.

Makes 6 servings.

Nutrient Value Per Serving:
167 calories, 4 g protein, 1 g fat,
38 g carbohydrate, 39 mg sodium,
3 mg cholesterol.

1½ cups lowfat vanilla yogurt
2   tablespoons chopped dried
     cherries OR: 2 tablespoons
     chopped pitted prunes

6   small bananas
6   slices (½ inch thick) fresh
     pineapple
6   mint sprigs, for garnish

1. Stir together the yogurt and the dried cherries or prunes in a small bowl and refrigerate the sauce.
2. Build a charcoal fire. Slice the unpeeled bananas in half lengthwise.
3. Place the pineapple slices on the grill rack and grill them for 2 minutes. Turn over the pineapple and add the bananas to the grill, cut side down. Grill the fruit for 2 minutes more.

4. Spread some of the cherry sauce on each of 6 individual dessert plates. Place a pineapple slice in the middle of each plate, with a banana half on either side. Garnish with a mint sprig.

Note: *The fruit also may be broiled.*

GINGERED FRUIT SALAD

LOW-FAT
LOW-CALORIE
LOW-SODIUM
LOW-CHOLESTEROL

Grated fresh gingerroot adds a touch of spice to the traditional summer fruit cup.

Makes 4 servings.

Nutrient Value Per Serving (with optional grapes and ½ cup of pineapple juice): 61 calories, 3 g protein, 1 g fat, 40 g carbohydrate, 20 mg sodium, 0 mg cholesterol.

CookSmart

Fruit for Thought

Blueberry: The most flavorful berries are available from June to August. The best blueberries are large, firm and unmarked. Refrigerate them for up to two weeks.

Mango: Fleshy mangoes come in many shapes and sizes, and range in taste from extra sweet to tart. Domestic varieties are available from June to August and imported varieties are in the markets year round. Pick firm, semi-ripe mangoes. To ripen them fully, leave the mangoes at room temperature; refrigerate them for up to two weeks.

Papaya: A tropical treat, papayas have a sweet pulp and a center cavity filled with black seeds. Available throughout the year, papayas are at their best in the spring and fall. Buy fruit that are fairly firm but just give to the touch. Ripen papayas at room temperature; refrigerate them for up to two weeks.

Raspberry: This delicately flavored fruit is at its peak from June to August. Look for firm, dry berries. Refrigerate them for up to two days.

Strawberry: Although available throughout the year, the best season for fresh strawberries is April through July. Select firm, dry, shapely, bright red berries. Refrigerate them for up to one week.

All fruits should be used as soon as possible after purchase for the best possible flavor and nutrient value.

½ large ripe cantaloupe melon, seeded, trimmed and cut into 1-inch chunks
½ ripe honeydew melon, seeded, trimmed and cut into 1-inch chunks
½ pint strawberries, hulled and halved, if large
2 ripe peaches, halved, pitted and thickly sliced
2 ripe nectarines, halved, pitted and thickly sliced
2 ripe plums, halved, pitted and sliced
1 cup seedless grapes (optional)
1 crisp apple, halved, seeded and chopped (optional)
Juice of ½ lemon
2 teaspoons grated fresh gingerroot, or to taste
Unsweetened pineapple juice

1. Combine the cantaloupe, honeydew, strawberries, peaches, nectarines, plums and, if you wish, grapes and apple in a large glass serving bowl. Sprinkle the lemon juice and the ginger over the fruit and toss the mixture gently.

2. Add just enough pineapple juice to moisten the fruit. Toss the mixture gently. Cover the bowl and refrigerate the salad for at least 1 hour. Serve the salad very well chilled.

PEARS IN RED WINE SAUCE

A simple-to-make dessert that will never fail to "wow" your friends and family.

Makes 2 servings.

Nutrient Value Per Serving:
190 calories, 1 g protein, 6 g fat,
36 g carbohydrate, 2 mg sodium,
0 mg cholesterol.

1 tablespoon unsalted
   margarine
2 firm, ripe pears, peeled,
   cored and quartered

1½ tablespoons sugar
2   bay leaves
¼   cup fruity dry red wine

1. Melt the margarine in a large skillet over medium heat. Add the pears, sugar and bay leaves and sauté for 1 minute.
2. Add the wine to the skillet. Bring the mixture to boiling and boil for 5 minutes or until the liquid is reduced by half.

3. Remove the bay leaves. Serve the pears topped with the red wine sauce.

FRESH FRUIT IN GRAND MARNIER

An elegant toss-together — try serving this colorful dessert in a glass or cut-glass bowl.

Makes 6 servings.

Nutrient Value Per Serving:
158 calories, 2 g protein, 1 g fat,
36 g carbohydrate, 6 mg sodium,
0 mg cholesterol.

1 cup seedless green grapes
1 cup seedless red grapes
1 pint strawberries, hulled
1 pint blueberries
3 ripe peaches, pitted and
   sliced

2 kiwifruit, peeled and sliced
2 carambola (star fruit), sliced
   Juice of 1 lemon
¼ cup Grand Marnier OR: other
   orange-flavored liqueur

1. Place the green and red grapes, strawberries, blueberries, peaches, kiwis and carambola in a large bowl.

2. Combine the lemon juice with the Grand Marnier or other orange-flavored liqueur in a small bowl. Pour the liquid over the fruit and toss gently to mix the ingredients. Cover the bowl and refrigerate the dessert until serving time.

CookSmart

Just Desserts: Light and Luscious Fresh Fruit

● Use fresh fruits only when they are perfectly ripe. Fruits at their peak require less sugar and allow you to enjoy more of their natural flavor.
● To enhance the natural flavor of fresh fruits, try adding a "flavor lift" by sprinkling them with fresh lemon, lime or orange juice. Then add an extra zing with a dash of spice, such as ginger, nutmeg, allspice or cinnamon.

SPICY WINE-POACHED PEARS AND CHERRIES

Be sure to let the poaching liquid cool before beginning to poach the pear halves, so they will cook evenly. The pears are refreshing when served icy cold, but they have more flavor at room temperature.

Makes 4 servings.

Nutrient Value Per Serving:
216 calories, 1 g protein, 1 g fat,
56 g carbohydrate, 6 mg sodium,
0 mg cholesterol.

CookSmart

Topping Tips

● To reduce the fat, but not the flavor, in fresh fruit cobbler biscuit toppings, use buttermilk or lowfat milk instead of cream or whole milk. If you're using buttermilk, which yields a tender crumb and a gentle tangy flavor, be sure to add a little baking soda along with the baking powder to neutralize the acid in the liquid.
The Calorie Countdown (per cup):
Heavy cream = 820
Whole milk = 159
Lowfat buttermilk = 99
If you don't have buttermilk on hand, substitute plain lowfat or nonfat yogurt, thinned with a little skim milk. Or add 2 tablespoons of lemon juice to one cup of skim milk and let the milk stand for a few minutes to thicken before using it.
● For light and fluffy fresh fruit cobbler biscuit toppings, try to handle the dough as little as possible. Instead of rolling out the biscuit dough, try patting it out between the two halves of a folded-over sheet of lightly floured wax paper.
● Keep thickening to a minimum in fruit fillings for pies and cobblers. The texture will be more delicate and you'll enjoy more pure fruit flavor.
● To serve fruit desserts à la mode, try topping them with lowfat or nonfat vanilla yogurt, frozen yogurt or ice milk instead of ice cream.
The Calorie Countdown (per ¾ cup):
Rich vanilla ice cream = 410
Lowfat vanilla yogurt = 200
Lowfat ice milk = 150
Nonfat plain yogurt with a couple of drops of vanilla extract = 110

1½ cups water
1½ cups white wine
⅓   cup honey
2   lemon slices
2   cinnamon sticks
¼   teaspoon ground allspice

4   firm, ripe Anjou pears
1   cup sweet cherries, pitted and halved
    Shredded lemon zest (yellow part of rind only), for garnish (optional)

1. Combine the water, wine, honey, lemon, cinnamon and allspice in a large saucepan. Bring the mixture to boiling over medium heat. Reduce the heat and simmer for 10 minutes. Cool the liquid completely. Remove the lemon and the cinnamon and discard them.
2. Halve, peel and core the pears. Place the pears in a wide saucepan and immediately pour the poaching liquid over them. Bring the mixture to boiling over medium heat. Lower the heat and simmer for 4 to 5 minutes or until the pears are just tender when pierced with the tip of a paring knife. Do not overcook the pears. Remove them with a slotted spoon from the poaching liquid to a bowl.

3. Add the cherries to the hot poaching liquid and simmer them for 5 minutes. Pour the cherries and the poaching liquid over the pears. Cool the mixture to room temperature. Then refrigerate to chill it.
4. At serving time, spoon 2 pear halves with some of the poaching liquid and cherries into each of 4 individual bowls. Garnish with lemon zest, if you wish.

Note: *Fresh raspberries can be substituted for the cherries in this recipe. If you use raspberries, add them to the bowl with the poached pears in Step 2. Simmer the poaching liquid for 5 to 10 minutes, then pour the liquid over the pears and raspberries.*

ORANGE SLICES IN BERRY SAUCE

This refreshing combination of fresh strawberries and raspberry purée served over orange slices tastes even better if it's removed from the refrigerator about 15 minutes before serving.

Makes 6 servings.

Nutrient Value Per Serving:
109 calories, 1 g protein, 1 g fat, 26 g carbohydrate, 2 mg sodium, 0 mg cholesterol.

1   **package (10 ounces) frozen raspberries in light syrup, thawed**
2   **navel oranges**

1   **tablespoon Grand Marnier**
1   **tablespoon 10X (confectioners' powdered) sugar (optional)**
2   **pints strawberries**

1. Place the raspberries with their syrup in the container of an electric blender or a food processor. Cover and whirl until the raspberries are puréed. Strain the purée into a medium-size bowl.
2. Grate ¼ teaspoon of the zest (orange part of the rind only) from 1 of the oranges. Stir the zest into the raspberry purée with the liqueur and, if you wish, 10X (confectioners' powdered) sugar.

3. Rinse, hull and halve the strawberries. Toss the strawberries with the raspberry purée. Cover the bowl and refrigerate the fruit mixture.
4. At serving time, peel, halve and slice the oranges. Arrange the orange slices on 6 small plates. Top them with the strawberries in purée.

RICOTTA-FILLED PLUMS

The plums can be filled in advance, but don't dust them with the powdered sugar until just before serving.

Makes 6 servings.

Nutrient Value Per Serving:
117 calories, 4 g protein, 5 g fat, 15 g carbohydrate, 35 mg sodium, 9 mg cholesterol.

⅔   **cup lowfat ricotta cheese**
3   **tablespoons finely chopped walnuts**
1   **tablespoon granulated sugar**
½   **teaspoon vanilla**
6   **ripe plums**

   Strawberries, orange zest strips and mint leaves, for garnish
2   **tablespoons 10X (confectioners' powdered) sugar**

1. Combine the ricotta cheese, walnuts, granulated sugar and vanilla in a small bowl until they are well blended.
2. Pit the plums. Spoon the ricotta filling into a pastry bag fitted with a large star tip. Pipe the filling into the plum cavities. (Or use a teaspoon to fill the plums.) Place the plums on a serving platter or on 6 individual dessert plates.

3. Garnish the plums with the strawberries, orange zest and mint leaves. Sift the 10X (confectioners' powdered) sugar over the plums just before serving.

BERRY FOOL

A "fool" is a traditional English dessert, made by folding together cooked fruits and lots of whipped cream. This adaptation has been lightened by replacing the heavy cream with lowfat yogurt.

HEALTH

Yogurt: Not Just for Waist-Watchers!

One cup of lowfat yogurt gives you a good amount of protein, zinc, folacin, B₁₂ (important for healthy blood and skin tone) and riboflavin (important for providing energy to skin cells). And the two key skin vitamins yogurt lacks — A and C — are a cinch to stir in.

HOTLINE

Makes 6 servings.

Nutrient Value Per Serving:
162 calories, 4 g protein, 1 g fat,
35 g carbohydrate, 53 mg sodium,
4 mg cholesterol.

1   **pint fresh blueberries,**
       picked over
1   **pint fresh blackberries,**
       picked over
⅓   **cup sugar**
½   **teaspoon ground cinnamon**

¼   **cup plus 1 tablespoon cold water**
2   **teaspoons cornstarch**
       Pinch freshly ground black
       pepper (optional)
1   **pint lowfat vanilla yogurt**

1. Place half the blueberries and blackberries in a medium-size saucepan with the sugar, cinnamon and the ¼ cup of cold water. Cover the saucepan and bring the mixture to boiling over medium heat, stirring it once or twice.
2. Meanwhile, stir together the cornstarch and the remaining 1 tablespoon of cold water in a small cup or bowl until a smooth paste is formed. Add this mixture to the boiling fruit. Cook, uncovered and stirring constantly, for 2 minutes or until the berry mixture thickens slightly. Remove the saucepan from the heat. Immediately place a piece of plastic wrap directly on the surface of the cooked berry mixture to prevent a skin from forming. Cool the mixture completely.
3. Set aside a few of the remaining berries for garnish. Stir the remaining berries into the cooled, cooked berry mixture. Add the black pepper, if you wish. Gently stir the yogurt in its container until it is smooth. Spoon some of the berry mixture into each of 6 tall parfait glasses and top it with a layer of the yogurt. Continue alternating the layers, ending with a layer of the cooked berries topped with a small dollop of the yogurt. Place 1 or 2 of the reserved berries on top of each glass. Refrigerate the glasses until serving time.

Note: *If desired, make the fool using only one type of berry, rather than a combination of the two. Plain nonfat yogurt, lightly sweetened with honey and a dash of vanilla, can be used instead of the vanilla yogurt called for in the recipe.*

LEMON BLUEBERRY SWIRL

Tangy lemon and sweet blueberries are blended together to create a lovely make-ahead dessert.

LOW-FAT

LOW-SODIUM

Makes 6 servings.

Nutrient Value Per Serving:
183 calories, 5 g protein, 2 g fat,
39 g carbohydrate, 43 mg sodium,
68 mg cholesterol.

1   **package unflavored gelatin**
¼   **cup cold water**
1   **bag (1 pound) unsweetened frozen blueberries**
1¼   **cups sugar**
1   **cinnamon stick**
½   **teaspoon vanilla**

2   **egg yolks**
¼   **cup lemon juice**
¼   **cup water**
2   **teaspoons grated lemon zest (yellow part of rind only)**
6   **egg whites**
   Lemon twists and blueberries, for garnish (optional)

1. Sprinkle the gelatin over the cold water in a small cup. Let the mixture stand for at least 2 minutes for the gelatin to soften.

2. Combine the blueberries, ¼ cup of the sugar and the cinnamon stick in a medium-size saucepan. Bring the mixture to boiling over medium heat (the berries will create their own liquid). Cook, stirring occasionally, for 4 to 5 minutes. Strain the mixture through a fine sieve over a small bowl. Press out all the liquid from the berries with the back of a wooden spoon. You will need 1¼ cups of blueberry juice. Return the juice to the saucepan. Add half the softened gelatin. Heat the mixture over low heat, stirring constantly, until the gelatin is dissolved, for about 1 minute. Stir in the vanilla. Pour the blueberry mixture into a medium-size bowl and set it aside.

3. Mix together the egg yolks, ½ cup of the sugar, the lemon juice, water and lemon zest in a medium-size saucepan. Cook the lemon mixture over medium heat, stirring constantly, just until it begins to boil. Remove the saucepan from the heat. Add the remaining softened gelatin and stir constantly until the gelatin is completely dissolved, for about 1 minute. Pour the lemon mixture into a second medium-size bowl.

4. Place both bowls in the refrigerator. Chill the mixtures for about 45 minutes, stirring every 15 minutes, or until the mixtures are the consistency of unbeaten egg whites. Remove the bowls from the refrigerator. (If the gelatin sets too much, place the bowl in a larger bowl of hot water for a few seconds.)

5. Beat the egg whites in a medium-size bowl until soft peaks form. Gradually beat in the remaining ½ cup of sugar, 1 tablespoon at a time. Continue beating until stiff, shiny peaks form.

6. Divide the beaten egg whites in half. Thoroughly mix about ½ cup of the beaten whites from one half into the blueberry mixture. Gently fold in the remaining part of the half. Thoroughly mix about ½ cup of the beaten whites from the second half into the lemon mixture. Gently fold in the remaining egg whites.

7. Pour the blueberry mixture into a large bowl. Pour the lemon mixture on top of the blueberry mixture. To create swirls, fold or stir only 2 times with a rubber spatula. Immediately pour the mixture into a 6½-cup clear soufflé dish or bowl. Refrigerate the swirl for 8 hours or overnight. Garnish it with lemon twists and blueberries, if you wish.

PEACH YOGURT SUNDAE

For a light lunch, double the quantities and serve with a pumpernickel raisin roll.

Makes 2 servings.

Nutrient Value Per Serving:
155 calories, 8 g protein, 3 g fat,
26 g carbohydrate, 87 mg sodium,
2 mg cholesterol.

1   cup plain nonfat yogurt
1   tablespoon honey
1   teaspoon vanilla
1   firm, ripe peach

1   tablespoon finely chopped
      walnuts
    Ground cinnamon

1. Beat ½ tablespoon of the honey and the vanilla into the yogurt with a spoon, stirring until the mixture is smooth.
2. Halve, peel and pit the peach. Cut it into chunks directly into 2 individual dessert bowls or glasses.

3. Spoon the yogurt mixture over the peach chunks. Top with the remaining honey, the walnuts and cinnamon.

FRESH FRUIT IN LEMON JUICE AND PORT

The combination of sweet and tart creates a very refreshing finish to a meal.

Makes 4 servings.

Nutrient Value Per Serving:
183 calories, 1 g protein, 0 g fat,
42 g carbohydrate, 6 mg sodium,
0 mg cholesterol.

6   tablespoons superfine sugar
⅓   cup fresh lemon juice (about
      3 lemons)
⅓   cup ruby port wine
⅛   teaspoon freshly ground pepper

1   cup cubed ripe mango
1   cup cubed ripe papaya
1   cup blueberries
1   cup raspberries

1. Combine the sugar, lemon juice, port and pepper in a medium-size bowl. Whisk to blend the ingredients.

2. Add the mango, papaya, blueberries and raspberries and stir gently to combine the ingredients. Serve the fruit at room temperature or chilled.

THE
BIG CHILL

Pear Champagne (recipe, page 225),
Lemon Blueberry Swirl (recipe, page 222)

PEAR CHAMPAGNE SORBET

This dessert calls for a celebration! Puréed pears mixed with champagne make a sensational sorbet.

Makes 6 servings.

Nutrient Value Per Serving:
145 calories, 0 g protein, 0 g fat, 31 g carbohydrate, 9 mg sodium, 0 mg cholesterol.

1 **can (29 ounces) pear halves in heavy syrup**
2 **tablespoons sugar**
1 **tablespoon lemon juice**

1 **cup champagne**
   Fresh mint sprigs, for garnish (optional)

1. Drain the pears, reserving 1 cup of the syrup. Dissolve the sugar in the reserved pear syrup. Add the lemon juice.

2. Place the pears in the container of a food processor. Cover and whirl until the pear purée is very smooth, for about 30 seconds. Mix the purée with the syrup mixture and the champagne in a large bowl. Pour the mixture into the container of an ice cream maker. Freeze the mixture following the manufacturer's directions. Garnish each sorbet serving with a mint sprig, if you wish.

BANANA ORANGE YOGURT POPS

Summer heat got you hot under the collar? Cool off with these yummy (and low-cal) pops. Tangerine juice can be substituted for the orange juice.

Makes 4 ice pops.

Nutrient Value Per Serving:
96 calories, 4 g protein, 1 g fat, 18 g carbohydrate, 41 mg sodium, 4 mg cholesterol.

1 **cup plain lowfat yogurt**
1 **banana, sliced**

1 **cup orange juice**
1½ **teaspoons vanilla**

1. Place the yogurt, banana, orange juice and vanilla in the container of an electric blender. Cover and blend until the mixture is smooth. Pour the mixture into 4 small paper cups and place the cups in the freezer.

2. When the pops are half-frozen, insert ice-pop sticks in the pops. Return the pops to the freezer and freeze them until they are firm.
3. To serve, run each cup under hot water just until the pop slips out.

COFFEE GRANITA

*This coarse-crystalled Italian ice has an intense coffee flavor.
Without the traditional accompaniment of lightly whipped cream, the
granita is a guilt-free refresher.*

LOW-FAT

LOW-CALORIE

LOW-SODIUM

LOW-CHOLESTEROL

Makes 4 servings.

Nutrient Value Per Serving:
100 calories, 0 g protein, 0 g fat,
26 g carbohydrate, 4 mg sodium,
0 mg cholesterol.

3 **cups very strong hot coffee,
preferably espresso
(decaffeinated coffee
also may be used)**

½ **cup sugar**

1. Dissolve the sugar in the hot coffee in
a small bowl. Cool the coffee mixture to
room temperature and refrigerate it until
it is completely chilled.

2. Pour the coffee mixture into ice cube
trays without dividers or into a pie plate.
Place in the freezer for 45 minutes or
until the coffee mixture is frozen around
the edges. Cut the frozen coffee into
coarse crystals, using 2 table knives,
and blend it into the liquid portion.
Return the mixture to the freezer.

3. Repeat the cutting, blending and
freezing 1 or 2 more times. The final
time, the mixture should be frozen
throughout.

4. At serving time, break up the frozen
mixture into large, even crystals using 2
forks or table knives. (Or place the
coffee mixture in the container of a food
processor and break it up by quickly
pulsing the machine on and off; do not
overprocess it.) Spoon the granita into 4
tall wine glasses and serve it
immediately.

Note: *The granita is best made shortly
before serving time. However, it can be
prepared a full day ahead and stored in
the freezer. Shortly before serving time,
place the granita in the refrigerator to
thaw slightly before breaking it up, but
avoid letting it melt.*

CookSmart

The Ice Man Cometh

● Granitas and ices should have a
much coarser texture than
sorbets, so just stir them gently
once or twice while they're in the
freezer.

● Sorbets, ices and granitas all
taste best served freshly made. If
you store them in the freezer,
remove them to the refrigerator to
soften, covered, for 15 to 45
minutes before serving.

CHOCOLATE GRANITA

LOW-FAT
LOW-CALORIE
LOW-SODIUM
LOW-CHOLESTEROL

A chocoholic's delight — cool, refreshing chocolate ice with a hint of cinnamon and orange.

Makes 6 servings.

Nutrient Value Per Serving:
108 calories, 1 g protein, 1 g fat,
23 g carbohydrate, 1 mg sodium,
0 mg cholesterol.

½ cup sugar
½ cup unsweetened cocoa
    powder
2 cups water
2 tablespoons crème de cacao
    liqueur

1 teaspoon vanilla
½ teaspoon ground cinnamon
1 teaspoon grated orange zest
    (orange part of rind only)

1. Combine the sugar with the cocoa in a medium-size saucepan, stirring well to eliminate all the lumps from the cocoa. Slowly add the water, beating with a wire whisk until the mixture is smooth.
2. Bring the mixture to boiling over medium heat, stirring to dissolve the sugar. Lower the heat and simmer the mixture for 5 minutes. Remove the saucepan from the heat. Stir in the crème de cacao, vanilla, cinnamon and orange zest.

3. Pour the mixture into an 8- or 9-inch metal baking pan. Place the pan in the freezer and freeze the mixture until it is firm but not solidly frozen. Break up the mixture into icy chunks with a fork and return it to the freezer. Freeze the granita for at least 3 hours or until it is frozen solidly.
4. At serving time, let the granita stand at room temperature for 5 minutes. Break up the frozen mixture with a fork. Spoon the chunks into 6 glasses and serve them immediately.

PINEAPPLE ORANGE ICE

LOW-FAT
LOW-CALORIE
LOW-SODIUM
LOW-CHOLESTEROL

Go Hawaiian! This tangy ice will whisk you off to the tropics with its blend of ripe pineapple, orange juice and rum.

Makes about 2½ pints.

Nutrient Value Per Serving:
75 calories, 0 g protein, 0 g fat,
16 g carbohydrate, 1 mg sodium,
0 mg cholesterol.

1 ripe pineapple, peeled,
    quartered, cored and cut into
    1-inch chunks (about 4 cups)

½ cup 10X (confectioners'
    powdered) sugar
1 cup orange juice
2 to 4 tablespoons white rum

1. Working in batches if necessary, combine the pineapple, sugar and orange juice in the container of a food processor. Cover and whirl until the mixture is puréed. Add the rum.
2. Pour the mixture into an 8-inch square metal pan. Freeze the mixture until it is almost frozen, for 2 to 4 hours. Stir the mixture several times so the ice freezes evenly.

3. Transfer the mixture to the container of a food processor or a large chilled bowl. Quickly process or beat the mixture until it is smooth and fluffy. Return the mixture to the pan and freeze it for 30 minutes more. Process or beat the mixture again.
4. Freeze the ice, tightly covered, until it is almost firm, for 1 to 2 hours. If the ice freezes solidly, soften it in the refrigerator for 30 minutes before serving.

THE
BAKE SHOP

Angel Food Cake with Berries
(recipe, page 229)

ANGEL FOOD CAKE WITH BERRIES

Heavenly fare in red, white and blue. To save time, use a store-bought angel food cake with fresh berries and homemade sauce.

Bake at 350° for 50 minutes, grill or toast for 2 to 3 minutes.

Makes 12 servings.

Nutrient Value Per Serving (with strawberries and blueberry sauce): 142 calories, 4 g protein, 0 g fat, 31 g carbohydrate, 53 mg sodium, 0 mg cholesterol.

Angel Food Cake:
1   cup sugar, divided
1   cup plain cake flour (not self-rising)
12 egg whites, at room temperature

1   teaspoon cream of tartar
1   teaspoon vanilla

   Blueberry Sauce (recipe, page 237)
1   pint fresh strawberries, rinsed, hulled and sliced

1. Prepare the Angel Food Cake: Preheat the oven to moderate (350°). Sift together 2 tablespoons of the sugar and the cake flour onto wax paper and set them aside.
2. Beat the egg whites in a very clean large bowl with an electric mixer at high speed until they are foamy. Sprinkle the cream of tartar into the bowl and continue beating until the whites are stiff but not dry. Beat in the vanilla, then slowly beat in the remaining sugar, 1 tablespoon at a time, until the mixture is stiff and glossy.
3. Gently fold the flour mixture into the egg whites. Quickly but carefully pour the batter into an ungreased 10-inch tube pan.
4. Bake the cake in the preheated moderate oven (350°) for 50 minutes or until the top springs back when lightly pressed with your fingertip. Invert the cake in the pan onto a bottle large enough to support it (a large soda bottle usually works well) and let the cake cool for 1 hour.

5. Loosen the cake from the side and tube of the pan with a long, narrow knife. Invert the cake onto a platter and remove the pan.
6. At serving time, cut the cake into 12 slices with a serrated knife (a regular knife will squash the delicate interior). Toast the cake slices for 1 to 1½ minutes per side or until they are lightly golden. Spoon some of the Blueberry Sauce onto each of 12 individual dessert plates. Top with the toasted slices of cake and the strawberries.

MOCHA MERINGUE KISSES

This recipe produces rich-tasting cookies that are chewy on the inside, crisp on the outside. Parchment paper is available in cookware stores and many supermarkets.

Bake at 250° for 25 to 30 minutes.

Makes 30 meringues.

Nutrient Value Per Meringue:
16 calories, 0 g protein, 0 g fat,
4 g carbohydrate, 3 mg sodium,
0 mg cholesterol.

2   **teaspoons instant espresso powder**
1   **teaspoon very hot water**
1   **teaspoon crème de cacao liqueur**

1   **teaspoon vanilla**
2   **egg whites**
½   **cup sugar**
2   **tablespoons unsweetened cocoa powder**

1. Preheat the oven to slow (250°). Line a large baking sheet with a piece of parchment paper.
2. Dissolve the espresso powder in the hot water in a cup. Stir in the crème de cacao and the vanilla. Cool the mixture to room temperature.
3. Beat the egg whites in a small deep bowl with an electric mixer at high speed until they are foamy. Gradually beat in all but 2 tablespoons of the sugar, 1 tablespoon at a time, alternating with a scant ¼ teaspoon of the coffee mixture. Continue beating until the meringue forms stiff peaks. Stir together the cocoa powder and the remaining 2 tablespoons of sugar in a small cup. Using a rubber spatula, fold the cocoa sugar into the meringue gently but quickly, to avoid deflating the beaten egg whites.

4. Drop the meringue by teaspoonfuls onto the prepared baking sheet.
5. Bake the meringues in the preheated slow oven (250°) for 25 to 30 minutes or until the kisses are firm on the outside but still a bit soft on the inside.
6. While the kisses still are hot, carefully remove them with a spatula to a wire rack and cool them completely. Store the kisses in a container with a loose-fitting cover.

CookSmart

Make Marvelous Meringue

● Choose a cool, dry day; humid air tends to soften meringues. Be sure your tools — non-plastic bowl and beater — are clean and dry. The tiniest speck of fat will spoil meringues.
● Egg whites will beat higher if allowed to stand at room temperature to warm slightly.
● Depend on your electric mixer, since long beating is a must to dissolve sugar completely and prevent meringue from "weeping." To test if sugar is completely dissolved, rub a bit of meringue between your fingers. The meringue should feel smooth.

LEMON ALMOND WAFERS

Crisp, delicate cookies that are perfect with lemon herbal tea for an afternoon treat.

Bake at 425° for 6 to 7 minutes.

Makes 2 dozen.

Nutrient Value Per Wafer:
66 calories, 1 g protein, 5 g fat,
6 g carbohydrate, 35 mg sodium,
8 mg cholesterol.

2　egg whites
½　cup firmly packed light brown sugar
6　tablespoons butter, melted and cooled
　　Grated zest (yellow part of rind only) of 1 lemon

¼　cup unbleached all-purpose flour
　　Pinch freshly grated or ground nutmeg
½　cup chopped unblanched almonds

1. Preheat the oven to hot (425°). Grease and lightly flour 2 baking sheets.
2. Beat together the egg whites and the brown sugar in a small bowl with an electric mixer at high speed until soft peaks form.
3. Stir in the butter and the lemon zest. Fold in the flour, nutmeg and almonds.

4. Drop the batter by teaspoonfuls onto the prepared baking sheets.
5. Bake the wafers in the preheated hot oven (425°) for 6 to 7 minutes or until they are crisp around the edges. Carefully remove the wafers with a metal spatula to a wire rack. Cool the wafers completely before packing them in an airtight container.

PEANUT BUTTER COOKIES

A cookie classic made with whole wheat flour and natural peanut butter for a nutrition-packed snack.

Bake at 375° for 10 minutes.

Makes 2 dozen.

Nutrient Value Per Cookie:
92 calories, 2 g protein, 6 g fat,
9 g carbohydrate, 40 mg sodium,
18 mg cholesterol.

1¼　cups sifted whole wheat flour
1　teaspoon baking powder
½　cup natural peanut butter
⅓　cup unsalted butter, softened

¼　cup honey
1　egg yolk
¼　teaspoon vanilla

1. Preheat the oven to moderate (375°). Grease 2 baking sheets.
2. Stir together the flour and the baking powder in a small bowl.
3. In another bowl, beat together the peanut butter and the butter with an electric mixer at high speed until light. Beat in the honey and the egg yolk and continue beating until the butter mixture is light and fluffy.
4. Add the vanilla to the butter mixture, then the dry ingredients, stirring just to blend them.

5. Drop the batter by teaspoonfuls, 1 inch apart, onto the prepared baking sheets. Flatten each cookie slightly with a crisscross of fork tines.
6. Bake the cookies in the preheated moderate oven (375°) for 10 minutes or until the cookies are golden and firm on top. Remove the cookies with a metal spatula to a wire rack to cool.

STRAWBERRY LAYER CAKE WITH FLUFFY FROSTING

This airy cake requires more experience in baking—but what a beautiful result!

LOW-FAT

Bake at 400° for 5 minutes.

Makes 8 servings.

Nutrient Value Per Serving:
190 calories, 5 g protein, 4 g fat, 32 g carbohydrate, 181 mg sodium, 137 mg cholesterol.

Cake Layers:
⅔ cup sifted cake flour (not self-rising)
1½ teaspoons baking powder
¼ cup sugar
1 teaspoon grated orange zest (orange part of rind only)
    OR: lemon zest (yellow part of rind only)
4 eggs, separated
⅛ teaspoon salt

Strawberry Filling:
1 envelope whipped topping mix
½ cup cold skim milk
¼ cup reduced-sugar strawberry spread

Fluffy Frosting:
⅓ cup sugar
2 tablespoons dark corn syrup
3 tablespoons water
2 egg whites

1. Preheat the oven to hot (400°). Grease three 8 x 1½-inch round nonstick layer cake pans. Line the bottoms with aluminum foil. Grease the foil.
2. Prepare the Cake Layers: Sift together the flour and the baking powder onto wax paper. Combine the sugar with the orange or lemon zest on a second sheet of wax paper. Beat together the egg yolks and the sugar mixture in a small bowl with an electric mixer at high speed for 7 minutes. Beat in the flour mixture; the yolk mixture will be very thick and sticky.
3. Beat together the egg whites and the salt in a clean bowl with clean beaters until soft peaks form. Stir one third of the whites into the yolk mixture; fold in the remaining whites. Divide the batter evenly among the prepared pans.
4. Bake in the preheated hot oven (400°) for 5 minutes or until the cakes pull away from the sides of the pans and spring back when lightly pressed with your fingertip. Loosen the cakes around the edges with a knife and invert them onto wire racks. Peel off the foil. Cool the cakes completely.

5. Prepare the Strawberry Filling: Prepare the whipped topping mix following the package directions, using the skim milk instead of whole milk. Fold in the strawberry spread. Refrigerate the mixture for 10 minutes to firm it up, if necessary.
6. Set one cake layer on a cake plate. Spread it with half the filling and top with the second layer. Spread the remaining filling and stack on the third layer. Refrigerate the cake for 1 hour before frosting it.
7. Prepare the Fluffy Frosting: Combine the sugar, corn syrup and water in a very small, heavy saucepan. Set the mixture aside.
8. Beat the egg whites in a small bowl until firm peaks form. Bring the syrup mixture to boiling. Continue boiling, without stirring, until the mixture registers 242° on a candy thermometer. With the electric mixer running, very slowly pour the hot syrup in a thin stream into the beaten whites, beating constantly. Continue beating on high speed until stiff, glossy peaks form. Frost the cake and serve it.

CookSmart

The Great Cake Bake

● If you want your cake to have the best volume, shape and texture possible, use the ingredients, measurements and pan size called for in the recipe.
● For easier egg separation, separate the yolks from the whites when the eggs are cold.
● Allow egg whites to come to room temperature for maximum volume when beating.
● Remember to preheat the oven to the proper temperature 10 minutes before baking.
● Cakes may turn out heavy and soggy if the oven temperature is too low.
● Cakes may fall if the oven door is opened too soon, if the oven is too hot or if there is not enough flour in the batter.

CHOCOLATE ROLL WITH ORANGE GINGER MERINGUE

Let this scrumptious rolled cake star at your next party — or just surprise your family with a special treat.

LOW-FAT
LOW-CALORIE

Bake at 375° for 10 to 12 minutes.

Makes 12 servings.

Nutrient Value Per Serving:
98 calories, 3 g protein, 2 g fat,
18 g carbohydrate, 85 mg sodium,
69 mg cholesterol.

Chocolate Roll:
   Nonstick vegetable cooking spray
½   **cup sifted cake flour**
3   **tablespoons unsweetened cocoa powder**
¾   **teaspoon baking powder**
3   **eggs, separated**
¼   **cup plus 3 tablespoons granulated sugar**

2   **tablespoons water**
1   **egg white**
⅛   **teaspoon salt**

Orange Ginger Meringue Filling (recipe follows)

1   **tablespoon 10X (confectioners' powdered) sugar**
   Orange twists, for garnish (optional)

1. Prepare the Chocolate Roll: Spray a 15 x 10 x 1-inch jelly-roll pan with nonstick vegetable cooking spray. Line the bottom of the pan with wax paper and spray the paper.
2. Preheat the oven to moderate (375°).
3. Sift together the cake flour, cocoa powder and baking powder onto clean wax paper.
4. Beat the egg yolks in a large bowl with an electric mixer at high speed until they are foamy. Gradually beat in the ¼ cup of sugar, 1 tablespoon at a time, until the yolk mixture is very thick, for 3 minutes. Add the water and beat the mixture well. Stir in the flour mixture until the batter is smooth.
5. Beat the 4 egg whites with the salt in a large bowl with clean beaters until the whites are foamy. Gradually beat in the remaining 3 tablespoons of sugar until soft peaks form. Fold one third of the whites into the batter to lighten it. Fold in the remaining whites until no streaks remain. Spread the batter evenly in the pan.
6. Bake the cake in the preheated moderate oven (375°) for 10 to 12 minutes or until the center springs back when lightly pressed with your fingertip.

7. Spray a sheet of wax paper with nonstick vegetable cooking spray. Loosen the cake around the edges with a knife and invert it onto the wax paper. Carefully peel the paper from the cake. Starting at the short end, roll up the cake and wax paper together. Place the roll, seam side down, on a wire rack and cool it completely.
8. Unroll the cake and discard the paper. Spread the Orange Ginger Meringue Filling on the cake and reroll it. Sprinkle the cake with the 10X (confectioners' powdered) sugar and, if you wish, garnish it with orange twists.

Note: *If you make the roll a day ahead, you will have a slightly "wetter" cake.*

Orange Ginger Meringue Filling:
Beat 3 egg whites with ¾ teaspoon of cream of tartar in a large bowl until the whites are foamy. Gradually beat in 3 tablespoons of sugar, a tablespoon at a time, until firm peaks form. Gently fold in 2 tablespoons of orange marmalade and 1 tablespoon (½ ounce) of chopped preserved candied ginger.

CHOCOLATE-TOPPED SPONGE CAKE

The more gently you fold in the egg whites, the higher and lighter the cake will be.

LOW-CALORIE

LOW SODIUM

Bake at 350° for 40 to 45 minutes.

Makes 16 servings.

7   egg whites
⅛   teaspoon cream of tartar
¾   cup sugar
3   egg yolks
1   teaspoon vanilla
1   cup sifted cake flour

Nutrient Value Per Serving:
115 calories, 3 g protein, 5 g fat,
16 g carbohydrate, 46 mg sodium,
57 mg cholesterol.

3   tablespoons butter, melted
     and cooled to lukewarm

   Chocolate Topping:
1½ ounces semisweet chocolate
2   tablespoons vegetable
     shortening

1. Preheat the oven to moderate (350°).
2. Beat the egg whites with the cream of tartar in a large bowl until the whites are foamy. Beat in the sugar, 1 tablespoon at a time, until the whites form stiff but not dry peaks.
3. Stir together the egg yolks and the vanilla in another large bowl. Fold in one third of the beaten egg whites. Fold in the remaining whites until no streaks remain. Sprinkle the cake flour over the top of the mixture and fold it in. Very gently fold in the melted butter; do not overfold. Turn the batter into a 9-inch tube pan, spreading it evenly.
4. Bake the cake in the preheated moderate oven (350°) for 40 to 45 minutes or until a wooden pick inserted near the center comes out clean.

5. Invert the cake in the pan onto a large funnel or bottle and let the cake hang until it is completely cooled, for at least 1½ hours.
6. Run a knife around the inner and outer edges of the cake. Turn it out onto a wire rack with the crusty portion up.
7. Melt together the chocolate and the vegetable shortening in the top of a double boiler over hot, not boiling, water, stirring occasionally, until the melted chocolate is smooth. Cool slightly. Spoon the melted chocolate evenly over the top of the cake, letting the excess run down the sides.

CookSmart

Done to Perfection

Cakes are done when:
● The cake shrinks slightly from the sides of the pan.
● A fingertip is lightly pressed on the top of the cake and the top springs back to shape.
● A cake tester or wooden pick inserted near the center of the cake comes out clean, with no batter or moist particles clinging to it.

PUMPKIN CHEESECAKE

A deliciously different way to use pumpkin, lightly spiced with cinnamon, ginger and nutmeg.

Bake at 350° for 45 minutes.

Makes 10 servings.

Nutrient Value Per Serving:
133 calories, 7 g protein, 2 g fat,
23 g carbohydrate, 276 mg sodium,
57 mg cholesterol.

HEALTH

It's the Great Pumpkin!

Pumpkin, the fruit of a vine of the gourd family, is native to Central America and was grown by American Indians long before the first colonists landed in this country. Indians boiled and baked pumpkins, and also dried them to use in the winter. Although pumpkin most often is used to make pies, it also can be used to make soups or breads and can be served as a vegetable. Pumpkin is a good source of vitamin A with only 33 calories in a 3½-ounce serving.

Fresh pumpkin is in season from September to December. The size and shape of pumpkin does not affect the taste; however, the smaller the pumpkin, the more tender the flesh. A 5-pound pumpkin will yield about 4½ cups of mashed, cooked pumpkin. When serving as a vegetable, allow ½ to ¾ pound for a serving. Fresh pumpkin can be kept in a dry, well-ventilated place for several months.

Pumpkin is available year-round cooked, puréed and canned. Pumpkin seeds are sold dried, unshelled or shelled and salted.

HOTLINE

Nonstick vegetable cooking spray
3   tablespoons finely crushed zwieback biscuit crumbs
1½ cups lowfat (1%) cottage cheese
1½ cups canned pumpkin purée (not pie filling)
½   cup granulated sugar
¼   cup firmly packed dark brown sugar

3   tablespoons all-purpose flour
2   eggs, slightly beaten
¾   cup skim milk
2   teaspoons fresh lemon juice
1   teaspoon ground cinnamon
½   teaspoon ground ginger
½   teaspoon salt
⅛   teaspoon ground nutmeg

1. Preheat the oven to moderate (350°).
2. Spray nonstick vegetable cooking spray on the inside of an 8-inch springform pan with a tight-fitting bottom. Sprinkle the pan with the biscuit crumbs.
3. Place the cottage cheese in the container of a food processor. Whirl until the cheese is very smooth, scraping down the sides of the container; there should be no lumps in the cheese.
4. Add the pumpkin purée, granulated and brown sugars, flour, eggs, milk, lemon juice, cinnamon, ginger, salt and nutmeg. Whirl until the mixture is smooth. Let the mixture stand in the processor container for 5 minutes. Ladle the mixture into the prepared pan.

5. Bake the cake in the preheated moderate oven (350°) for 45 minutes; the outer edge will be set but the center still will be soft. Turn off the oven and let the cake stay in the oven for 30 minutes.
6. Cool the cake slightly in the pan on a wire rack. Lightly cover the cake and refrigerate it overnight or until it is well chilled. To serve, run a sharp knife around the outer edge of the cake and remove the pan side.

TOP
IT OFF!

The berry best in toppings!

BLUEBERRY SAUCE

*If you cannot find fresh blueberries, substitute frozen ones.
Eliminate the sugar from the sauce if the berries were frozen with
added sugar.*

Makes about 1 cup.

Nutrient Value Per Tablespoon:
12 calories, 0 g protein, 0 g fat,
3 g carbohydrate, 1 mg sodium,
0 mg cholesterol.

2   **cups fresh blueberries**
2   **teaspoons sugar**

Place the blueberries and the sugar in
the container of an electric blender or a
food processor. Cover and whirl until
the mixture is puréed. Pour the sauce
into a small bowl. Cover the bowl and
refrigerate the sauce.

STRAWBERRY SAUCE WITH COGNAC

*A refreshing combination that is superb on ice cream, cold citrus
soufflés or sponge cake.*

Makes 2 cups.

Nutrient Value Per ⅓ Cup Serving:
39 calories, 0 g protein, 0 g fat,
7 g carbohydrate, 1 mg sodium,
0 mg cholesterol.

2   **cups hulled and sliced fresh
      strawberries**
1   **to 2 tablespoons superfine
      sugar**
2   **tablespoons cognac**

1. Place the strawberries, sugar and
cognac in the container of an electric
blender or a food processor. Cover and
whirl until the mixture is puréed.

2. Transfer the sauce to a bowl. Cover
the bowl and refrigerate the sauce for
several hours so the flavors blend.

STRAWBERRY SAUCE

A wonderful way to take advantage of strawberries in season. This sauce is great on just about anything, from pancakes to frozen yogurt.

Makes 3 servings.

Nutrient Value Per Serving:
53 calories, 1 g protein, 1 g fat,
12 g carbohydrate, 2 mg sodium,
0 mg cholesterol.

1½ pints fresh strawberries
2 tablespoons fresh orange
   juice
1 tablespoon sugar (optional)

1. Rinse, hull and halve the strawberries. Place one third of the strawberries in a bowl and reserve them for serving. Place the remaining strawberries in the container of a food processor.

2. Add the orange juice and, if you wish, sugar. Cover and process until the mixture is puréed. Transfer the sauce to a bowl. Cover the bowl and refrigerate the sauce and the reserved strawberries until serving time.

FRESH MINT SAUCE

Splash a bit of this piquant sauce onto fresh fruit compote or over ice cream.

Makes about 1 cup.

Nutrient Value Per Tablespoon:
8 calories, 0 g protein, 0 g fat,
2 g carbohydrate, 0 mg sodium,
0 mg cholesterol.

1 cup fresh mint leaves, rinsed
   and patted dry
2 tablespoons sugar
½ cup hot water
⅔ cup cider vinegar

1. Place the mint leaves and half the sugar in a mortar. Pound and tear the leaves with a pestle until they are well bruised. Alternatively, pound the leaves with the side of a chef's knife and then chop them; transfer the leaves to a small bowl.

2. Add the hot water and the remaining sugar, stirring until the sugar dissolves. Add the vinegar and stir to combine all the ingredients. Transfer the sauce to a bottle and seal the bottle. Let the mixture stand at room temperature for up to 1 week.

DOUBLE BERRY SAUCE

Double the berries, double the fun — and the taste! Without the liqueur, this sauce is perfect on pancakes; with liqueur, it's an elegant dessert topping.

LOW-FAT
LOW-CALORIE
LOW-SODIUM
LOW-CHOLESTEROL

Makes about 2 cups.

Nutrient Value Per ¼ Cup Serving:
7 calories, 0 g protein, 0 g fat,
2 g carbohydrate, 0 mg sodium,
0 mg cholesterol.

1   **pint ripe strawberries, hulled**
1   **pint ripe raspberries, picked over**
    Few drops fresh lemon juice

1   **to 2 tablespoons fruit brandy or crème de cassis (optional)**
    Superfine sugar, to taste (optional)

1. Place the strawberries and slightly less than half the raspberries in the container of a food processor. Cover and process until the mixture is puréed. Force the purée through a fine sieve with the back of a spoon or a rubber spatula into a medium-size bowl.

2. Stir the remaining raspberries, the lemon juice and, if you wish, fruit brandy or crème de cassis into the strained purée. Taste and add sugar, if you wish. Cover the bowl and refrigerate the sauce for up to 3 days.

HEALTH

Strawberries: Incredible Collagen Boosters

These luscious berries are an excellent source of vitamin C, the vitamin critical to the formation of collagen — a key element of the connective tissue that keeps skin firm. Vitamin C also helps prevent the tiny capillaries beneath the skin's surface from breaking, and it promotes healing of wounds. One cup of strawberries provides over 125% of your RDA of vitamin C, for only 45 calories. And strawberries are rich in potassium, which helps regulate the body's water balance. They contain a fair amount of iron and fiber, too.

HOTLINE

CALORIES COUNT

Fruit

	CALORIES	PROTEIN (grams)	FATS (grams)	CARBOHY-DRATES (grams)	SODIUM (milligrams)	CHOLESTEROL (milligrams)
Apple						
fresh, 1 medium	81	Trace	1	21	0	0
Applesauce						
unsweetened, 1 cup	105	Trace	Trace	28	5	0
sweetened, 1 cup	194	Trace	Trace	51	8	0
Apricots						
fresh, 3 medium	51	1	Trace	12	1	0
dried, raw, ½ cup	155	2	Trace	40	7	0
dried, cooked without sugar, 1 cup	213	3	Trace	55	8	0
dried, cooked with sugar, 1 cup	306	3	Trace	79	8	0
Banana						
fresh, 1 medium	105	1	1	27	1	0
Blackberries						
fresh, 1 cup	75	1	1	18	0	0
frozen, unsweetened, 1 cup	97	2	1	24	2	0
Blueberries						
fresh, 1 cup	82	1	1	20	9	0
frozen, sweetened, 1 cup	187	1	Trace	50	3	0
Cantaloupe						
½ medium	93	2	1	22	24	0
Casaba Melon						
1 wedge	43	1	Trace	10	20	0
Cherries						
raw, sweet red, 1 cup	104	2	1	24	0	0
canned, sweet, in light syrup, 1 cup	169	2	Trace	44	8	0
Coconut						
1 tablespoon fresh, shredded	18	Trace	2	1	1	0
Currants						
dried, 1 cup	408	6	Trace	107	12	0
Dates						
4 dried	91	1	Trace	24	1	0
Figs						
dried, 1 medium	48	1	Trace	12	2	0
fresh, 1 medium	37	Trace	Trace	10	1	0
Grapefruit						
fresh, ½ medium	38	1	Trace	10	0	0
Grapes						
American, fresh green seedless, Delaware, etc., 1 cup	58	1	Trace	16	2	0
European, fresh Thompson, Emperor, etc., 1 cup	114	1	1	28	3	0
Honeydew						
1 wedge	45	1	Trace	12	13	0
Kiwi						
1 medium	46	1	Trace	11	4	0

	CALORIES	PROTEIN (grams)	FATS (grams)	CARBOHY-DRATES (grams)	SODIUM (milligrams)	CHOLESTEROL (milligrams)
Lemon						
1 medium	22	1	Trace	12.	3	0
Lime						
1 medium	20	Trace	Trace	7	1	0
Mango						
fresh, 1 whole	135	1	1	35	4	0
Nectarine						
fresh, 1 medium	67	1	1	16	0	0
Orange						
fresh, peeled, 1 medium	69	1	Trace	17	0	0
Papaya						
fresh, 1 medium	119	2	Trace	30	9	0
Peaches						
fresh, peeled, 1 medium	56	1	1	15	0	0
dried, uncooked, 1 cup	382	6	1	98	11	0
canned, without sugar 1 cup	59	1	Trace	15	7	0
Pears						
fresh, unpeeled, 1 medium	98	1	1	25	0	0
dried, 1 medium	92	1	Trace	24	2	0
Pineapple						
fresh, 3½″ x ¾″ slice	41	Trace	Trace	10	1	0
canned in juice, 1 cup	150	1	Trace	39	3	0
Plum						
fresh, 1 medium	36	1	Trace	9	0	0
Pomegranate						
fresh, 1 medium	105	1	Trace	26	5	0
Prunes						
dried pitted, 10 medium	201	2	Trace	53	3	0
dried, cooked without sugar, 1 cup	227	2	Trace	60	4	0
Raisins						
seedless, 1 cup	435	5	1	115	17	0
Raspberries						
fresh, 1 cup	60	1	1	14	0	0
Rhubarb						
cooked with sugar, 1 cup	278	1	Trace	75	2	0
Strawberries						
fresh, whole, 1 cup	48	1	1	11	2	0
frozen, sweetened, sliced, 1 cup	246	1	Trace	66	8	0
Tangerine						
fresh, peeled, 1 medium	37	1	Trace	9	1	0
Watermelon						
1 slice	152	3	2	35	10	0

Vegetables

	CALORIES	PROTEIN (grams)	FATS (grams)	CARBOHY-DRATES (grams)	SODIUM (milligrams)	CHOLESTEROL (milligrams)
Alfalfa Sprouts						
1 cup, raw	10	1	Trace	1	2	0
Artichoke						
1 medium	53	3	Trace	12	79	0
Asparagus						
fresh, cooked spears, 4 medium	15	2	Trace	3	2	0
frozen, cooked cut & tips, 1 cup	52	6	Trace	10	44	0
Avocado						
fresh, ½ medium	162	2	15	7	10	0
Beans, fresh						
green, cooked, ½ cup	22	1	Trace	5	2	0
lima, cooked, ½ cup	105	6	Trace	20	14	0
sprouted mung, raw, ½ cup	16	2	Trace	3	3	0
wax, cooked, ½ cup	22	1	Trace	5	2	0
Beans, frozen						
green, cooked, 1 cup	35	2	Trace	8	18	0
Beets						
canned diced, 1 cup	53	2	Trace	13	401	0
fresh, cooked, 1 cup	53	2	Trace	11	83	0
Broccoli						
cooked, 1 large stalk	52	5	1	10	20	0
frozen, cooked, chopped, 1 cup	52	6	Trace	10	44	0
Brussels Sprouts						
fresh, cooked, 1 cup	61	4	1	14	33	0
Cabbage						
raw shredded, 1 cup	17	1	Trace	4	13	0
cooked, 1 cup	32	1	Trace	7	29	0
Carrots						
raw, 1 medium	31	1	Trace	7	25	0
fresh, cooked, sliced, 1 cup	70	2	Trace	16	103	0
Cauliflower						
fresh, cooked, 1 cup	30	2	Trace	6	7	0
frozen, cooked, 1 cup	34	3	Trace	7	32	0
Celery						
raw, 1 stalk	6	Trace	Trace	1	35	0
Cilantro						
½ cup fresh	2	Trace	Trace	Trace	2	0
Collards						
frozen, cooked, 1 cup	61	5	1	12	85	0
raw	35	3	Trace	7	52	0
Corn						
fresh, cooked, 1 ear	77	3	1	17	14	0
frozen, cooked, 1 cup	133	5	Trace	34	8	0
Cucumbers						
raw, 1 medium	31	1	Trace	7	5	0
Eggplant						
boiled, 1 cup	27	1	Trace	6	3	0

	CALORIES	PROTEIN (grams)	FATS (grams)	CARBOHY-DRATES (grams)	SODIUM (milligrams)	CHOLESTEROL (milligrams)
Endive						
1 cup	9	1	Trace	2	11	0
Lettuce						
Boston or Bibb, 1 cup	10	1	Trace	2	5	0
Iceberg, 1 cup	10	1	Trace	2	5	0
Romaine, 1 cup	9	1	Trace	1	4	0
Mushrooms						
canned, 1 cup	37	3	Trace	8	624	0
fresh, 1 cup	18	1	Trace	3	3	0
Onions						
raw, chopped, cup	52	2	Trace	12	3	0
green, raw, chopped, 1 cup	25	2	Trace	6	4	0
Mint						
½ cup fresh	5	Trace	Trace	10	NA	0
Parsley						
10 sprigs	3	Trace	Trace	1	4	0
Parsnips						
fresh, cooked, 1 cup sliced	109	2	Trace	26	13	0
Peas						
green, fresh, cooked, 1 cup	134	9	Trace	25	5	0
green, frozen, cooked, 1 cup	125	8	Trace	23	139	0
Peppers						
green, 1 medium	19	1	Trace	4	2	0
red, 1 medium	19	1	Trace	4	2	0
hot, chili green, canned, 1 cup	34	1	Trace	8	830	0
Potatoes						
baked in skin, 1 medium	220	5	Trace	51	16	0
boiled in skin, sliced, 1 cup	136	3	Trace	31	6	0
Radishes						
raw, 10 medium	8	Trace	Trace	2	11	0
Spinach						
raw, 1 cup	12	2	Trace	2	44	0
frozen, cooked, 1 cup	53	6	Trace	10	163	0
Squash						
winter baked, 1 cup	129	4	1	32	2	0
Sweet Potatoes						
fresh, baked in skin, 4 oz.	117	2	Trace	28	11	0
Tomatoes						
raw, 1 medium	23	1	Trace	5	10	0
canned, 1 cup	48	2	1	10	391	0
paste, ¼ cup	55	2	1	12	517	0
sauce, ½ cup	37	2	Trace	9	738	0
Turnips						
steamed, 1 cup cubes	28	1	Trace	8	78	0
Watercress						
1 cup	4	1	Trace	Trace	14	0

Legumes, Nuts & Seeds

	CALORIES	PROTEIN	FATS	CARBO	SODIUM	CHOL
Beans, dry						
chick peas, cooked, 1 cup	269	15	4	45	11	0
lentils, cooked, 1 cup	230	18	1	40	4	0
lima, cooked, ½ cup	105	6	Trace	20	14	0
navy or pea, cooked, ½ cup	129	8	1	24	1	0
red kidney, cooked, ½ cup	112	8	1	20	2	0
Beans, canned						
red kidney, 1 cup, includes liquid	207	13	1	38	888	0

	CALORIES	PROTEIN	FATS	CARBO	SODIUM	CHOL
Almonds						
whole, 1 cup	766	26	68	27	14	0
slivered, 1 cup	795	27	70	28	15	0

Legumes, Nuts & Seeds (continued)

	CALORIES	PROTEIN (grams)	FATS (grams)	CARBOHY-DRATES (grams)	SODIUM (milligrams)	CHOLESTEROL (milligrams)
Cashew Nuts						
dry roasted, salted, 1 oz.	163	4	13	9	181	0
Filberts						
shelled, chopped, 1 cup	727	15	72	18	3	0
Peanut Butter						
1 tablespoon, smooth	95	5	8	3	76	0
Peanuts						
dry roasted, salted, ¼ cup shelled	203	9	18	8	317	0
dry roasted, unsalted, ¼ cup shelled	203	9	18	8	0	0
Pine Nuts						
shelled, 1 oz.	146	7	14	4	1	0

	CALORIES	PROTEIN (grams)	FATS (grams)	CARBOHY-DRATES (grams)	SODIUM (milligrams)	CHOLESTEROL (milligrams)
Pumpkin Seeds						
1 cup, with shells	285	12	12	34	12	0
Tahini (Sesame Paste)						
1 tablespoon	89	3	8	3	17	0
Soybean Curd (Tofu)						
regular, 1 oz.	22	2	1	1	2	0
firm, 1 oz.	41	4	2	1	4	0
Sunflower Seeds						
hulled, dry roasted, salted, 1 cup	745	25	64	31	998	0
Walnuts						
black, shelled, 1 cup	759	30	71	15	1	0
regular, shelled, 1 cup	770	17	74	22	12	0

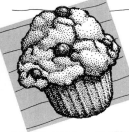

Grains & Grain Products

	CALORIES	PROTEIN (grams)	FATS (grams)	CARBOHY-DRATES (grams)	SODIUM (milligrams)	CHOLESTEROL (milligrams)
Barley						
3 oz. dry	303	10	1	64	8	0
Bulgur						
1 oz. dry	102	2	Trace	23	1	0
Breads						
bagel, 1 plain, 2 oz.	150	6	1	30	352	NA
bagel, pumpernickel, 2 oz.	160	6	1	31	369	NA
French, 1″ slice	102	3	1	19	203	1
hoagy, 1 medium, 11½″	392	12	4	75	783	4
Italian, ¾″ slice	83	3	Trace	17	176	Trace
oatmeal, 1 slice	70	2	2	13	185	NA
pita, 1 small plain, 2 oz.	174	5	Trace	37	363	NA
pita, 1 small whole wheat, 2 oz.	167	6	1	35	364	NA
pumpernickel, 1 slice	79	3	Trace	17	182	Trace
raisin, 1 slice	66	2	1	13	91	1
roll, hard, 1 medium	156	5	2	30	313	2
rye, 1 slice	61	2	Trace	13	139	Trace
white, enriched, 1 slice	65	2	1	12	122	1
whole wheat, 1 slice	56	2	1	11	121	1

	CALORIES	PROTEIN (grams)	FATS (grams)	CARBOHY-DRATES (grams)	SODIUM (milligrams)	CHOLESTEROL (milligrams)
Couscous						
2 oz. dry	199	7	0	41	NA	0
Crackers						
graham, 2	55	1	1	10	95	0
melba toast, 3	50	2	0	10	NA	NA
Noodles						
egg, enriched, cooked, 1 cup	200	7	2	37	3	50
Oats						
dry rolled, 1 cup uncooked	311	13	5	54	3	0
oat bran, 2 oz. dry	219	11	5	32	2	0
oatmeal, 1 cup cooked	145	6	2	25	2	0
Pasta						
enriched, cooked, 1 cup	155	5	1	32	1	0
Rice						
brown, cooked, 1 cup	232	5	1	50	0	0
white, cooked, 1 cup	223	4	Trace	50	0	0
Wheat						
wheat bran, unprocessed, ¼ cup	42	2	Trace	7	1	0
cream of wheat, 1 cup cooked	133	4	1	28	3	0
wheat germ, 1 tablespoon	27	2	1	4	Trace	0

Fats & Oils

	CALORIES	PROTEIN (grams)	FATS (grams)	CARBOHY-DRATES (grams)	SODIUM (milligrams)	CHOLESTEROL (milligrams)
Butter						
lightly salted, 1 tablespoon	102	Trace	12	Trace	117	31
sweet, 1 tablespoon	102	Trace	12	Trace	2	31
whipped, 1 tablespoon	68	Trace	8	Trace	78	21

	CALORIES	PROTEIN (grams)	FATS (grams)	CARBOHY-DRATES (grams)	SODIUM (milligrams)	CHOLESTEROL (milligrams)
Lard						
1 tablespoon	116	0	13	0	0	12
Margarine						
regular, 1 tablespoon	102	Trace	11	Trace	134	0
Oils, Vegetable						
1 tablespoon	120	0	14	0	0	0
Vegetable Shortening						
solid, 1 tablespoon	113	0	13	0	0	0

Fish

	CALORIES	PROTEIN (grams)	FATS (grams)	CARBOHY-DRATES (grams)	SODIUM (milligrams)	CHOLESTEROL (milligrams)
Anchovies 2 oz. can, drained	95	13	4	0	1651	25
Catfish raw, 4 oz.	132	21	5	0	71	66
Caviar black or red, 1 tablespoon	40	4	3	1	240	94
Clams raw shucked, 1 pint	336	58	4	12	254	154
canned, drained, 1 cup	237	41	3	8	179	107
Cod broiled fillet, 4 oz.	119	26	1	0	88	62
Crab canned, blue, 1 cup	134	28	2	0	450	120
Flounder baked, 4 oz.	133	27	2	0	119	77
Halibut broiled, 4 oz.	158	30	3	0	78	46
Lobster cooked meat, 1 lb.	445	93	3	6	1725	327

	CALORIES	PROTEIN (grams)	FATS (grams)	CARBOHY-DRATES (grams)	SODIUM (milligrams)	CHOLESTEROL (milligrams)
Salmon Atlantic fillet, raw, 4 oz.	161	23	7	0	50	62
Sardines canned in oil, drained, 1 oz.	59	7	3	0	143	40
Scallops bay and sea, raw, 4 oz.	100	19	1	3	183	37
Shrimp raw, ½ lb.	241	46	4	2	336	345
Swordfish broiled, 4 oz.	176	29	6	0	130	57
Trout raw, 4 oz.	168	24	8	0	59	66
Tuna chunk, canned in oil, drained, 3 oz.	168	25	7	0	301	55
chunk, canned in water, 3 oz.	111	25	Trace	0	303	36
fresh, broiled, 4 oz.	208	34	7	0	57	55

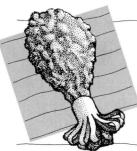

Meat & Poultry

	CALORIES	PROTEIN (grams)	FATS (grams)	CARBOHY-DRATES (grams)	SODIUM (milligrams)	CHOLESTEROL (milligrams)
Bacon cooked, 2 medium slices	73	4	6	Trace	202	11
Canadian, cooked, 1 oz.	52	7	2	Trace	433	16
Beef, braised, simmered or pot roasted						
chuck, stew meat, 3 oz.	301	23	23	0	50	84
corned beef, 3 oz.	213	15	16	Trace	964	83
hamburger lean, 3 oz. broiled	231	21	16	0	65	74
liver, 3 oz.	137	21	4	3	60	331
rib roast, 3 oz.	306	19	25	0	54	72
sirloin steak, 3 oz. broiled	277	20	21	0	51	71
Chicken, cooked						
light meat, without skin, 4 oz.	196	35	5	0	87	96
dark meat, without skin, 4 oz.	232	31	11	0	105	105

	CALORIES	PROTEIN (grams)	FATS (grams)	CARBOHY-DRATES (grams)	SODIUM (milligrams)	CHOLESTEROL (milligrams)
Chicken, cooked *(continued)*						
livers, 4 oz.	178	28	6	1	58	716
Frankfurters 1 all beef, 2 oz.	179	7	16	1	582	35
Lamb, cooked						
roasted leg, lean, 3 oz.	153	24	6	0	56	74
loin chop, broiled, 3 oz.	183	26	8	0	71	80
stew meat (shoulder), 3 oz.	287	18	23	0	45	83
Pork, cooked						
ham, roasted, 3 oz.	151	19	8	0	1276	50
boneless center loin chop, trimmed of fat, broiled, 3 oz.	196	27	9	0	66	83
spareribs, braised (8 oz. as purchased)	351	26	27	0	82	107
Turkey, roasted						
light meat, 3 oz.	131	25	2	0	58	59
dark meat, 3 oz.	157	24	6	0	70	75
Veal, cooked						
boneless, cutlet, fried, 3 oz.	155	28	4	0	69	112
loin chop, rib, roasted, 3 oz.	143	22	6	0	87	108
loin chop, braised, 3 oz.	185	28	7	0	76	138

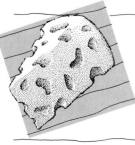

Dairy

	CALORIES	PROTEIN (grams)	FATS (grams)	CARBOHY-DRATES (grams)	SODIUM (milligrams)	CHOLESTEROL (milligrams)
Buttermilk 1 cup	98	8	2	12	257	10
Cheeses American, 1 oz.	106	6	9	Trace	405	27
blue, 1 oz.	100	6	8	1	395	21

	CALORIES	PROTEIN (grams)	FATS (grams)	CARBOHY-DRATES (grams)	SODIUM (milligrams)	CHOLESTEROL (milligrams)
Cheeses *(continued)*						
camembert, 1 oz.	85	6	7	Trace	239	20
cheddar, 1 oz.	114	7	9	Trace	176	30
cottage (4.5% milk fat) creamed, regular, 1 cup	216	26	9	6	851	32
cottage, lowfat, 1 cup	163	28	2	6	918	9
cottage, unsalted, dry curd, 1 cup	123	25	1	3	19	10
cream cheese, 1 tablespoon	49	1	5	Trace	42	16
parmesan, grated, 1 tablespoon	23	2	2	Trace	93	4
ricotta, 1 oz. whole milk	49	3	4	1	24	14
ricotta, 1 oz. part skim	39	3	2	1	35	9
Swiss, 1 oz.	107	8	8	1	74	26

Dairy (continued)

	CALORIES	PROTEIN (grams)	FATS (grams)	CARBOHY- DRATES (grams)	SODIUM (milligrams)	CHOLESTEROL (milligrams)
Cream						
half & half, 1 tablespoon	20	Trace	2	1	Trace	6
heavy, 1 tablespoon	51	Trace	6	Trace	6	20
light, 1 tablespoon	29	Trace	3	1	6	10
Eggs						
white, 1 large	16	3	0	Trace	50	0
yolk, 1 large	63	3	6	Trace	8	272
whole, 1 large	79	6	6	1	58	272
Ice Cream						
regular, 1 cup	269	5	141	327	116	60
soft frozen, French vanilla, 1 cup	377	7	23	38	153	153

	CALORIES	PROTEIN (grams)	FATS (grams)	CARBOHY- DRATES (grams)	SODIUM (milligrams)	CHOLESTEROL (milligrams)
Ice Milk						
1 cup	183	5	6	29	105	18
soft, 1 cup	223	8	5	38	163	13
Milk						
whole, 1 cup	149	8	8	11	120	34
skim, 1 cup	86	8	Trace	12	127	5
lowfat (2% fat), 1 cup	122	8	5	12	122	20
condensed, sweet, 1 cup	982	24	27	166	389	104
nonfat instant powder, 1 cup	243	24	Trace	35	373	12
Yogurt						
plain, whole, 8 oz.	155	8	7	11	104	29
plain, lowfat, 8 oz.	143	12	4	16	159	14
plain, nonfat, 8 oz.	127	13	Trace	17	172	8

Beverages

	CALORIES	PROTEIN (grams)	FATS (grams)	CARBOHY- DRATES (grams)	SODIUM (milligrams)	CHOLESTEROL (milligrams)
Alcohol						
80 proof (gin, rum, vodka, whiskey), 1 jigger (1½ oz.)	97	0	0	0	0	0
Apple Juice						
canned, 1 cup	117	Trace	Trace	29	7	0
Beer						
12 oz. can	146	1	0	13	18	0
Coffee						
black, 1 cup	5	Trace	0	1	5	0
Cranberry Juice Cocktail						
1 cup	144	0	Trace	36	5	0
Grapefruit Juice						
fresh, 1 cup	96	1	Trace	23	3	0
frozen, unsweetened concentrate, diluted, 1 cup	102	1	Trace	24	2	0

	CALORIES	PROTEIN (grams)	FATS (grams)	CARBOHY- DRATES (grams)	SODIUM (milligrams)	CHOLESTEROL (milligrams)
Grape Juice						
canned or bottled, 1 cup	154	1	Trace	38	8	0
frozen, sweetened concentrate, diluted, 1 cup	127	Trace	Trace	32	5	0
Lemon Juice						
fresh, 1 tablespoon	4	Trace	0	1	Trace	0
bottled, unsweetened, 1 tablespoon	3	Trace	Trace	1	3	0
Orange Juice						
fresh, 1 cup	112	2	1	26	3	0
canned, unsweetened, 1 cup	105	1	Trace	25	5	0
frozen concentrate, reconstituted, 1 cup	112	2	Trace	27	2	0
Peach Nectar						
canned, 1 cup	124	1	Trace	35	17	0
Pineapple Juice						
canned, unsweetened, 1 cup	140	1	Trace	35	3	0
Prune Juice						
canned, 1 cup	182	2	Trace	45	10	0
Tea						
brewed, 1 cup, unsweetened	2	0	0	1	7	0
Tomato Juice						
canned, 1 cup	41	2	Trace	10	881	0

INDEX